AMY WINEHOUSE — THE UNTOLD STORY

BY CHLOE GOVAN

This edition first published in 2013 by:

Thistle Publishing
36 Great Smith Street
London
SW1P 3BU

For Khalid, who matches Blake in both ill-fatedness and intensity. For better or for worse, love is a Class A drug – the most potent and poisonous of them all.

PREFACE

There are many ways to remember Amy Winehouse. A troubled young woman falling face down into a pool of vomit, her perilously high heels discarded beside her. A lost soul clinging frantically to her ex-husband as blood, tears and eyeliner streak her haunted face. A fragile girl recoiling from dozens of intrusive camera flashes as she stumbles around Camden High Street, her tortured life all too often resembling a soap opera. Or perhaps an innocent, unspoiled school girl with fantasies of relieving the world's pressures by putting her life to a melody – one for whom the strongest poison was a bottle of illicit vodka; someone who openly shunned Class A drugs.

Later came a woman determined to beat her demons, shakily taking to the stage on methadone to claim her prize – no fewer than five Grammys – and breaking a world record in the process. And then the 'final frame' – which came all too soon – accompanied by the words 'Amy Winehouse died today'. There was a brutal finality about it – the pictures of her tiny, frail frame hidden under the burgundy coloured cloth as she left her Camden flat for the last time, in a body bag.

Back in the beginning, things had been very different. Amy was all about the music and she'd mocked the fame. She refused to play up to illusions of polished perfection, preferring to appear as herself. What was more, she refused to be styled and she wrote her own songs. In Amy, the music world had just found themselves a new alien.

She wasn't a fame hungry media whore desperate for publicity and she didn't want to grace the front cover of a magazine or sing lead vocals on a CD if it meant compromising her credibility. In a world of rabidly determined *X-Factor* and *Fame Academy* contestants, that made her unique.

She displayed a brand of jaw dropping honesty that would see the average showbiz 'talent' instantly dropped from their label. She then called S-Club 7 'shit', denounced Dido as 'the soundtrack to death' and claimed she was praying for Britney Spears to have more children if it would retire her from the music industry. For Amy, good grace paled in comparison to raw honesty – and that made interviews with her extremely lively. She wasn't looking for approval – either followers could like her voice, look and behaviour or lump it and – if an audience criticised her – in typical Amy style, she simply branded them 'monkey cunts'.

She showed little respect for manager Simon Fuller either, insisting he was 'smart enough to know he can't fuck with me'. To her, music bosses were merely a necessary evil – a means to an end – and that end was performing music without boundaries. On the PR circuit, she was the kind of weapon of mass destruction that would have bosses wincing – and she was unrepentant too. Back in her younger years, she'd joked: 'I won't ever be a mass artist, so I don't think I'll ever have to say sorry for the things I've said.'

How wrong she was – in fact, her next album would go on to sell millions of copies. However, as her fame grew, her openness and lack of inhibitions took on a more sinister turn. Whether it was needle trackmarks on her arms, carpet burns on her elbows and knees or blood from self-harm streaming down her skin, Amy was astonishingly unselfconscious.

At the start, her debauchery had been dismissed as a carefully calculated publicity stunt. It's not hard to guess why. Ashtrays and pint glasses were sold as novelties at her online merchandise store, while 'Rehab' gags were standing jokes around the world. However, it quickly became clear that Amy was genuinely suffering. It started with performances where she could barely stand, let alone sing, where she was reduced to a slurring wreck in front of millions on live television. She then seemed to be singlehandedly saving her local Hawley Arms pub from the perils of the recession. What was worse, she was on that crusade during working hours too – after cancelling shows, an allegedly ill Amy would be seen in supermarkets stocking up on wine or cider, or raucously hollering into her mobile phone, with that distinctive Cockney twang, to make social arrangements for the same evening.

She'd win awards but fail to arrive at the ceremony, leaving others to collect them, where they often ended up languishing in the toilet cubicles of seedy bars. Things were about to get a lot worse too. Amy then embarked on a passionate self-destructive marriage with a man she called the love of her life – Blake Fielder-Civil. Things became obsessive and the pair quickly became as addicted to drugs as they were to each other. Blake introduced her starry-eyed lover to heroin – and what had once been flirting with danger for a taste of the rock 'n' roll lifestyle would soon turn more sinister, seeing her hurtle down a highway to hell.

The music she'd once adored took a back seat to attending to Blake. She began to loudly proclaim she'd never wanted fame – but just to be a wife and a mother. She even insisted: 'If I had another life, I'd be a housewife' and 'I wasn't put on this earth to sing'. Millions of fans begged to differ – but she was no longer listening. Rehab wasn't just a catchy song anymore – it had become the soundtrack to her life.

There was the love rehab. An obsessive Amy had taken to caving her beloved's name into her flesh with shards of glass and, in some interviews, would talk only of him – or her much loved hair. Then there were the tearful showdowns in Eurostar terminals when Amy would cry hysterically at the prospect of leaving her lover, even for just 24 hours. She was a no-show at her own video shoot once, which was abandoned at a cost of £70,000, just so that she could be with Blake.

Then there was the drug rehab and the overdoses. She would punch the wall with her fist, slurring incoherently, tears streaming from her eyes – and, the next day, would be bundled into a wheelchair barely conscious, the victim of yet another night of over-indulgence.

Amy might have been rock 'n' roll, but her excesses were now far from music to the ears of industry bosses. To them, there was a fine line between publicity-touting, headline holding debauchery and downright self-destruction – and Amy had crossed it. What was more, the drug-taking was no longer glamorous, fun, or symbolic of simply hard partying.

Put simply, she wasn't having fun anymore. She was desperately unhappy and was intoxicating herself to take away the pain. Yet, paradoxically, without the pain, she felt some of her most loved songs could never exist.

If Amy was a car and life was a highway, her biggest mistake was never applying the brakes. She played out a humiliating public demise from behind the lens of hundreds of cameras. Full scale media bidding wars were launched for pictures that portrayed her slumped in a heap outside her house – or, even, innocently and innocuously buying beer from her local Tesco. The Sun newspaper was prompted to launch a Wino Watch column on their showbiz pages to monitor her increasingly erratic behaviour and express their concern.

Amy endured meltdown after meltdown, cancelling a UK tour after Blake was sentenced to time in prison. That would be the last UK tour she'd ever schedule. As she took time out for rehab, her life began to overshadow her music. With her unkempt beehive, blackened fingernails and bloodstained ballet pumps, Amy was more renowned for not changing her clothes for five days running than she was for any burgeoning sense of style. Flaunting her figure and hollering loudly about the size of her breasts in her distinctive Cockney accent in restaurants, she wasn't top of the class for her etiquette either. But it was the drugs that really infatuated the media.

Totally ill-equipped for a life of fame – one she said she had never wanted – she played out her car-crash lifestyle like a fragile moth seduced by a bright light and blinded by the bulb. Inevitably, a day would come when Amy would burn out altogether.

And that day promised to be sooner than anyone had thought. As the years passed, it had seemed she was getting better – recording new material, sunning herself on beach holidays and even mentoring her god daughter's musical career. Reports by her father suggested she hadn't touched drugs for months, if not years. Then a disastrous show in Serbia grinded the illusions to a halt – where Amy falteringly sang her hits, forgetting some of the lyrics, and looked tearful and distressed when the crowd booed. Her European tour that summer was cancelled, but still, no one had realised the full extent of her problems. The following month, she allegedly blacked out three times in one week from vodka binges – and Priory staff darkly warned that her heart would not take any more alcohol.

Yet a hopelessly addicted Amy had been seen buying – and downing – an entire bottle of vodka on her way to the clinic. Musically she had shown flashes of brilliance, reminding audiences exactly why they loved her, before descending back into the depths of addiction and becoming unreachable. Did Amy have no idea that, towards the end, each bottle of vodka could be her last?

Originally, this book was to be called *Survivor* and would have been an account of how, against all odds, Amy had conquered her demons with drugs to make a triumphant return to the stage in 2011. Alas, it was not to be. On July 23, Amy's heart stopped beating – just two months short of her 28th birthday.

At that moment, a light went out for all those whose lives she had touched. It wasn't just her family and friends that grieved – followers camped outside her house to pay tribute. That day, 20 million people spoke of her on Twitter. Many would feel denial, disbelief and a sense of devastating injustice. Amy had achieved more in her short 27 years than many achieve in a full lifetime – yet there were still many things she had never achieved, such as the child she longed for, which many think could have been a stabilising influence in her life.

Plus there's always the nagging suspicion that there was much, much more music to come from her. Just a day earlier, she'd been cheerily terrorising the neighbours with her new drum kit – and the same week she'd supported her god daughter Dionne in concert. Yet now, inextricably, she was gone.

To her fans, she was uncompromising, defiantly honest and effortlessly talented. Fiercely loyal, she would also have died for love – and she composed many a song about the headaches and heartaches that position brought on. Ultimately for Amy, not just love, but life, was a losing game. She lost her battle – but her legacy will live on.

CHAPTER 1

From angelic soul singer, orthodox Jewish girl, unconventional sex symbol and immaculate jazz princess to tearful and deeply troubled drug addict – not to mention love addict – Amy Winehouse was a complex enigma. Whether she was playing the role of sell out singer or self-destructive temptress, her life – painfully short - made headlines the world over. Yet who was the real Amy and where did her journey begin?

Stepping back in time to east London in the 1950s, the way was already being paved for Amy's arrival. Like Amy, her father Mitchell Winehouse – better known as Mitch – was quite a character. He began his life in a large four storey house in the east end's Tower Hamlets. In the style of a Jewish kibbutz, several members of the extended family lived together, including his mother Cynthia and her twin sister, his grandmother and great uncle, and a Holocaust survivor who had earlier fled Germany. He recalled of his time there: 'All I remember since day one was music. Jazz, swing, lots of Sinatra. When it was quiet, my mum and my auntie would ballroom dance together across the floor. We lived above this place with aunties, uncles, grandparents, great grandparents. Every floor had different music. We were singing all the time; together, on our own. I mean, it was a poor world, no indoor toilets, kids still died of rickets through poor diet. But when I look back, the music soundtracks a happy time. It's a way of life that's gone forever but the memories are the wonderful people and music. It oozes through these songs.'

Back then, Tower Hamlets was poverty stricken, with more than a third of all households out of work, but the Winehouses stuck together. The family consisted of cab drivers, tailors and barbers, all keen to earn their crust and they soon moved to a more affluent area to seek work. Unfortunately they would also experience anti-Semitism. 'When we moved to Southgate in North London, we were the only Jewish family there and [people] thought Jews had horns on their heads or something – so I was fighting all the time. That's what you did, when we were kids. I'm not a tough guy or anything like that, but I knew how to protect my family,' Mitch told the *Huffington Post*.

Fortunately he had work from an early age to build his identity and get him through the tough times. Growing up, his first job was a stint proof-reading and editing features for the Jewish Chronicle, a local faith newspaper also based in east London. Tiring of typewriters, he then became a double glazing salesman, using his cheeky Cockney charm and persistence to win over buyers. It was whilst in this profession that his life changed. His best friend from school had an enticing yet forbidden cousin called Janis who, in 1975, became his new love interest.

Loud, rowdy and passionately obsessed with performance, it was a surprise to the family of the more reserved Janis when the two got together. Hailing from a respectable family in Brooklyn, New York, who also had roots in Miami and Atlanta, the quiet and refined Janis came from a science background and couldn't have been more different from the extroverted Mitch. She had put herself through Open University before going on to work in the pharmaceuticals industry as a lab technician.

Some of Janis's family were instantly suspicious of Mitch and his working class roots, suspecting that he was a philanderer and begging her to marry the type of suit-wearing professional that they felt she deserved. Nevertheless he had charmed Janis into ignoring this advice and the two were soon married.

Janis gave birth to the couple's first child, Alex, in 1979 and the headstrong Amy followed four years later, on September 14th 1983. This marked the beginning of a troubled yet tantalising era the Winehouses would never be able to forget.

Amy, a Virgo, was blessed with a double dose of musical DNA – not only were two of Janis's uncles professional jazz musicians, but her paternal grandmother Cynthia had also been an aspiring jazz singer in her youth.

An 18-month old Amy knew nothing of her family history when she would help her father belt out the lyrics to Frank Sinatra's 'I Only Have Eyes for You', but she knew she loved to sing. Her desire to be heard matched her father's and he would sing out the verse: 'Are the stars out tonight? I don't know if it's cloudy or bright, because I only have eyes for...' while Amy chimed in '...YOU!' Mitch recalled of his daughter: 'Amy had a very similar upbringing [to mine] - always aunties, uncles, grandparents and friends around... and always music.'

When Mitch was at work during the week, Amy would continue to sing, composing her own verses to the cries of 'Shut up!' from her frustrated mother. To Janis back then, her daughter's irrepressible urge to break into song was nothing more than an irritant – little did she know that the same voice would one day become an internationally admired multimillion pound money maker. On Mitch's return home, there was no respite either – he and Amy would sing Beatles tracks and alternate the verses between them. In fact, it was a standing joke in the family that Amy had learnt to sing before she had learnt to talk.

Not just irritating to the less musically inclined in the household, the increasingly accident-prone Amy was also a cause for concern. She almost choked to death at age two on account of trying to eat cellophane, and alleged that she 'cut off one of my toes opening cat food' at the tender age of four.

Wilful, manipulative, naughty and easily bored, it was a relief to everyone concerned when it was time for Amy to start her education. The young Amy's first taste of school life was at the state-owned Osidge Primary School in Southgate. It once hit the headlines for the 'appalling quality' of its canteen food, when top chefs were called in to replace the fried chicken and greasy sausage diet with healthier alternatives. The food might not have been top notch, but Osidge was the location where a four year old Amy would meet her future best friend and partner in crime, Juliette Ashby.

Inseparable from the start, their misdemeanours included relentlessly teasing the boys in their class, forcing one to pull down his pants in public if he wanted to retain their friendship. 'We told this boy if he didn't pull his pants down, we wouldn't be his friends anymore and he did it,' cackled Amy to *The Observer*.

The pair became so renowned that their parents begged teachers not to let them sit together, knowing that wherever the twosome went, trouble would surely follow. However, even when apart, the cunning pair's appetite for mischief never receded and they soon found a way to be together again. 'You'd get sent to the school reception if you were naughty,' Amy remembered, 'and we were always meeting up there.'

Even in her younger years, Amy had already made a name for herself as a bit of a handful. However, according to a male classmate, Amy was merely mischievous. 'Osidge was a middle class suburban school and Amy wasn't forever in trouble,' he revealed to the author. 'She was pretty lively, boisterous, confident, a bit bossy – but she wasn't ever a tearaway.'

The pair first met when Amy attended his fifth birthday party and they later appeared together, aged seven, in a performance of *Joseph and the Technicolour Dream Coat*. Then, in the summer of 1995, the entire year group put on a production of *Grease: The Musical*. As a humble school leaver's play, it didn't have the £6 million budget that the original play had commanded, but Amy was looking forward to it nonetheless and was determined to clinch the lead role. To her horror, she was usurped by a more popular classmate and it was not Amy but one of her best friends, Lauren Franklin, who secured the part.

'It was always a given that Lauren would end up playing Sandy,' the classmate continued. 'She had a great voice as a kid.' However *The Sun* didn't share his opinion when they hosted a video of the school play on their website, advising viewers to turn off the sound 'after Amy exits and the unfortunately voiced schoolgirl starring as Sandy starts in on [the song] 'Hopelessly Devoted To You'.'

Amy's refusal to heed rules and decorum was illuminated in her portion of the video. While the spotlight shifted onto Amy's singing companion, she was filmed casually wiping her nose on her sleeve. Nonchalant and without a hint of embarrassment, she seemed oblivious to the camera. This led *The Sun* to rather cruelly report that – even in her early years – she had not given her nose a much needed break.

Amy's classmate continued: 'She wasn't forever the star of the school play. You wouldn't have said at primary school that this was a girl marked out for fame. She didn't stand out as a star of the future and I was surprised by just how successful she became.'

However Amy was a dark horse and was secretly building up a collection of CDs that she would listen to avidly and try to emulate.

It was whilst at primary school that Amy discovered music, but at that time she adored artists that today would have made her cringe – Madonna being one example. 'From the age of six, I listened to the Immaculate Collection every day,' she grimaced. This would continue for the next five years until Amy 'grew up' and abandoned the Italian-American songstress and her other favourite, Kylie Minogue, sneering of the latter: 'She's not an artist – she's a pony – a beautiful, cute little pony.'

However in the meantime, at age eight, Amy would enter a recording studio for the first time ever, a stint that would put her efforts in the same league as Michael Jackson and Stevie Wonder. Both were Amy's idols, whose songs she later went on to cover, and both had their first taste of stardom, like her, at eight years old. She and equally dedicated Juliette Ashby hit the recording studio with the producer Alan Glass, a family friend keen to give them their first taste of the music world. He had previously sent tracks sung by Aretha Franklin to the top of the charts, so whilst the sessions were short, Amy's talents had been in good hands.

With all of this to occupy her, Amy had been a happy-go-lucky and mischievous child, until disaster struck. The Winehouses had been harbouring a dark secret – there was a third person in Janis and Mitch's marriage. Since Amy was just 18 months old, Mitch had been openly dating a woman named Jane whom his children knew as 'Daddy's work wife'.

This caused come confusion for a young Amy about matters of monogamy. Envisaging her mother as the unlikely leader of a male harem, she asked, 'Mum, why don't you marry [TV presenter] Phillip Schofield?', only for a bemused Janis to reply, 'Amy! I'm married to your dad!' In fact, Phillip had a striking resemblance to Mitch, although he was more than a decade younger. In spite of the comedic undertones to Amy's request, her father's affair was no laughing matter. By all account, it had wreaked havoc on the family.

Following a passionate seven year affair, emotions were running high and the complicated love triangle had to end. Mitch knew he had to choose and he did, divorcing Janis and leaving the family home in 1993. Amy was just nine years old.

Previously a bright and inquisitive child, Amy's world descended into chaos. She remembered forgiving her father quickly for his infidelities, commenting to *The Times*: 'Why should I be angry with my dad just because he has a penis?'

However, inevitably, the pain ran deep. Devastated and anxious, a nine year old Amy began to self-harm, cutting her arms with razor blades and shards of glass. 'I had a morbid curiosity to know what it felt like,' she told *Scene* magazine. 'It's probably the worst thing I've ever done.' In moments of frustration, she would also bang her head against her bedroom wall repeatedly, causing Juliette to panic during sleepovers. Amy later explained simply, 'I like pain. It relieves you.'

The BBC Health website confirmed this as a typical reason for self-harm, stating: 'Your feelings of anger and tension get bottled up inside until you feel like exploding. Self-harm relieves this tension.' Indeed, self-harm is commonly described as a way of expressing extreme emotional distress that cannot find an outlet in the harmer's every day life or be channelled in conventional ways. Whilst causes can include self-loathing and a desire for attention, experts say it is just as commonly a way to express pent up anger when the victim lacks coping strategies.

Self-harm expert Marilee Strong, author of the book *A Bright Red Scream: Self Mutilation And The Language of Pain*, suggests that most self-harmers are women who were emotionally, sexually or physically abused during childhood.

Indeed, Mitch shouldered responsibility for some of Amy's emotional grief, claiming to the BBC show *One Life: Rock Star Parents*, 'It is easy for me to say it was my fault [for leaving] and that had I been a better parent, this would not have happened. But who knows?'

Yet Charley Baker, a self-harm expert and psychology lecturer at Nottingham University, contested the childhood abuse model. She told the author, 'Without clinically interviewing Amy herself, it is difficult to comment on, but although major life events can be a trigger for self-harm to begin with, equally periods of stress or depression can be enough to start it, without any significant life event… Similarly the message that self-harm is rooted in childhood and/or associated with abuse in childhood is fiercely contested. For some people who self-harm, difficult childhoods might be apparent, but for many it's a reaction to adult life events, emotional stressors or relationships.'

Tragically in Amy's case, her self-harming had actually begun in childhood. She was one of many troubled celebrities who had succumbed to self mutilation, although her experiences were perhaps among the earliest in terms of life years. Actor Johnny Depp acquired eight scars on his left arm from knife cuts as a teenager, each marking grief-ridden milestones in his life, while Richie from the rock band Manic Street Preachers once carved the word 'Real' into his arm during a radio show. Other well-known self-harmers have included Angelina Jolie, Courtney Love and even the late Diana, Princess of Wales.

The princess revealed her secret to the world in 1995 on a BBC interview, claiming: 'You have so much pain inside yourself that you try to hurt yourself on the outside because you need help.'

It was an unsophisticated but understandable way for Amy to deal with her raw emotion. Fortunately for her, she was increasingly finding solace in music. In Cyprus, during the last holiday that the Winehouses had enjoyed together as a family, Amy had attended a talent contest and blown away onlookers with her sound. Mother Janis had initially been bemused at her keenness to enter, but soon realised there was more to Amy's enthusiasm than she had thought.

Consequently, Amy's grandmother Cynthia, who had been engaged to infamous jazz singer Ronnie Scott in her earlier years, suggested that Amy attend the Suzi Earnshaw School to build on her aptitude as a singer and actress. Characteristically head-strong Amy listened to very few people in her life, once claiming only to listen to her inner child, but there was one special woman who commanded her unreserved attention - and that was Cynthia. As she had once been a devoted singer herself, she related to Amy's passion to succeed. Recognising something truly special in the youngster, she channelled it early, arranging herself for Amy's first taste of the performing world. She duly began at the school, which, according to its mission statement 'encourages students to look beyond the norms and dare to dream of new ways of contributing to the performing arts industry'.

Amy thrived on this new and unexpected outlet for her pain. She was soon sent to audition for the part of the feisty yet deeply troubled Annie in the musical of the same name - a character not unlike Amy herself.

In the musical, Annie is left on the doorstep of an orphanage at birth with a note from her parents promising that one day they will return to claim her. Tired of living in vain hope, Annie decides to escape to find her birth parents by herself and, via a stay in a kind billionaire's mansion, the adventurous 11-year-old is finally reunited with them.

Unfortunately for Amy, she performed her piece off-key and endured criticism from her mother, despite assurances that the school had merely sent her out to get practise. The experience highlighted that few people were aware of Amy's aptitude at that time. A daunted Mitch, watching by the side of the stage, had remarked to his new wife Jane despairingly 'At least she can have a career as an actress!'

It must have been humiliating for Amy to see Mitch criticise her in front of the woman who'd replaced her mother in his affections. What was more, these events had a chilling resonance with Harvard psychiatrist Edward Khantzian's theory about the childhood experiences of drug addicts.

'Mothers – and no doubt many fathers – of frequent drug users have been described as "relatively cold, unresponsive and under-protective",' he explains. 'Regarding their children's accomplishments, they send a very mixed message – they're pressuring and overly interested in their children's performance, yet rarely offer them encouragement.'

What was more, perhaps their hesitance of congratulate her and their lack thereof when it came to highlighting her failures, contributed to Amy's flagging self-esteem. For, like them, she was equally modest about her abilities, later telling *The Telegraph*: 'I was good at singing, but I was also good at sewing - do you know what I mean? I never thought I would get anywhere.'

Yet music had quickly become Amy's reason for existence. Thankfully for her, her 'embarrassing' penchant for pop princesses had not lasted long. She had once belted out Ironic by Alanis Morissette for an audition, yet later belittled the Canadian as 'shit'. Meanwhile Madonna, once her cherished favourite, was soon described as 'an old lady'. She instead developed an infatuation with Michael Jackson. 'I could never decide whether I wanted to be Michael Jackson or marry him. I don't care what people say about him now because he's a fucking genius,' she told *The Guardian*.

Another rite of passage for Amy in her quest to discover 'real music' was an obsession with Salt and Pepa. The shamelessly straight-talking, sexually explicit all-American female rap duo became Amy and best friend Juliette's new heroines. As front women they were unafraid of frankness and excess and this was exactly how Amy herself aspired to be. Whilst tame in today's musical climate, at the time of its release the song 'Push It' with the words 'Can't you hear the music pumping hard, like I wish you would?' was groundbreaking and raunchy, with few competitors daring to be so sexually provocative, upfront and open. The duo might have raised a few eyebrows – and sparked outrage in more conservative families - but they instantly started selling records. Like Amy, they were trend-setters, and they were the inspiration that truly made her acid tongue come alive.

She and Juliette began a group of their own called Sweet and Sour – Amy, naturally, was Sour – modelled on the rap duo. One of their tracks was called 'Spinderella', named after the DJ that once collaborated with Salt and Pepa.

However edgy popular music was not Amy's only sphere of interest. She also listened initially to jazz and soul classics Thelonious Monk, Dinah Washington, Sarah Vaughan and Ella Fitzgerald. Unfortunately Amy's chart-worshipping friends did not share her obsession. 'I would say that jazz is my own language,' she had mused. '[My friends and I] all love Timbaland and Magoo, we all love Stevie Wonder, but no-one shares my taste for the old stuff.'

Yet it was a passion that she did share with her father Mitch and music brought the two - now living apart - closer together. Mitch had loved singing from a very early age, recalling to *The Telegraph*: 'I always wanted to sing at every opportunity - weddings, parties, bar mitzvahs - I would be up there.' He added of his childhood 'I grew up in the pre television age so at home it was always music. That's how people entertained themselves – playing piano, singing and dancing.'

At first it might have seemed as though Amy's early life had been as care-free as her father's – full of joyful voices, uninhibited dancing and parties with the extended family – complete with a musical soundtrack to suit every occasion. Yet, according to a close friend from her youth, beneath the façade, Amy was desperately unhappy. In fact, by the age of ten, she had been ready to take her own life.

'By tradition, most Jewish families are very close-knit and a value is put on seeming respectable. Divorce is considered shameful, so Amy went through a lot of pain at her parents' separation,' her anonymous friend explained to the author. 'She might have put on a front like she didn't care, but to her, seeing her father leave her for another woman was the ultimate abandonment.'

'Amy had also attended some classes to study the Torah, but she stuck out like a sore thumb amongst all the religious families and I guess that's where the feeling of not belonging really began,' she added. 'Amy was never your archetypal good Jewish girl. She had the type of personality where, depending on how strait-laced people were, they would either react with a wry smile or complete and utter horror. She was rouble and there came a point when she stopped seeming endearingly naughty and started being downright out of control. If I could compare her childhood personality to anyone else's, it would be Russell Brand.'

She continued: 'As Amy grew up, things didn't get much better and actually the divide between her and these types of good Jewish families got even bigger. By ten she'd had her first spliff and, in some people's eyes, was on a bit of a road to ruin."'

While Amy had already learnt to cook, bake cakes and sew, sometimes spent weekend mornings giving her beloved grandmother pedicures and seemed to be the perfect Jewish housewife in training, there was another side to her – perhaps borne out of childhood trauma – that she struggled to control. What was more, her father's absence had provided a convenient way for her to wreak havoc and get away with it. 'Amy would boast about how, now that her dad had moved out, she could get away with murder! I felt like that was maybe a front to make herself look like she wasn't hurting, but then Amy got attention for acting up, so she would act up even more. She had quite a reputation!'

Amy's identity with her peers was that she was the funny one, the perpetual cheeky troublemaker – something which her friend believed she may have used to cover up her feelings of inadequacy in other areas of life. 'Amy had some gorgeous childhood friends that she couldn't quite compete with,' she revealed. 'She blossomed into a real beauty in her late teens, but earlier on she hadn't really grown into her looks. She was seen as a bit of an ugly duckling and she felt awkward around some of the others. It didn't help that she never cared for tidiness, so by the end of the day she would look like a scarecrow. She was still a cute child, but she told me on more than one occasion that she felt ugly.'

Clearly, the passage from child to teenager was proving more difficult for her than most. Amy was also a renowned tomboy and was more often content playing outdoors and getting covered in mud than she was joining her beauty-conscious friends for a makeover. Suffice it to say, Amy wasn't the type of girl who could have been found trying on her mother's lipstick and high heels whilst practising salacious poses in the mirror. Feeling increasingly alienated from the preteen pageant queens and pink-adorned princesses clutching Barbie dolls – on Amy's part, she'd rather have been mutilating one than playing with it – she fell into depression.

Amy had been desperate to break away from her background, feeling that the strict Jewish society she'd been raised in was too limiting for her. Plus not only did she not feel at home around her peers – some of whom had little patience for her hell-raising – she was still feeling the pain of her parents' separation.

'In my opinion, most of Amy's pent-up anger was directed towards herself,' her friend claimed. 'She had an inferiority complex. She felt she wasn't good enough – if she had been, why would her father have left her?'

Whatever the cause, within just months of reaching double figures, Amy's anxiety had reached fever pitch. She'd already been slashing her arms and wrists with compasses, razor blades and shards of glass – but the worst was yet to come. 'Amy was such a smiley, happy girl on the surface – maybe she was a good actress as well as a good singer – so it came as a surprise,' revealed her friend. 'I only knew how bad things had become when she overdosed.'

She continued: 'That day, I found Amy clutching her stomach in agony. She'd started foaming at the mouth and her eyes were rolling. It was easily the most terrifying thing I'd ever seen. She'd overdosed on pills because she didn't want to live. She told me she'd wanted to go for a long sleep. I stayed with her until it wore off because she begged me not to tell anyone. Plenty of people would say I was a bad friend for not raising the alarm but I was truly scared.'

She'd been close to revealing her friend's secret, but she had been successfully persuaded otherwise. Rooted to the spot and paralysed with fear, she listened as Amy promised that it was an one-off mistake she never wanted to repeat. 'When I asked her what had made her do it, she said it was nothing and she'd just been really stupid,' she explained. 'She swore blind it was the last time.'

Fortunately, Amy was telling the truth. Dissuaded by the agonising stomach cramps the overdose had left her with, she instead sought solace in her first love – music. Fast forward 12 years and the sensational quote 'If it wasn't for music, I'd be dead by now' was emblazoned across nearly every celebrity gossip website in the country. Yet behind the headlines, few people knew just how true to life that sentiment really was. Not only did the rhythms of her favourite bands soothe her pain, but it was a way for Amy to bond with her estranged father again. Music had been a second language that they shared – one that anyone could listen to but that they felt only the two of them could fully understand.

'Amy adored her father,' explained Amy's anonymous pal. 'They were both into music so I think that's what broke the ice between them again.'

According to her, Amy's talent for composition had already shown itself too. Aside from jokey lyrics produced with her friend Juliette, a song about her father was to be the first serious song she'd ever written. 'Amy was never a touchy feely emotional person who liked to talk about her feelings,' her friend continued. 'It was awkward for her so she'd laugh it off, but for everything she couldn't or wouldn't put into words, she found that there was a song.'

She added: 'It started out with other songs mimicking how she felt either in their lyrics or their melody, until one day that wasn't good enough and she wanted to write her own. I wish I could remember lyrics. But music saved Amy's life – without it, she might have been dead 17 years earlier.'

Amy was finally entering a happier phase in her life, pouring her emotions out with song and perhaps exorcising the negative ones forever. She hadn't stopped listening to a range of music either. While her friends might have stared blankly, when it came to jazz, her father could sing along to every tune – and Amy never hesitated to join him.

What was more, while her father was content merely to entertain workmates with her voice, singing loudly and controversially in his sales office, Amy was determined to make something more of the talent she'd been blessed with – and she never gave up on her dream of seeing her name in bright lights.

However, her wishes were temporarily thwarted when she began at the local comprehensive, Ashmole Academy. Its education-focused ethos was about to bring Amy back down to earth with a bang.

Located on Cecil Road in Southgate, the school had a heavily academic reputation, with a 2009 Ofsted report claiming that it 'consistently exceeds its targets'. It specialised in providing a scientifically rich learning environment, with medicine, maths and IT included – all of Amy's worst nightmares at once! Her one consolation was that she would be attending with best friend Juliette.

However, throughout, Amy had left no-one under any illusion about the type of career she wanted to pursue. 'She had a passion to be a pop singer,' head teacher Derrick Brown explained simply in an interview with the author.

Luckily, despite disguising itself well as a science-based school, Ashmole was also the starting point for several talents in the musical world, with the faculty website stating 'The benefits of musical education stay with students for life.'

'Rachel Stevens from S Club 7 studied here,' Derrick confirmed, 'but she wasn't such a soloist in terms of individual performance and she certainly didn't have quite the unique quality that Amy had.' Evidently Amy agreed, as just a few years later she would make a public service announcement that S Club 7 was 'shit'. Avoiding the computer rooms and the laboratory like the plague, Amy instead attended optional singing classes.

'We had quite a strong singing group of Amy and three others, all of whom were really talented,' Derrick remembered. 'One wanted to become an artist, the other two were into drama, but Amy stood out because I remember her describing to me that she wanted to sing for a living.'

Fortunately for her, the school was hiding a strong musical focus. 'We recognise where pupils have talent and give them the opportunity to develop that talent,' Derrick stated. 'This helped Amy shape her performance for later on in life.' Students were able to perform in weekly assemblies representing each year group. However, knowing the temperament of girls like Amy, the school postponed the assemblies until the afternoons. 'At 8:40am, students go straight into lessons, as we know they tend to concentrate better in the mornings,' Derrick chuckled. 'The assemblies start at 2:00pm.'

There was also a drama studio at the school where small-scale concerts were staged. 'We would do *Ashmole's Got Talent* type shows at Christmas, and Amy was often involved,' he claimed. 'I recall the first time she did a solo song – it was a trendy young jazzy-folk type song, which was very much her style, and I can remember being totally wowed by the performance she gave.' He added 'Hopefully we did our bit to help Amy realise her ambition.'

Whether or not Ashmole was responsible, her time there was certainly characterised by a desperate desire for her voice to be noticed – and by her third year, Amy had taken that desire a step further forward.

Due to some ingenuity on her part, her stay at Ashmole was to be short-lived and, in Year 9, replaced with real life performance. The 13-year-old took it upon herself to apply for entry to the fiercely competitive Sylvia Young stage school in London, which was world renowned for its calibre.

As part of her application, she wrote a short essay demonstrating why she wanted to be part of the school. Rather than strategic business speak calculated for maximum effect, Amy's note was unsophisticated, free from formalities and totally from the heart. It was also sarcastic, entertaining and – like the name of her first album - frank. There were no airs and graces and no cover ups as she joked about her family and her bad school reports both for behaviour and academic work. The essay read as follows:

'All my life I have been loud, to the point of being told to shut up. The only reason I have had to be this loud is because you have to scream to be heard in my family. My family? Yes, you read it right. My mum's side is perfectly fine, my dad's family are the singing, dancing, all-nutty musical extravaganza. I've been told I was gifted with a lovely voice and I guess my dad's to blame for that. Although unlike my dad, and his background and ancestors, I want to do something with the talents I've been 'blessed' with. My dad is content to sing loudly in his office and sell windows. My mother, however, is a chemist. She is quiet, reserved. I would say that my school life and school reports are filled with 'could do betters' and 'does not work to her full potential'. I want to go somewhere where I am stretched right to my limits and perhaps even beyond. To sing in lessons without being told to shut up (provided they are singing lessons). But mostly I have this dream to be very famous. To work on stage. It's a lifelong ambition. I want people to hear my voice and just . . . forget their troubles for five minutes. I want to be remembered for being an actress, a singer, for sell-out concerts and sell-out West End and Broadway shows. For being just... me.'

CHAPTER 2

This casually penned but passionate essay would spell a new era in Amy's life. In spite of her self-confessed troubles, the note seemed compellingly honest to Sylvia and she was invited for an audition. Allegedly 400 applicants were vying for each place, but - determined to win a scholarship - Amy approached her father for help in crafting the perfect audition. Mitch tirelessly helped his daughter rehearse Ella Fitzgerald's 'Sunny Side of the Street'. He would advise: 'We'll listen to the record, listen to where Ella takes a breath and work it out from there.'

On judgement day, Amy offered a rendition of both the Ella Fitzgerald track and 'What About Us' by Michael Jackson. The school's founder Sylvia was instantly impressed. 'She struck me as unique, both as a composer and as a performer, from the moment she came through the doors,' she revealed.

One thing was for sure - Amy certainly stood out. Among the rows of perfectly poised young ladies, her innate awkwardness and kooky grin set her apart from the rest and her east London twang stood out miles away. Yet it was her performance above all that had the tutors talking and Amy was instantly accepted.

The rebellious young woman with a formidable voice, an acid tongue and a broad Cockney accent, someone who had been described as 'symbolically working class' would now descend on a world of wealthy teenagers with professional parents, country mansions, bulging bank balances and – beyond that - seemingly infinite trust funds. Her own parents could scarcely have afforded the £10,000 per year admission fees, but the young starlet had been awarded a scholarship on the grounds of raw talent.

Attending school without Juliette for the first time ever, Amy needn't have been nervous - despite being known as the 'weird kid', she was accepted straight away. One of the girls to share a class with the youngster was Jodi Albert. The would-be star later went on to earn a place in the Channel 4 teen soap *Hollyoaks* after achieving a top 10 chart position with one hit wonder *Girl Thing*. Like Amy, her father had once been a taxi driver struggling on a meagre wage to support the family. Whilst Amy was granted a scholarship, Jodi's dedicated parents remortgaged the family home to give her a chance of attending the prestigious stage school. Neither of the girls were typical 'rich kids' and the pair bonded in their uniqueness. Jodi's modest background but rabid desire for fame complemented Amy's own clear cut ambitions.

However, that was where the similarities between the two ended. Jodi, who had acted in the stage play *Les Miserables* at the tender age of 10, starring as Young Cozette, was one of the girls Amy would later witheringly describe as 'totally insufferable kids who'd come into class and announce "My mummy's coming to pick me up for an audition at 3 o' clock."'

The differences between Jodi and Amy were to become even more apparent in later life. While Amy suffered from cripplingly low self esteem, describing herself as 'ugly', Jodi on the other hand had no qualms about becoming the scantily clad cover girl of Maxim. Some described her poses as 'soft-core pornography' whilst others, including Jodi herself, saw it as 'fashion modelling'.

However, there were advantages to Amy's friendship with Jodi. Her best friend at school was Matt Willis, who would later become a member of the teen rock group Busted. Amy had harboured a secret crush on him throughout her time at school and although the pair rarely socialised, they saw each other almost every day. Jodi was her strongest link to Matt. It was reportedly fantasising about him that kept Amy going, especially in the part of the week dedicated to academic work, which she loathed.

A notorious trouble maker, she was frequently 'on report' where teachers commented on their classroom behaviour in every lesson and records of her attendance were regularly sent to the head. 'With me it was like "Came into the classroom with a safety pin in her ear. Didn't want to remove it and then cried in front of everyone,"' Amy chuckled. 'I would look around at my fellow pupils and think "Everyone's working. They're not trying to talk on the phone or anything – what's wrong with them?"'

Amy's tutors would wryly remark that she did not adapt well to being institutionalised. Her beaming response? 'All the teachers hated me.' Her appetite for mischief continued when she would pretend to be a witch and claim to have put spells on her classmate Billie Piper, famed for a career in 'cheesy pop' that made even Billie herself cringe, a marriage to the much older radio and TV presenter Chris Evans and her starring role in ITV drama *The Secret Diary of a Call Girl*.

Other classmates for Amy included the singer Gem Allen, who went on to support X-Factor winner Shayne Ward on his UK arena tour. Sadly, she failed to achieve the dizzying heights of stardom she had always longed for, and in later years she wrote on Twitter in protest: 'Gamu [Nhengu, a 2010 X Factor contestant] not even in X Factor anymore and she still gets more media attention than me. Does anyone know if this voodoo thing really works?' She was a fiercely competitive drama student and Amy – talented yet more laid back and modest – occasionally felt uncomfortable in her presence. Nonetheless, the two enjoyed a significant friendship.

Amy also studied with future McFly star Tom Fletcher, who was several years younger. 'She had a reputation even back then for being pretty wild,' he recalled. 'I know she was extremely talented.'

As well as her new network of friends, Amy continued to keep in touch with Juliette, despite their different phases in life – Amy was now a 'grunger' who shopped in Camden Market for clothes and collected piercings while Juliette proudly labelled herself 'a rude girl'. On one of their meets, she was horrified to see that the artistic Amy had acquired a self-designed nose piercing. 'You pierced your own face!' she had bawled at her friend. Boasting a 'very high' pain threshold, Amy was accustomed to alarming her friends with her new body work.

She would have been quite at home at the Phuket Vegetarian festival in Thailand where, during annual parades, participants self-pierce their cheeks, backs and necks with skewers and swords to demonstrate their religious faith, claiming to feel no pain. Curiously competitive, natives boast up to dozens of large incisions.

Back at the strict Sylvia Young School, tutors were less impressed with Amy's piercings, insisting that she take them out. Yet despite her deliberate disobedience, she and Sylvia carved out a fond mutual respect for one another and Sylvia was horrified to learn that the principal at the time had telephoned Amy's parents and asked them to place her elsewhere. Noticed for her brilliance yet attracting attention from the academic principal for very different reasons, Amy's time at the school was about to come to an end.

Most pupils were high achievers, and all were expected to attain a balanced academic diet – of both the performing arts curriculum they adored and the scholarly tasks that girls like Amy merely tolerated. Students routinely achieved A★-C grades in their GCSEs, but – due to lack of interest and motivation – it became clear that Amy was not going to scrape the necessary grades. While she immersed herself thoroughly in performance, she was very reluctant to do schoolwork.

Anxious to maintain its reputation as a school that achieved academic success, the principal made a frantic telephone call to Amy's mother, recommending that she be removed with immediate effect. This was in direct opposition to Sylvia's declaration that Amy was too bright to even need to study. She had already been placed a year above her chronological age and Sylvia strongly believed it was a lack of interest, rather than ability, that led to bad grades.

Amy was not formally expelled but, according to the school's prospectus, simply fitted one of the categories for exclusion – 'when a child is withdrawn by a parent in concerns over their work, attitude, progress or behaviour' – which is exactly what happened in Amy's case.

The principal who made the decision was fired soon afterwards, but it was too little, too late. Amy was devastated, crying every night in indignation. 'I've never been to a school that I came away happily from, ever,' she told *The Word*. 'With Sylvia Young's, it wasn't a monstrous, call my parents in, scream the school down thing. It was quiet and underhanded. I was devastated leaving there. Of all the schools, I would have stayed there happily.'

She continued wistfully: 'It's not a shit school. They've got a reputation because they are the best. It's not a pop star factory, they channel your creativity and you learn how to use it. For every precocious kid, there were kids who really worked… I learnt a lot of important things.'

Of the five schools she had already attended in her short life, the Sylvia Young School was the one that had built her character, pushed her as a performer and allowed her to flirt with acting and singing, the only thing she enjoyed about school life.

Amy's father Mitch later insisted that she had been expelled. However Sylvia told the *Daily Mail*: 'There is one persistent myth I would like to tackle. I want to make it absolutely clear that she was not expelled from the school… behind my back, the academic head rang Amy's mother and told her she would fail her GCSEs if she remained at the school as she was too easily distracted. I knew that wasn't the case, but as a result of the conversation, Amy's mother decided to send her elsewhere.'

She added: 'If I met her today I would give her a big hug and say "My dear Amy, you were never expelled. Instead you were admired and loved… I remember that you don't like being told what to do. But think back to the time when you wrote that what you really care about is people hearing your voice.'

The highlights of her time at the school included appearing in a TV production. She was awarded a small part on *The Fast Show*, a national TV series screened on November 21st 1997. As part of the comedy's Competitive Dad sketch, Amy appears in *A Midsummer Night's Dream* as the fairy Peasblossom, before her archetypal pushy stage dad, not content with heckling her from the side of the stage, gatecrashes and joins in the performance with his own rendition of how it ought to be done. Amy stages a stunned look of surprise to peals of laughter from the audience. She had been cast as a virginal figure, dressed in an elegant beige gypsy top and a long flowing skirt. However, the earlier performance of *Grease* had been much more congruent with Amy's fashion preferences. '[Since] I played in *Grease* as a kid at school… I've always worn bowling shirts and things like classic trench coats,' she told *Artist Direct* later.

However, Amy's parents were unimpressed with her acting gigs and instead wanted her to achieve good grades. Anxious that Amy would fail at school altogether, Janis immediately enrolled her daughter in a Mill Hill based Jewish private school for girls named The Mount. She desperately hoped that a religious all-girls environment would tame Amy's rebellious ways. However, this was not to be. Aged 15, the flamboyant teenager illegally got her first tattoo – a Betty Boop figure on her backside. It was to be the first of many.

Stifled by her time at the Mount and declaring that gender-segregated schools were 'backward' and 'boring', Amy left at 16, passing just five GCSEs. Her most enduring memory of the school was coming in every morning and seeing the distinctive brown uniform, which she believed made crowds at the school gates resemble '300 turds all coming in at once'.

She pressurised her parents to give her another chance in the world of fame and, GCSEs out of the way, they reluctantly agreed. She embarked on yet another stage school journey, this time at the Brit School in Croydon.

An unassuming and almost ugly plain brick building, it was housed in a poverty-stricken suburb on the outskirts of London. One nearby wall was plagued with green mould, whilst another had a 'Skeg List' scrawled across it of girls who the graffiti writer believed to be whores. What was more, the list of names was increasing daily.

Despite the dismal surroundings, Amy believed the school was a haven of creativity and it marked the spot where she was finally able to pursue her calling. She chose the musical theatre course, just as graduates such as Kate Nash, The Feeling, The Kooks, *X-Factor* winner Leona Lewis and soul songstress Adele had done. Yet, her parents believed, not one of them was as magical as Amy.

Equipped with state of the art mixing suites, rehearsal studios and industry-standard recording studios, the school was a fame seeker's playground – and best of all, it was state-funded, meaning that Amy could take advantage of the facilities absolutely free. She finally had all the tools for success at her fingertips. She trained in jazz dance, ballet dance and choreography alongside singing and classic theatre courses. Equal attention was paid to acting, choral singing and composition and Amy regularly wrote her own songs here.

However, the Brit School was nothing like Sylvia Young. Amy saw her new stage school counterparts as 'precocious' and 'spoilt kids' whereas Amy herself had often been described as 'working class'. She also decried the school for failing to provide enough male love interests. Ballet dancing and theatre were not typically male domains. Without men to titillate and tease – or at the very least fantasise about – Amy was thoroughly bored.

There was still a fair share of 'cheesy musicals like *Flashdance'* – which centres around a woman desperate to win a scholarship at a performing arts school – and ironically Amy's former crush Matt Willis went on to star in the very same show at London's Shaftesbury Theatre in 2010. Critics queried whether the musical, already very familiar from his performances at school, was truly a challenge for Matt.

Meanwhile Amy, as always, had stood out as a candidate for more diverse tunes. 'If there was a jazz song, or a sexy husky song, they'd give me the solo in that,' she recalled.

There was no uniform at the Brit School and students could address tutors by their first names. However this might give the marijuana loving Amy a false sense of security – far from the liberated haven it appeared, deep down it was like any other school where the rules were concerned. Nick Williams, the principal, told BBC Newsbeat: 'Our drugs policy would be the same as any other school… and we enforce that.'

Amy enjoyed performance but nonetheless she was desperately unhappy at the Brit School. She cursed its lack of male students, failed to relate to the female ones, and consequently was forced to find solace by spending lunchtimes alone, locked away in the music rooms. This voluntary imprisonment worked well for Amy, as it gave her the opportunity to practise her piano skills. Nevertheless, she chose to leave after just a few weeks.

Seeking something to fill her empty days, a brief flirtation with fashion followed. She took out a subscription to *Vogue*, which for the jobless and penny pinching Amy was one of her biggest weekly indulgences. Surviving on an allowance from her father, some might have wondered how Amy could ever afford the elitist designer threads she found inside the pages. Yet she devoured each issue, slowly transforming herself from grunger girl to designer label princess. However, although she had a keen interest in labels like Louis Vuitton, she had an archetypal Jewish thriftiness and she shunned the expensive originals in favour of market stall fakes.

Her approach to fashion remained unconventional. 'I don't want to be the prettiest or the sexiest,' she declared defiantly. 'I just want to be different and to look like me.'

Several dead-end jobs followed her time at the Brit School, including one in fashion retail. She also did a stint of reception work at both a tattoo parlour and a piercing clinic, both of which matched Amy's appetite for body modification. 'I did all kinds of work – I'm not a snob,' she recalled of her secretarial times.

However, she refused to toe the line there as well, as her ego stood in the way of most menial tasks. 'I was the sort of secretary where it'd be "Amy, make me a cup of tea." "No, fuck off!"' she told *Pop Justice*. '"You should call Rymans for their catalogue,"' she continued as an example. "Hang on, are you taking the piss out of me? You fucker! Really?" "Call Rymans, or…." "Are you being serious? Just go to another secretary and get her to order it."'

Unsurprisingly, Amy's work with the public did not last long. However, salvation came in the form of best friend Juliette and her father Jonathan Ashby. He secured Amy a job in his news agency *WENN* (World Entertainment News Network) which sent news bulletins out to MTV and the BBC among others, and she became a trainee music journalist.

She was first put to work as an office junior, running errands and making endless cups of tea. However when the agency found she had an aptitude for writing, she began to assist the journalists with research and before long she was writing her own news stories.

The agency released around 100 stories each day – but even the fast-paced frenzy of the news room wasn't enough to distract Amy from her first love, singing. According to some sources, barely an hour went by without succumbing to a melody – even when she was making the tea.

However, being on the bottom rung of the ladder in a company that employed 60 people often meant that singing her heart out had to take a back seat to hard graft. At first, Amy's attitude at the news network had been much the same as in her schooldays – she was rebellious, anti-authority and a perpetual daydreamer.

At times she inhabited a fantasy world of her own, one that consisted purely of men and music. She openly despised and sneered at what she called "corporate bullshit" and would hum distractedly to get her through the day.

It resembled a scene from Britney Spears's debut music video 'Hit Me Baby One More Time', where a bored school girl sits in a classroom and staring listlessly into space, her eyes fixed on the clock as she waits for the bell to ring so that she can escape and break into song.

The start of the video sees Britney incessantly tapping her heel against her desk as if paying tribute to some unheard rhythm, killing time until the song begins. This embryonic moment was symbolic of Amy's own path, sleepwalking through life and waiting for her big break. As she gradually took on more serious responsibilities at WENN, she started to knuckle down.

Unfortunately for Amy, there was another distraction in the shape of Chris Taylor, an older boss at the network who was seven years her senior. Chris ran the London Newswire Desk and was responsible for several employees, but underneath his professional stance, he too was hiding a passion for music.

With this in common, romance blossomed and Chris – a guitarist – would become her first serious boyfriend. Tall, thin and average looking, Chris was widely considered at WENN to be no Brad Pitt, but he was edgy and shunned the mainstream – qualities that would fit his personality with a quirky Amy's completely.

Yet again, hard work gave way to sexual fantasies, secret flirtations and eventually a clandestine affair for Amy. What was more, beneath the frivolity of workplace romance, it was becoming serious. "It was definitely a love thing," revealed one friend who worked with the pair. "They were obsessed with each other. One time I believe they even had sex in the staff toilets. Chris was always a serious type, and Amy brought out a hidden side to him. But there'd be arguments too. He was very sensitive, considerate, quite passive – to some girls he'd have been the perfect boyfriend, but Amy was addicted to danger. She'd actually rather have had an abusive man than a kind one because she thrived on the drama. That was just Amy – crazy."

The friend added, "In many ways, she wasn't a girly girl at all. She wasn't interested in love letters, flowers and romance. She didn't have time for it and regarded it as soppy. She didn't want the kid gloves approach either, like having doors opened for her. She had a very male attitude to affairs of the heart. She fell in love deeply, yes, but she wasn't the type to talk about her emotions. Yet in some ways, she WAS very female – and Chris, being very laid back, wouldn't take charge as she had hoped and let her enjoy that feminine role."

Amy, who saw herself as "a man's man", was becoming increasingly frustrated by her passivity. She saw him as perfect in every other way, but couldn't get past his effeminate nature in relationships. It wasn't just affairs of the heart that were floundering for Amy, either – her six month apprenticeship at WENN was about to come to an end too.

Towards the end of her stint with the agency, menial duties such as opening the mail, filing documents and making tea had been upgraded to bona fide journalism jobs – but it wasn't enough. She'd been occupying herself by creating short news stories and uploading them to the Internet, where they were syndicated worldwide. However, she quickly tired of reporting other people's successes, preferring to achieve her own. It was her name that she felt deserved to be in bright lights, yet she found herself writing congratulatory stories about rival singers instead. Perhaps it was time to make a clean break.

The restless Amy's resignation from her father's business did not distress Juliette – as she told *The Observer*, 'I'd have to shoot her boyfriend [for us to fall out.]' Indeed, the pair's friendship had remained solid even in spite of Amy's many changes of school. 'I always said that if Amy was a black man, we'd be married,' Juliette added. 'We're that close.'

However most were sad to see her go – and friends predicted a double-edged sword for a "tortured soul", both a bright future in music and a dark journey battling her personal demons.

However, it wasn't to be – and, based on his fleeting experience of her, Lloyd predicted a double-edged sword, both a bright future in music and a dark journey battling her personal demons.

Amy certainly had some demons during her time at WENN, but she was drawn to music to dull the pain. Consequently she turned her attention to performing again, encouraged by her ex school teacher Sylvia Young. She arranged for her to do an audition for the National Youth Jazz Orchestra, which she passed with flying colours.

In an interview with the author, the orchestra's founder Bill Ashton confirmed Amy's 'brilliance' but confessed to mixed feelings about her four months with them. 'She's probably the best singer, technically, that we've ever had. But she had no manners, no self-control, and was altogether a bit of a waste of time. I knew her very well – she was just an ill-mannered, surly North London girl, who only got worse.'

His first recollection of her was equally colourful. 'She came in and said "Ello, my name's Amy Winehouse, and that's a Jewish name." I knew she'd be good because her father's a North London Jewish taxi driver and they have immensely good musical taste – what goes into your head tends to come out of it.'

Yet Amy's single-mindedness and refusal to conform collided badly with the no nonsense approach of Bill, who believed in obedience and had previously been in the notoriously strict air force. He also found himself infuriated that – despite paying no attention to his instructions – she still excelled at live shows.

'She came in, sat in the corner and smoked – she didn't apply herself or involve herself at all – and then she came in and sang all of the songs perfectly.' He added 'One time, Amy went to sing the concert on the steps outside. There was a 22-piece band in there and she was sitting on the pub steps singing to herself. She had no interest at all in the group.'

She also raised eyebrows when she arrived 'bringing a young boy of about 16 along who she claimed was her manager'. It has since been speculated that the boy in question was fellow musician friend Tyler James. With him in tow, Amy wasn't paying much attention. 'She treated the whole thing as if it was her own year group,' Bill recalled incredulously.

'She was a graceless girl – and still is. She went to great extremes. She's exactly the same age as my daughter – and I wouldn't want her for a daughter.'

Despite his reservations about her manners, he was seduced by her musical excellence when he first heard her sing 'Who's Blue', a song composed by Bill himself.

Like Sylvia Young, he believed that Amy had effortless, innate talent that barely needed to be nurtured. While Sylvia had claimed that Amy barely needed to study for her GCSEs, Bill remembered Amy perfecting his songs in the space of just half an hour.

'One day I phoned her because the singer for that Saturday wasn't available and I asked her to come in. She said "But I don't know your repertoire!" I said I would get someone else then and she said "No, I'll do it, I'll learn the songs on the tube on my way over."'

Anyone else might have been nervous about her lack of preparation – Amy wasn't for the faint-hearted – but Bill knew her better than that. Despite her obvious distaste for her, he knew she had effortless musical intellect.

It was her other vices that concerned him the most. He believed that, influenced by the antics of Frank Sinatra who 'drank too much, smoked too much and thought he knew it all', Amy too was becoming a wild character. 'I only spoke to her mother once on the phone and she just said, helplessly, "Can you stop her smoking so much?"'

He later found it maddening to hear her comments on performing with his beloved group. The orchestra had appeared on the nationally screened Royal Variety Performance in 1978 and in 2010 had maintained its high standards with one musician being invited to play live at Buckingham Palace for its 45th birthday celebrations. However, the orchestra's pedigree was entirely lost on Amy.

'We gave Amy her first experience [of performance] and she described it as being in a pub performing to a room full of old people,' he exclaimed in disbelief.

Bill was very proud of his group and her remark had stung. The National Youth Jazz Orchestra had started out as a wish to form a band for just one person 'and his like', a talented pupil at the Rising Hill school in Islington, which has since closed. Bill was an accomplished musician who at the time had been teaching French there, alongside working as a tri-lingual translator.

During a stint of National Service in the air force, alongside learning Russian, Bill had armed himself with a saxophone and begged his band-master to teach him how to play. Thinking he'd be given a thorough grounding in the basics, he was astonished to hear the instant response 'You're in the band'. He protested that he couldn't read music, but was accepted with open arms nonetheless, and the rest was history.

Forming his own group at university later and then becoming a professional musician, he never forgot his roots in music. When he formed the orchestra for his French pupil, it was the start of a primarily instrumental based group with a smattering of vocals that would travel the world in the name of sharing their songs. The group performed in Portugal, Malta, America, Australia and Turkey to name just a few.

However, the restless Amy did not share his pride in the internationally acclaimed group. She once commented to him: 'I thought in coming here that I'd be doing standard songs, but I'm singing Bill Ashton songs. I wanted to write my own.'

By this point, the relationship between Amy and Bill had become a little frosty. He criticised her 'lack of decorum' and claimed that she had 'no respect for adults'. In spite of all this, he still felt that she was the best singer they'd had, with the possible exception of his favourite vocalist, Emma Smith.

Talking of the storm of interest after she became famous, Bill argued: 'She's one out of thousands of talented people, who people want to talk about because they've seen her in *The Sun* with her boobs hanging out. We're the best big band in the world, we've been around for 45 years and all people want to talk about is one surly, bad mannered, churlish North London Jewish girl.'

Bill might have been insistent on her conforming to the group, but Amy soon found an outlet for her individuality when she joined a group called the Bolsha Band. Instead of performing with them, Amy was able to take to the stage separately both before and after their sets, instead of getting lost in the crowd. It was an auspicious arrangement for more reasons than one, too. Their rehearsal spot, Mill Hill Studios in Mill Hill East, was also the location where Amy would meet the man who become a close friend and her formal backing vocalist, Ade Omotayo.

'Most of the guys in the band were doing A-Levels at that time, just playing to mates in North London,' he explained to the author. 'At my first rehearsal, I arrived before everyone else and, as the band walked through, I saw this tiny girl wearing a trilby to the side, showing a lot of attitude.'

That tiny girl turned out to be Amy Winehouse. The two hit it off instantly – in Ade's case, he couldn't help but love her as she continually showered him with praise for his voice. 'She loved praising my singing,' he recalled. 'She kept saying "You sound wicked!" Then when it came to her turn to sing, I was hoping I'd be able to give her a genuine compliment but it was way beyond that. It was special. For such a tiny person, her voice was absolutely incredible. 'I went home that night and told my brothers to look out for her. I was saying: "Watch for Amy Winehouse! She's gonna be massive!"'

Over the months that followed, the group covered numerous cover tracks – particularly by bands such as Stevie Wonder and Marvin Gaye. Amy even took to the stage with some of her own compositions, as the band toured anywhere they could around the country – but she was in for a disappointment. 'People didn't really respond to her songs because they didn't know them that well,' Ade revealed. 'She'd sometimes get a polite round of applause or at times nothing at all.'

Did the deafening silence crush Amy's spirit? According to Ade, while it might have been momentarily embarrassing, nothing could repress her enthusiasm for music. She loved to perform – and the pair continued to play with the band as often as possible. That was when a warm friendship began to develop.

'There was a mutual respect for our talents and our tastes were quite similar,' Ade explained. 'She had a great love for music at such a young age and that amazed me as well. She'd borrow my guitar and take out a 2p coin as a plectrum and go "I wanna jam, let's jam!"'

As well as impromptu jamming sessions, Amy also shared with him her crusade against TV talent shows. She felt that they gave a select few accolades if they fitted the pop star mould but robbed the average would-be singer of a chance of success. 'We often critiqued modern day acts we liked or didn't like, but Amy saw Pop Idol and shows like that for what they were,' Ade recalled. 'It was just a TV show for her, but she did feel that not enough talent was being rewarded – she felt it was entertainment. That's why later, most of the people in her band were handpicked by her and were people she thought deserved to be heard and discovered.'

She and Ade would play music and talk about acts they admired several times a week – and his affection for her grew. 'She was an impish character, with so much energy, always hopping about – but she was actually very loving,' he recalled. 'She had a bit of attitude and a very short fuse though. I just remember she always used to like smoking weed and drinking alcopops and I'd always see her with a bottle of WKD.'

She could also add to the list of attributes a biting sense of humour. 'One time in Brighton on stage, the drummer was drumming really fast and she just stopped him before he had a chance to get into the song and went "Frank, slow down – that's why you're single!"' Ade chuckled. 'That's Amy – very, very quick-witted.'

In fact, her jokey putdown was just one in a long list of quick-witted conquests. She'd scorned Bill Ashton's NYJO to the point that he turned purple with rage and ridiculed TV talent shows, becoming the type of person that Simon Cowell might, with a dramatic roll of his eyes, have declared 'a nightmare to work with'. Amy knew it, though – and she loved it. In fact, in spite of her irrepressible naughty streak, she was already heading for her big break in music. When it all took shape, she'd been almost ready to give up.

For one thing, she'd been consumed by fears over her mother's worsening health. Although no-one knew why, it was beginning to deteriorate rapidly and, as an unconventional family holiday comprising of both Janis and Mitch's new wife Jane would prove, things were about to come to a head.

Janis, who'd been suffering from the painful symptoms of undiagnosed multiple sclerosis (MS) since before Amy was born, found that for the duration of the ten day break in Italy, she could barely stand up. She was nauseous, dizzy and found it increasingly difficult to control her limbs. Humiliatingly, as her former love rival showed off a series of glamorous dresses, she struggled just to be mobile. Initially she dismissed her symptoms as a bad case of flu, but by the end of the holiday, things had worsened to the extent that she could no longer scale the steps to disembark from the aeroplane. As they touched down in Stansted Airport, she sank to her knees and collapsed.

A horrified Amy raced to help her mother up, but the complications were worse than she'd imagined. This was no mere dizzy spell - on her return home, she'd finally be diagnosed with MS. A degenerative muscular disease, no-one could predict whether she'd lead a normal life for years or whether she'd be confined to a wheelchair within weeks. There were no concrete rules.

A family girl at heart, Amy devoted herself to taking care of her mother – who was becoming increasingly immobile as the condition took hold – and her dreams of musical success slowly began to slip away.

Despite having been desperate to make stage school, she was beginning to abandon music as a full time career. In fact, she was seriously considering becoming a roller waitress instead.

She had decided against sending out demos, telling the *Belfast Telegraph*: 'I wouldn't bother sending anybody your tape. People get tapes by the sack load and a lot of the time they don't care.'

Amy was right. Not only was the music industry notoriously difficult to break into, especially for an artist without management, but the policy of most record companies was to refuse to accept unsolicited demo tapes. Many required a known agent or manager who represented the artist to submit the demo on their behalf. In fact for that matter, Island Records, the company Amy ultimately signed with, state on their website: 'If you're determined to make sure we hear your music, we would have to receive it from a recognized lawyer or manager, as we don't accept unsolicited demos.'

Amy clearly needed a helping hand and, one weekend when performing with the National Youth Jazz Orchestra, she got it. Tyler James, one of her best friends from the Sylvia Young School, had put in a word in for Amy at his management company, 19. Despite the fact that young Tyler had not so much as clinched a record deal yet, his influence was enough to persuade the company to listen to her extraordinary voice and manager Nick Godwin was delighted with what he heard.

By coincidence, shortly afterwards, 19 contacted Bill Ashton asking him to recommend some of his singers. 'This is a multi-million pound company and they're asking me for arrangements,' Bill recalled incredulously. 'I suggested some singers and, as an afterthought, said "I'll give you Amy – you deserve each other" – as they were ill-mannered too.'He added 'They never even said out of courtesy "Do you want a glass of wine?" but just came and scribbled a list of names down.'

As a result of that meeting, two reps – Nick Godwin and Nick Shymansky – made their way down to the National Youth Jazz Orchestra, allegedly accompanied by CEO Simon Fuller, for a second encounter with the young Amy Winehouse.

The pioneering force behind both the Spice Girls and the lucrative TV series *Pop Idol*, Simon Fuller of 19 was the manager for only the most up and coming young stars. *Pop Idol* had been syndicated to dozens of different countries by the time he met Amy, so his interest was pedigree indeed. Plus he already managed Will Young and S Club 7, who had become overnight superstars. The opportunity was clear, but would there be a personality clash?

Unlike his other protégé, the headstrong 17 year old already had song writing experience and a larger than life personality. She was stubborn, outspoken and defiant. In fact, some might say she was the complete antithesis of the manufactured pop acts Fuller had enjoyed success with thus far. Had she told him she was trouble?

Amy saw his artists as desperately fame hungry manufactured pop acts, willing to sacrifice their individuality and integrity for a fleeting chance of chart success. What's more, she wasn't afraid to say so. According to Amy, the Spice Girls, whose first hit Wannabe had hit the Number 1 spot in 34 different countries thanks to Fuller's management, were 'diabolical'. She also believed TV shows aimed at discovering new talent – *Pop Idol* inclusive – were 'damaging'.

She then dismissed how Fuller might feel about her belittling his acts by audaciously implying he was wealthy enough to take the risk. 'I don't think he cares if he gets a return on me,' she chuckled later. 'He's smart enough to know he can't fuck with me.'

For all of these reasons, Amy was reluctant to seal the deal. Fuller's right hand men Nick Shymansky and Nick Godwin had been blown away by her jazz performance and had been pursuing her ever since, but she was cautious. 'I wouldn't sign for a year,' she revealed, 'because I was convinced they would say something like "You can completely make the album you want to make" and then, as soon as I'd signed, go "Right, this is Simon, he's going to style you, he's going to give you a perma-tan and hair like his!"' She paused for effect, before dissolving into giggles at her manager's 'Ken-doll' appearance.

Her honesty, cheerful disregard for protocol and refusal to court the companies who offered her success made Amy a terrifying prospect for some, but for Fuller it seemed to make her all the more alluring.

While she was dangling them on a string, Amy jetted off to China with drummer Brad Webb of Bill Ashton's second band NYJO2, where she was working on the rhythm section. Brad would later go on to join the Jamie Cullum band. It was a successful performance but, remembering how much she longed to write and record her own songs, she came back to the UK keen to seal the deal with 19. On her return, a friend of Amy's allegedly told her in reference to the Spice Girls, 'Fuller gave a band that was quite frankly atrocious mass market popularity – what could he do for you? It would be crazy not to sign.'

At the age of 18, Amy finally swallowed her embarrassment at being connected to the Spice Girls and signed on the dotted line to Brilliant 19, a subsidiary of the parent company 19 Management. On hearing her new management claim that Amy was extremely talented and had a strong chance of success, bewildered father Mitch blurted out: 'Is she?' However, there was no doubt in Fuller's mind and the ink had barely dried on the contract before Nick Shymansky had encouraged her to drop into the studio and start recording. Thus began a new chapter in Amy's life.

CHAPTER 3

After receiving Amy's musical hand in marriage, 19 was keen to introduce her to key players in the industry – ones who could make or break her first album. They needed little persuasion as, for those in the know, Amy's name had been on everyone's lips.

What was wowing everyone about Amy Winehouse was her unique ability to mix vintage jazz classics with contemporary street sounds. That gave her an old-world edge whilst still guaranteeing her the chance of mass-market appeal. In contrast to niche artists like Norah Jones who achieved short-lived success in the commercial market, it was believed that Amy could command long-term success by writing for the mainstream.

Manager Nick Shymansky knew he needed to get Amy into the studio fast, as he was 'working with gold-dust'. Moreover he feared her other career plans. 'I couldn't believe how good she was,' he recalled, '[but] I asked Amy what she wanted to do with her life and she said she wanted to be a waitress.' In his role of manager, Nick was understandably appalled by the news that she intended to 'fritter her life away' as a roller waitress and he immediately set about putting the time she had spent in stage school to good use.

He sought the perfect producer for her to initially experiment with and his prayers were answered in the form of north-west Londoner Major. He was new blood on the production scene, but Nick needn't have worried. Major clicked with Amy instantly because they shared the same musical diet – Amy had listened to her father's Sinatra records alongside the hip-hop beats that were popular with her class-mates and liked to combine the two. Major also had extensive experience of the new stuff, as he'd toured the country as a DJ and MC and had successfully put on a party for R & B crooner P Diddy. He was in touch with the streets, which was important- without that link to modern music, the finicky Amy might have ridiculed him. Yet whilst he might have passed the test on having the modern touch, he also understood Amy's range of older influences and – like her – was loathe to limit himself to just one genre. It was a match made in heaven.

Nick and Major arranged to meet up on September 11th 2001 to discuss Amy's sound, but it was a date they were to remember for all the wrong reasons. It was the day that extremist Muslim fundamentalists would set fire to the twin towers of New York's World Trade Center, killing 2752 victims. The bombings marked war on the west and although Amy and her people were safely in the UK, many Londoners were tearful and traumatised, fearing a similar attack back home.

Yet as soon as Nick played Major some samples of Amy's recording voice that day, it wasn't just the New York skyline that had burst into flames, but Major's inspiration. He instantly accepted the invitation to work with her.

Less than a week later, Major was welcoming Amy into his home studio in Kensal Rise. The two selected around four tracks that were the most representative of Amy's sound and agreed to work on them before recording them as demos.

'Alcoholic Logic' was the first of these to come to fruition. It had first come to life on a rickety National Rail train from Southampton to London one Monday morning, underwear discarded in her bag as Amy ended a party-fuelled weekend to visit Major and begin the recordings. It simply described the events of her weekend, having an impulsive one night stand with a 'one of a kind' man, her thoughts blurred by 'alcoholic logic' and hoping he will get her number so that they can take the experience further. Some of the lyrics included: 'As I write this on the train, Victoria's Secret in my bag, and my thighs ache again, last night tips into my mind.'

She continued that while her friend had tried in vain to stop her, her unfamiliar surroundings had left her keen to try something new. While the man in question wasn't her type, there was something about him that prompted her to "subconsciously on purpose" leave her coat behind.

This light-hearted girlish take on events and her frank depiction of what they meant to her was exactly what Major was looking for and from the infant stages of her feverish scribbling on the train, the final version was committed to tape within half an hour.

She was demonstrating the effortless ability that producers would come to know Amy for and would rave about time and again. Her ability to complete a tune within minutes astonished Major as much as Bill Ashton before him. Both had been won over.

Another song, 'When My Eyes', was equally personal, offering an insight into the mindset of an as yet unsigned Amy. 'Waitress on skates in training' was in the first verse, a nod to Amy's early aspirations to be a roller waitress, and showed how early the song had been composed. The lyrics 'Sinatra is always singing and you do all the clinging' were a nod to Chris, the over-emotional boyfriend who would also appear in Stronger than Me and the passion fuelled and anger fuelled nights they spent together to the sound track of the Sinatra album he had bought for her.

Towards the end, the line: 'When I drop it lyrically, words evolve generically and I don't ever need to collapse in tears' is one of the earliest indications that music was therapeutic for her. Extremely flowery and poetic, but as yet lacking a clear structure, it nonetheless 'bursted with raw talent' and showed her managers that they had a candidate well worth honing.

Ian Barter, another friend of Nick Shymansky's, also worked with Amy on several songs. One, 'Jewel', was about 'old jazz tunes from the 50s and her take on them', whilst 'Lucky Trainers', featuring a materialistic girl, was 'about being a shopaholic'. Others included 'Life Lesson', 'Trilby' and 'Matter of Time'.

Ian had worked with Paloma Faith, Neneh Cherry, Darius and later X-Factor hopeful Katie Waissel ('not a patch on Amy vocally!') but there was something different about Amy. Seduced by her rendition of songs like George Gershwin's Summertime and even more impressed by her own lyrical compositions, he threw himself into the role of working with her 'wholeheartedly'.

'Recording wise I would write the music and she would write lyrics and melody over the top on every track,' he told the author. 'I was quite surprised how, at 17 years old, when we first worked together, how good she was at lyrics and yeah, a phenomenal singer! But I guess there was inexperience in other areas, such as she would write really long verses!'

That sentiment was shared by Nick Godwin the first time he heard her work, who described the songs as 'eight or nine minute poems' with 'quite awkward guitar playing'.

Yet Ian was only too happy to remedy that, expanding her knowledge by teaching her jazz guitar. 'She could play a little already but she wanted to learn jazz chords,' he explained. 'Her management always wanted me to get her to put down the guitar, but she never wanted to!' Indeed, Amy ended up playing guitar on six of the tracks of the finished album.

After the demos were complete, Major let one of his best friends in the industry in on the secret, playing Alcoholic Logic to him over the phone. Darcus Beese, a senior A & R manager at Island Records, was enchanted the moment he heard it. The rhymes apparently showed a slight immaturity and a raw unpolished sound but, in Beese's eyes, the potential was glaringly obvious. There was by now a bidding war to be the first to sign Amy and, according to Mitch, 'five or six record companies' were already queuing up for the privilege. Darcus knew he had to act fast. He arranged a covert meeting with Amy via Major to propel himself to the front of that queue.

The Times had listed Darcus as one of the UK's 'Top 10 Star Makers', claiming that after snapping up pop group the Sugababes, he had 'helped give them a life span beyond all expectations'. Despite the trace of sarcasm in that sentiment, the message was clear – and as Darcus's colleague at Island, Lucian Grange, had made the number one spot on that list, Amy couldn't have placed her talent in better hands. Yet Darcus wasn't prepared to leave the possibility of a musical union to chance.

Unable to get the demos out of his mind and convinced her management had been 'keeping her a secret', Darcus surreptitiously sneaked into the 19 offices to make contact himself. 'I'd never heard a woman who lyrically put the shit together like she did,' he recalled to US magazine *Spin*, 'and I knew I had to have her.'

While the finishing touches were being put on the deal with Island, Amy was working hard in Mayfair Studios, west London, with two promising young songwriters who would help prepare for the possibility of a debut album.

Matt Rowe and Stefan Skarbek were experienced producers who had enjoyed enormous success, between them crafting chart-topping songs for Sophie Ellis Bextor, the Spice Girls, the Sugababes and East 17. However, despite their reputation, Amy was less than thrilled. On paper, she was far from keen to have the company of bubble gum pop producers in the studio. It was a genre she wanted to distance herself from.

The two were joined by another song-writer called Felix Howard, who had entered the business via TV presenting and modelling. Amy was equally skeptical about his 'disposable pop' past. He had first shot to fame in 1998 when he appeared in Madonna's video for the single 'Open Your Heart'. He then became a presenter on the Channel 4 music show *The Tube*, which received very mixed reactions. One anonymous viewer complained on an internet forum: 'He had a very short-lived career.... even by *The Tube's* incredibly low standards of professionalism, he was too awful to be allowed to continue, having babbled nonsense... and bemused Paul McCartney. No matter how "cute" he may have been, 13-year-old boys do not make good music presenters.'

When he entered the world of song-writing, he began producing for artists such as Kylie Minogue and Holly Valance. Amy was dubious - she might have adored Kylie as a child but she now yearned to be taken seriously as a singer and she felt connections with Kylie might not be the best way to achieve that.

However, whilst Amy was unsure, Felix was far from it. Brimming with enthusiasm, he told *The Guardian* 'When she showed up for her first session, she was wearing a pair of jeans that had completely fallen apart with 'I Love Sinatra' embroidered on the arse. That's so Amy - I just fell in love with her.' He also knew she was in a different league from his former protégé, adding, 'She has the power to scare the shit out of some very seasoned jazz people. I was doing her session with some very serious players, and when she started singing, they were like "Jesus Christ!"'

His positivity paid off and the trio won Amy over. They officially began their studio sessions in the spring of 2002. One of the locations for writing was the legendary Chateau Marmont in Los Angeles, following a concert there. The hotel was a fairytale castle cut into the hillside – so close to and yet so disconnected from the chaos and writhing traffic of the Sunset Strip below. Despite its bustling location, perched up in the Hollywood Hills, it was as secluded as they came.

However the hotel suited Amy's creative, rebellious and at times self-destructive streak down to a T and, with her later lifestyle in mind, it was an apt place for her to launch her decadent spirit and write some demos. The founder of film company Columbia Pictures, Harry Cohn, once said, 'If you must get into trouble, do it at the Chateau Marmont', while the hotel review website Frank Camel praised: 'This IS the world's number one rock and roll hotel. It may not have seen more celebrity excess and self destruction than Caligula's boudoir, but it's a close run contest.'

'That place induces decadence,' Stefan shuddered to the author in memory of it, 'and I try to stay away from it as often as possible… [but] Amy is a classic self-sabotager. The edge is where the magic is.'

From the outside, it might have seemed innocent, resembling a perfectly packaged Disneyland castle, or a Hollywood Neuschwanstein, but within its four walls, it breathed glamour, decadence and rock and roll. At this point, as a fresh-faced and voluptuous 18-year-old, Amy was innocent on the outside too, although –according to Stefan Skarbek – the cracks were already beginning to show. He told the author: 'I wasn't surprised to hear about her later drug problems – there were already indications of it when I knew her.'

The hotel quickly became one of Amy's favourites, unsurprisingly given its rich history. Complete with a smoky, musically buzzing jazz bar, the website claimed it was 'mindful of history, but always in the moment – it is as contemporary as tomorrow morning'. With that in mind, the hotel was just like Amy herself, complementing her mixture of modern, 21st century style and husky old school jazz sound.

Chateau Marmont was also a haven for aspiring libertines and Amy certainly fitted that description. The hotel was Courtney Love's abode of choice when she surfaced from her bedroom for an interview with a newspaper high on a cocktail of alcohol and anti-depressants – and completely naked. It was the location where Led Zeppelin rode into the lobby on motorbikes to the tune of adoring groupies' screams. Actor James Dean made a dramatic entrance to the auditions for *Rebel Without A Cause* – by leaping in through an open window. Jim Morrison had a near death experience, losing 'the eighth of my nine lives' when he fell from the roof of the property. The Red Hot Chilli Peppers used their suite as a studio to record hit song 'By the Way', while band member John Frusciante took part in an interview while in residence that would see him described as 'a skeleton with thin skin'. Arms riddled with heroin track marks, he was banned from the hotel altogether by the next day.

The hotel's darker side further emerged when musician, actor and comedian John Belushi died of a drug overdose in one of the Bungalows, and a fashion photographer had a drug induced fatal car crash in its driveway. The hotel was also famed for its obsessive love trysts – according to Johnny Depp, he and Kate Moss christened nearly every room with their love-making. Meanwhile actress Vivien Leigh plastered her suite from head to foot with photographs of estranged husband Lawrence Olivier. This addictive love affair mirrored an experience that Amy would later face with equally estranged husband Blake.

In more recent times, the hotspot was Lindsay Lohan's first night out after leaving rehab – and she loved it so much, she didn't leave until she had found a home of her own just down the road. Britney Spears was ejected from the hotel for smearing gourmet food across her face in a style that onlookers deemed would even embarrass unruly children in a fast food joint. Other celebrity guests over the years included Marilyn Monroe, Errol Flynn, Colin Farrell, Christina Ricci and John Lennon with Yoko Ono.

It was a love nest for celebrity couples, a millionaire's hideaway for shamelessly bad behaviour and a place for creative people to indulge in their most hedonistic fantasies while they worked at their craft. Boasting excess at both its best and its worst, it was a place where creative flames would both ignite and burn out – and despite the death and debauchery, some of the most creative writers in the world had composed songs while in residence there, concurrently battling their penchant for danger. Lily Allen wrote 'Batman, Guess Who?' at the hotel, while Judy Garland sang by the lobby's grand piano, exclaiming, 'Let's just sing real loud!' That was exactly what Amy hoped to do.

The website said, 'This great castle on the hill is the set of a film waiting for someone to call "action". This is the place where things happen.' It was a location of heart-break, hedonism and decadence – and Amy was right in the midst of it.

As the location for her first serious song-writing endeavours, it was as good a place as any for her to spread her wings. The film director Sofia Coppola said of her stay there, 'It's a rite of passage – it is linked with making it… while showing that you're still down to earth.'

This was exactly where Amy was at right now. She'd been given the opportunity of a lifetime in the form of a record deal, but she was still an ordinary girl without pretenses. Stefan was also new to the song-writing process. 'I was just out of school and stumbling into situations without experience,' he recalled. Yet the pair quickly made up for in enthusiasm anything they lacked in expertise. Their sessions at the Chateau Marmont, accompanied by Courtney Love and a sprinkling of other celebrities, were among the most enjoyable sessions of all. 'My last enduring memory of Amy is of the lift door closing at Chateau Marmont… at 6am while she was strumming a song we'd written and begging me not to go.'

Unfortunately not all of their studio locations were as glamorous. It was back in rainy England that the group wrote 'I'm a Monkey Not A Boy', inspired by a trip to the primate section of the zoo. 'We ran out of ideas in the studio in Primrose Hill and London Zoo isn't far, so we went there,' Stefan said. 'It was raining terribly. All the animals were hiding away and Amy kept rattling the cages. We went into the monkey enclosure and she was singing at them and I said 'You're a monkey, not a girl', then we changed it and wrote it up later that day. It was my favourite song, but it never got released.'

In those early days, whilst Amy and her team worked hard, they also played hard. Typical afternoons would consist of Amy enthusiastically dragging her producers around Camden on 'days out'. The expeditions were not all play, as the foursome found vintage records in charity shops to listen to and inspire their subsequent recordings. They also found time for some naughtiness, ending in Amy's arrest and removal to a police station. 'Amy flashed a policeman on Primrose Hill and got taken away,' chuckled Stefan. 'She struck me as funny, smart, sassy and pretty bitchy - a bit of an owl in the body of a porcelain doll. A pretty dirty one though.'

Despite spending lazy days in the pub, at the zoo, or drinking cocktails on Primrose Hill, the group would then head to the studio and create entire songs in a matter of moments, tricking her managers into believing they had been working on them all week. Some of these songs included 'The Ambulance Man', a tribute to Amy's grandmother who had been taken ill, and 'Ease Up On Me', an honest account of the pressure of troubled relationships.

Meanwhile, 'October Song' was a tribute to Amy's dearly departed pet bird, who died in October 2001. Overwhelmed by the fast-paced world of showbiz, Amy had forgotten to feed the canary before leaving home for a weekend away in Southampton. Her career was just starting to take shape and it wasn't until after her first studio session with Major the following Monday that Amy finally returned home to find the bird lifeless in its cage.

Consumed with guilt at the canary's unfortunate demise, Amy buried her in a Chanel sunglasses case, claiming that her avian friend 'had to depart in style'. Stefan Skarbek reassured her that the bird had died of natural causes, whilst *The Times* had a very different theory on the matter. It said: 'Winehouse insists that the bird, which she would fasten with her fierce, dark eyes while singing old standards "very slow and loud" in the bedroom they shared, died of natural causes. But after listening to [her] stripped-down, jazzy dissections of relationships, sexual betrayal and romantic jealousy, it is tempting to conclude that the poor thing one day saw Winehouse bearing down on her yet again and simply opted for the easy way out.'

'Amy Amy Amy', meanwhile, was a tale of frivolous fun in the workplace. Unable to concentrate on her former job as a journalist at *WENN* due to the distractions of her older boyfriend Chris, a hormone-ridden

Amy was prone to fantasising about the flesh of her new crush. The chorus line first took shape when Amy was later complaining to her producers about her fraught relationship with the same man and her desire to dump him. Stefan expressed his fatherly concern by groaning 'Amy, Amy, Amy!' and a new song was born.

'Amy didn't like that song,' he added, 'probably because it's weird to sing your own name three times.' However Stefan had wanted to capture this youthful side to Amy on CD, before her growing maturity made her too 'serious and intense'. 'They waited too long to release the album,' he lamented, 'and she lost her youthfulness. 'I'm A Monkey Not A Boy' and many other songs we did didn't make the cut. I think she got a bit serious and we never really saw her funny nature after that.'

The delay was due, of course, to tension and rivalry within the studio. Not only did Amy resent the pop emphasis of her management, but the producers themselves had some power struggles. 'Simon Fuller was a pop pop pop man,' Stefan recalled. She didn't like that and probably wondered why she was working with the Spice Girls producer. She wasn't happy and unfortunately I was just a guest at the table and didn't have the power to change a thing.' However he did offer his sympathies. Despite his back catalogue including some pop CDs, he secretly shared Amy's ambivalence for the genre. 'I worked with all the Spice Girls independently and don't know what I was thinking,' he confessed. 'I think I was stoned.'

Amongst the Spice Girls fans in the studio, Stefan stood out and became a good friend to Amy. He advised her to work with 'anyone but Kanye West', an artist that he felt was too 'predictable'. 'We had a lot of fun, we had a no regard for convention and in the nicest possible way, looked down on the world, usually through a White Russian or two. [Like me], Amy was not there to please anyone and didn't really care what people said or thought… however there was, as with most aspects of Amy, more to her than meets the eye.'

Stefan saw through the tough, ballsy rock chick that was her public face in her teenage years to the sensitive, insecure young woman within, trying to find her way. 'Amy is an old soul with the same problems any growing person has. She just could rise above them but they still were there,' he recalled. She is sensitive but can channel that into many emotions – that's song-writing.'

Other tensions in the studio involved negotiating with Matt Rowe, a co producer who loathed sharing the tracks with others. 'We had a rough patch because Matt felt the production was being taken away from him… they had multiple studios and producers and Matt's feelings got hurt a little,' Stefan continued. 'In hindsight, I wish he'd just buckled in and let the fresh blood in – we would have ended up working on 80% of the record had that been the case. Matt and Amy were kinda like trying to put a square through a circle.'

Another studio worker, who did not wish to be named, revealed: 'Matt wouldn't let his ego take a back seat. If he'd been willing to compromise, he'd have been working with Amy right through to the end.'

However, as the months passed, Amy's song-writing evolved. She wanted to be known for being a credible artist, not for songs about monkeys and shopping addictions. She wanted to get down to the nitty-gritty of why she really wrote music and why she sang - as a sophisticated form of pain relief, handling diverse emotions of heartbreak and hurt. If she was an entertainer, she wanted to be a meaningful one. She had once said, 'Dido is background music - the background to death' - and indeed, Amy would rather die than not make soul music.

The record company agreed. There had been three producers for one set of songs, all vying to take the music in different directions - yet ironically none of these visions totally matched Amy's. The result was chaos - and questions were raised about the quality of her demos. It was time, then, to say goodbye to the light-hearted popular music pioneered by Skarbek, Rowe and Howard, and to try again to make the ideal debut album.

Searching further afield for the perfect producer, Amy's management connected with Miami-based Salaam Remi, who was renowned for having some of the most sophisticated recording equipment in the USA. Better still, he was in tune with Amy's street vibe, having worked with Nas, one of her favourite artists of all time. After flying to Florida to meet him, Amy shared their enthusiasm.

It finally seemed as though things were looking up for Amy. What was more, her managers had secured her a lucrative publishing deal with EMI. No longer relying on her father for hand-outs, Amy could be financially independent. She received a £50,000 advance and, the moment the cheque cleared, arranged to move into a flat in Camden with her best friend Juliette. Rebelling against her father by shunning work in his news agency empire, Juliette was now an overworked telesales marketer, but she still lived for music in her spare time.

She and Amy were living in the heart of north London's Camden Town. A paradise for alternative people, the scent of fried noodles from Chinese takeaway stalls competed with the sound of death metal, rap and reggae blaring out from every shop doorway. This part of the city also smelt of leather, cigarettes and, if one ventured close enough, the algae-sodden aroma of the river.

Camden played host to every type of person imaginable - as long as they were different. With its tattoo studios, piercing parlours, record shops, live music venues, gothic clothes fairs, vintage thrift stores and stalls dedicated just to the knee high socks that Amy had told the media were her top accessory for spicing it up in the bedroom, Camden suited her down to a T.

It was all black eyeliner and unconventional 40s fashion from the same era as Amy's voice. Yet after dark, there was a serious element to Camden's streets where, alongside the pounding beats of late night clubs, drugs ranging from marijuana to heroin were freely peddled on corners. Amy and Juliette often partook in the former. 'Amy worked hard and smoked hard,' an anonymous friend told the author. 'After a day in the studio, she'd always like to unwind with some weed.'

Inspired by her surroundings and the joy of getting high with her favourite childhood buddy, Amy began to pen a new song called 'Best Friends'. 'That's about the time [Juliette and I] first lived together,' she recalled to *The Observer*. 'It's like, I hate you but I love you. The tempestuous times have had the effect of making us closer.'

The song charted the spiral of their friendship from a strong bond to resentment and back again. 'I had love for you when I was four,' Amy crooned into a microphone one night when trying to vent some post-argument frustrations, 'and there's no-one I wanna smoke with more.' Yet

who never sings the same tune the same way twice. Each performance is a different perspective on the song depending on the mood they are in.'

Not only did Jack look up to Amy's vocal prowess, but he also appreciated the part she played in kickstarting his career, transforming him from an enthusiastic amateur at the tender age of 15 to a fully fledged producer whose protégé had a record deal. He recalled: 'If it wasn't for Amy, I would never have broken into the industry as young as I did. After we did the session with John, I got a call from Amy's manager at the time, Nick Shymansky, asking me to come in for a meeting. Amy took me and we met in Pizza Express at Battersea. Nick told me how he believed in John as an artist and wanted to help us develop the project. Amy was very instrumental in using her influence in the industry to help us get things off the ground and eventually John got a record deal with Sony... I signed a publishing deal at the age of 15. If it wasn't for Amy's belief in me at first, I would never have had the opportunity.'

Amy had also been instrumental, of course, in introducing John to the contacts he needed to start out in the business. The dream he'd had in his bedroom of becoming an artist was now a reality. The subjects he tackled in his music, such as a thorny childhood, were meaningful to Amy and she was not just on the same wavelength but fully supportive. Perhaps it was inevitable, given how much they'd opened up to each other, that a sexual element would creep into their attraction.

Both just 18 at the time, Amy and John found they had a lot in common, although bizarrely Amy claimed she respected him too much to move into the realm of romance. Both had been hurt in their lives and she valued him not just as a sexual partner but as a soul mate with whom she could make tunes.

'There is definitely a chemistry between us,' she confirmed to *The Guardian*. 'There's not a lot of men who make me feel shy but he does. I can have sex with my boyfriend, I can have sex with John. I can make a tune with John but I couldn't make a tune with my boyfriend... it's like a deeper connection. I think I'm closer to him than I could be with any partner.'

It was no surprise, then, that Amy defended him with fierce loyalty when he failed to make the grade musically. Feeling he had strong potential, Amy had introduced him to 19 Management, which resulted in the young rapper being signed. However it was debatable whether that had been a wise decision. Despite early attention from the *NME*, John struggled to gain credibility in the hip-hop world, which often sneered at the opinions of mainstream music tabloids. The website *UK Hip-Hop* claimed his second single 'Put Your Hands Up' was 'entirely disposable', while *Designer* magazine was equally unimpressed when one of their reviewers caught him live, citing him 'the most atrocious crime committed to hip-hop ever – he takes all the worst elements of every single bad hip-pop record and multiplies them by a zillion'.

Good press was almost non-existent for John, but he had the ferocious Amy on hand to be his metaphorical bodyguard. She claimed she hated seeing him 'lazily compared to Eminem' simply because the two shared the then unlikely combination of a Caucasian skin tone and a career in rapping.

John and Amy had their own controversial views about music and she had helped him craft an early song, 'Pop Idle', which poked fun at 'talentless' artists who take part in shows such as *Pop Idol* and *Britain's Got Talent*. 'There was an obscene video to go along with it too,' Jack recalled.

John felt himself lucky that her anger never turned on him, remarking of Amy's ballsy attitude: 'If you say something that pisses her off, she'll eat you alive.' Fortunately John had never been the victim of one of Amy's mood swings. Her time with him not only helped him to further his own career, but also shaped Amy's own musical aspirations, giving her a clearer idea of the artist she ultimately wanted to be. Touched by his honesty in the songs, she already knew one thing – she wanted to match that candour and write music not for entertainment but from the heart. This was no *Pop Idol* contestant.

She also had valuable experience in the form of her first professional live show, aside from a very short performance at the East Finchley Fair, at the Torrington in North Finchley. The tiny pub was highly regarded by locals as a place to watch up and coming undiscovered talent, before its closure in 2004. A reveller wrote of its demise on London website *Beer in the Evening*, claiming: 'This was one of the few real pubs in Finchley, with a back room which was almost an institution, the kind of place where you'd go to see your mates' bands play and where they used to have record sales. It's now turned into yet another Starbucks. Who the hell gave planning permission for that?' Yet two years earlier, the low-key pub that revellers had adored had still been very much in action.

Photographs from the night depicted an elegantly dressed Amy in a beige 40s style evening dress, clutching her purse anxiously as she arrived at the venue. Others from later in the evening showed her back at home – young, fresh-faced and without a care in the world, clad in navy blue ripped tracksuit bottoms.

The then clean living Amy's humble beginnings saw her perform stone-cold sober. Nick Godwin allegedly said of those early shows: 'She never performed drunk or even tired… when she went home, she'd drink water then go to bed.' He added: 'Amy used to laugh at anyone who took Class A drugs.'

By this time, fuelled by the highs of first time live performance, Amy was ready to begin recording in earnest. Her management accordingly made enquiries. Salaam Remi, a producer with an enterprising rap background and a youthful modern approach – he was just 30 when he first heard Amy's work – was keen to welcome her back to his studio, Creative Space. He had to compete for her attentions with Gordon Williams – also known as Commissioner Gordon – who had been approached to handle her in New Jersey. The album would be divided between the two producers, meaning Amy's two mentors were a five hour flight away from each other. Having just finalised her contract, Amy was now officially signed to Island Records and was free to absorb herself with the studio sessions.

No longer a fledgling artist, new to the studio and experimenting with different beats, Amy was done with demos and was ready once and for all to make her first ever studio album.

CHAPTER 4

In the final recordings, Amy continued to struggle with her overwhelming desire for creative control. Unlike Fuller's previous conquests, she was no star-struck teenager – and she expected to get her own way. She envied artists like Timbaland, producers turned performers, who could create, mix and mould the same songs they sang on, to their own specification. Amy strived for that level of dominion in her own work.

The cheeky lyric on Timbaland's album *Shock Value* 'I'm a real producer and you're just a piano man' seemed to sum up Amy's attitude to the musicians and writers she shared the studio with. Yet while she craved the same unconditional control, she lacked the experience of her producers in creating a hit record and so, reluctantly, had to take a step back and let them work their magic.

This arrangement was not without difficulty. One of the issues was that Amy's management wanted her to sing catchy pop choruses, whilst she longed to be an edgy jazz performer. While she wanted personal fulfilment, they sought chart success.

Island and 19's collective goal was to rein in Amy's penchant for long guitar ballads and to transform her ideas into something short and snappy; the latest hits. They hoped to hone her work into a commercially viable, radio friendly pop package.

Yet producer Ian Barter believed that Amy, not Island, was the mastermind behind what made a hit. 'She was very strong-minded but I don't think that's a bad thing,' he told the author. 'An artist can have a lot of good people around them at their label and management but they are the ones who have to go out there and sing the songs for the next two years or longer, and a lot of the time artists listen to a lot more music and are a lot more plugged into what people like, I think, than the industry. So she had a few arguments with label and management. She is a sweet person with a big heart [but] is definitely good at standing her ground.'

In Amy's eyes, she had every right to do just that. While her management was running a commercial enterprise, Amy was not motivated by money. She sought not fame and riches, but the sheer joy and excitement of being in the studio, making the music she wanted to make. 'If someone offered me £3 million to make a Rachel Stevens cover record, I'd take it,' Amy guffawed sarcastically in a nod to her former Ashmole Academy classmate, before retracting her statement, adding, 'Money isn't important to me like music is. I'd go and live in a hole in the ground if it meant I could meet [musician] Ray Charles, you know what I mean?' Readers might have done, but her concerned management most definitely did not.

Amy was frustrated not just at the focus on pop music and profit and at her secret phobia that they'd turn her into a manufactured sex symbol for teenagers, but also at the endless stream of songwriters invited in to help record the album she'd been told was hers. Looking around her, Amy rebelled in indignation.

'I probably earned a reputation as a difficult person because I wrote my own songs and I didn't need people in the studio with me,' she told *The Word*. 'Not to be rude, but these people would be trying to write pop songs! And I would say, "Who are you writing for? What session are you on? Get out." But then I'd waste a day trying to be nice to the person. I'd waste studio time letting them do what they wanted, because I thought it would be the polite thing to do. You learn as you go along.'

She hadn't been exaggerating – no fewer than nine song-writers made the final credits of one track, 'What is It About Men'. 'I think she was generally unhappy with how the album sounded,' Ian recalled of her sessions in the crowded rehearsal room. 'She would sometimes snap at people… I was not in the studio sessions with various people but she said to me afterwards that she wasn't so happy and ended up finishing it just to get on with it.'

By her own admission, Amy was not a good collaborator. She told *The Word*, 'I know what I want to do before the other person is even in the room… maybe in years to come I will be a good collaborator but at that point I was like "Look, here is my music. We need brass on this, or that needs to be faster – and I don't want strings. If you want to work with me and you love strings, go home!'"

Whether she was seen as single-minded and feisty or just plain bratty, she was a force to be contended with. *The Independent* acknowledged that when they reported: 'Understandably [19] think Winehouse is a startling new talent which probably explains their ability to deal with the more wayward aspects of her personality.'

Playing down rumours of the altercations in the studio, her manager Nick Godwin confirmed: 'I don't have an issue with her frankness. She's a real artist… someone passionate who speaks their mind and isn't interested in money.'

Emotions were running high but fortunately, for every preacher of pop in the studio, there was another talented musician that Amy felt was worthy of her respect. Her label had wasted no time in hooking her up with some of the most renowned artists around. They boosted the love side of their strained love-hate relationship with the singer when they introduced her to saxophonist Jamie Talbot.

A former member of the National Youth Jazz Orchestra like Amy herself, Jamie had previously worked with many of her idols – Ella Fitzgerald, Aretha Franklin, Frank Sinatra, Moody Blues and Lou Reed. His jazzy influence would layer her tracks with a sophisticated sound. Asked what drove him, Jamie had replied: 'The knowledge that I could be much better'. For Amy, who had once insisted: 'It's a constant thing for me to better myself', this was an admirable sentiment and one that matched her own.

Other artists invited to stamp their personalities on the album included the Jamaican reggae guitarist Earl Chinna Smith, who had once worked with Bob Marley and the Wailers, and Neal Sugarman from the jazz band Sharon and the Daptone Kings, who gave out exactly the sound Amy was looking for.

However the atmosphere soon turned sour. According to her management, the irrepressible Amy 'would write '19 or 20 minute folk ballads with no chorus if she was allowed to' – and their differences of opinion soon came to a head. Despite Amy's renowned frankness and protestations of 'I always get my way', she hadn't been able to talk the label out of its love for her original demos – ones that she now felt lacked class and charisma.

'We just loved those songs,' an anonymous worker in the studio told the author, 'but we couldn't convince Amy. To her, they were old hat. She would shudder with embarrassment if she so much as heard their names.'

The three that made the final cut were 'Amy Amy Amy', 'October Song' and 'You Sent Me Flying'. The first two were included on the album against Amy's will, as she felt she'd outgrown them. To her, a song full of grief-stricken guilt about the demise of her pet canary wasn't exactly the mature and sophisticated image she now hoped to project. She hadn't bargained for the persistence of industry moguls anxious for a new hit, however. She was eventually persuaded but, in an act of defiance, refused to play the songs at any of her subsequent live shows – a move calculated to show 19 who was really boss.

Amy's dream to indulge her passion for music had come true, but studio life had quickly become her worst nightmare. Yet if Ian's advice was anything to go by, her original style and spirit would shine through regardless of any 'musical sabotage' from outsiders. 'Her vocal is definitely the best I've ever worked with and it lends itself to many styles – from jazz to reggae to hip-hop to funk to R & B,' he claimed reassuringly. 'I think she can pretty much do any style that she puts her mind to.'

It was these encouraging words that soothed Amy through the remainder of the sessions. By this time she had humiliated her label by publicly denouncing them as 'fucking morons' and, in private, had let loose an even harsher string of obscenities. Yet Amy's feisty straight-talking approach was why they loved her – wasn't it? It was a theory she had only just begun to put to the test.

Fortunately she was happy to smooth over the tension of sweet – but entirely insincere – words of apology. In memory of this time, she recalled: 'My management tell me off [and] say "Go and apologise to these heads at the record company." I'm like, "Oh, fuck it, cool – let's go." I'll apologise – I don't give a shit. Sorry, sorry, sorry, sorry – it's just a word, innit?' After the feature was printed, one suspected Amy might have yet more apologising to do.

Arguments aside, the skeleton of a 12 track album had now been produced. In the next song, 'Stronger than Me', a co-effort between Salaam and Amy, she addresses a passive partner seven years her senior and wastes no time in demanding that he lives up to his role. Continually disappointed by the man who she feels has illegitimately stolen her heart without earning it, she questions why he always puts her in control. An alpha female by nature, Amy implores ex-boyfriend Chris not just to match but to exceed her strengths because she feels he pales in comparison to the tower of strength he believes her to be. Dominant by nature, she is seeking a man who can be even more so. When her man doesn't get it, she publicly chastises him with a characteristic lack of tact, taunting 'Are you gay?'

'I'm screwy,' Amy later revealed by way of explanation. 'I need someone I can kick about a bit.'

The song shows several sides to Amy. First she vents her frustration at having to take the lead role, verbally assassinating her opponent with jaw-dropping ease. Next, she defiantly, unapologetically speaks out in defence of promiscuity and fulfilling urges of the flesh, spitting: 'I'm not gonna meet your mother any time, I just wanna rip your body over mine.' She pokes fun at the strait-laced sensibilities of her lover with caustic put-downs, asking why he thinks being a red-blooded woman with irrepressible desires is a crime.

Finally she shows the side of an insecure girl stuck in an alpha-female role, one who - underneath her ballsy attitude – disguises a longing for support and protection. Listeners are reminded of Amy's past claims that she could be more open in music than she ever could in partnership, revealing a secret, unspoken side of herself through song.

She presents herself as icy and cold-blooded, someone who doesn't care to talk problems through, yet reveals a softer side of herself with the admission that she needs her lover to comfortingly stroke her hair. Despite her feminist demeanour, her stereotypes of male-female relationships are, perhaps surprisingly, very traditional. Yet the paradox is typically Amy.

She sported the velvety vocals of an angel, but equally boasted the acid tongue of a devil – and one with some serious vengeance on her mind. She delivered caustic taunts akin to dunking someone in a vat of acid, yet teasingly combined them with a heart-soaring tune and an uplifting vocal. And underneath all of this pent-up frustration is a classic jazz tune with a modern, almost punky twist. A song that even finicky Amy found no fault with, it seemed a fitting way to preface the remainder of the album.

The next tune, 'You Sent Me Flying', is adapted from an original demo penned by Amy with Felix Howard. Not to be dismissed as just another pop producer, Felix hit back at Amy's low expectations by co-creating this dizzying soul track – which, of all the original demos, was the only one Amy didn't threaten to have erased.

In it, she cheekily bears more than a passing resemblance to the favourite artist she name-checks, Erykah Badu. The song's combination of buoyant piano chords and soul-penetrating vocals offer a more sophisticated sound than the original, with the last verse rising to a satisfying crescendo.

Here, the tables have turned on Amy in the game of love. She describes the humiliation of rejection, consoling herself with the defence that she doesn't want the object of her affections as much as it might appear. Despite conceding that he is nothing in the scheme of her years, he has made quite an impact on this seemingly cold, impenetrable girl.

'I'm not frightened of appearing vulnerable,' she told *The List* by way of explanation. 'I write songs about stuff that I can't really get past personally – and then I write a song about it and I feel better.'

Consequently this song spans various emotions from faltering uncertainty to raw pain to euphoric happiness – and by the end of it, her listeners feel better too.

At the tail end of the track, Amy pays a touching tribute to an all important tool of her trade – her guitar. Tucked away unassumingly between tracks two and three, the ballad could almost have gone unnoticed were it not for its arresting vocal.

Amy feels she can be more intimate in music than with her loved ones and her guitar, Cherry, is the ultimate cure for her self-enforced loneliness. To some a mere inanimate object, a lump of wood with bright red paintwork, Amy feels differently, pouring out her love with the words to her best friend: 'Maybe we could talk 'bout things, if you was made of wood and strings.'

As the final bars of the ode to Cherry ring out, 'Know You Now' is introduced. With the help of guest guitarist Earl Chinna Smith, Amy is freed up from her favourite instrument to concentrate on a challenging jazzy vocal. Her tale of unstoppable love at first sight will resonate with the romantics among her listeners. Impulsively drawn to a man beyond all logic, she tells of how she has to know him now, lest they never meet again. Magnetised by someone who her common sense would dismiss as 'just a little boy', she pursues him despite all advice to the contrary. An honest account of throwing caution to the winds, tinged with the anticipation of loss and regret, its guitar beat sets a relentless pace.

The next track, 'Fuck Me Pumps', is loaded with full throttle satirical humour, Amy style. The song is an ode to girls Amy ridicules – those whose dream in life is to marry a millionaire and thrive on undeserved luxuries. She name-checks shallow women who value big breasts, high heels, Gucci handbags and bulging bank balances above all else – 'At least your breasts cost more than hers'.

She also suggests that the reality for these women is often somewhat different from the fantasy image they portray. They might be flaunting fake tan a deeper shade of orange than an Easyjet flight to Ibiza, but even that fails to win favour. Amy teasingly pinpoints their failures as their attempts to attract men end in nothing more than one night stands. Mocking penniless Chanel purses, she toys with the paradox of outdoing friends in the appearance stakes, but having no coins left in that expensive designer handbag. One line asks women to refrain from jealousy simply because they are pushing 30 and their old tricks no longer work. The remark was met with collective outrage from some of the media. 'Trying to look good at 30? Heaven forbid!' stormed a journalist at *The Independent*. However, Amy dispelled the rumours of ageism by answering, when asked how old was too old to pull off a micro mini-skirt, 'If you've got it, flaunt it!'

She later added: 'I'm not trying to be negative about anyone – I just think that some girls waste their potential.' In another article, she claimed 'These girls think they're validated by a wedding ring or having a rich boyfriend – but they're not things you should strive for.'

With 'Fuck Me Pumps', Amy takes time out from the ill-fated relationships focus of the album, instead replacing it with a light-hearted dose of Winehouse humour. Gone is Amy's trademark jazz style, replaced instead with a pounding dance beat that wouldn't be out of place in the nightclubs frequented by the socialites she speaks of.

The observant listener might notice that the pictures in the album's lyric booklet, perhaps as an elaborate tease, follow a similar theme to the song – from adding the final touches to her makeup in the mirror to frowning contemplatively into 'that big empty purse'. If any further proof was needed, the teasingly ambiguous image of a pair of sexy heels abandoned at the side of a house completes the sequence. She is parodying the good-time girl.

Amy portrays herself as an inconsolable romantic, yet a serial adulterer by the same token – and this paradox is never more prominent than on 'Love Is Blind'. This track is where the two unlikely bed-fellows collide. 'It's not cheating, you were on my mind', Amy pleads to her betrayed lover in a bid to excuse her infidelity. In the eyes of her loved one, the girl who once told the media that cheating came as naturally as smoking a spliff is swiftly losing ground.

Amy bubbles with barely disguised fury towards her man for leaving her alone – and, in a subconscious bid for attention, seeks out a man of his mirror image. She then gives in to blissful temptation, excusing herself by promising she was thinking of him when she came.

The song struggles with two opposing instincts – her overwhelming guilt for betraying him versus her resentment that he has abandoned her, driving her into the arms of another man. This pitiful paradox plays itself out to the tune of a tortured guitar.

The only song on the album written exclusively by Amy, it combines her vocal with the sounds of the electric upright bass – courtesy of Salaam – and three different types of horn, commandeered by former Nas collaborator Bruce Purse.

The next song sees a swift change of pace. Amy switches from faithless philanderer to tender hearted soul diva with only love on her mind for the ballad 'Moody's Mood for Love'. Gone is the sarcasm, sadism and self-deprecation, only to be replaced by uncomplicated pledges of love and loyalty.

'No Greater Love' is equally persuasive in its role as an unconditional love song. Whilst discussing this song, Amy once brazenly asked an interviewer: 'Have you ever made love to my album?' She's clearly on a mission of languorous seduction, aided by the ultimate weapons for an auditory orgasm – generous helpings of flute, saxophone, guitar and piano.

However the tender Amy is quickly replaced by her hard-hearted twin on 'In My Bed', where lingering love is the last thing on the singer's mind. 'The song 'In My Bed' actually came about after I'd had sex with an ex-boyfriend,' Amy told *Blues and Soul* magazine. 'I was like "Now get out of my bed and take a cab home!" Then, when he said he had no money, I gave him a tenner and told him "Goodbye!"'

Perhaps the ultimate anti-romance tune, it features such charming lyrical endearments as 'The only time I hold your hand is to get the angle right'. This coarse sentiment led reviewers to condemn it as merely 'a song about a finger fuck' but Amy felt differently. 'I think the message of the song is "Even though you're familiar with me physically and you know what I like, it doesn't mean that you're welcome in my bed whenever you think you can come round,"' she explained. 'I'd always wanted to write a track on the theme of having sex with an ex and about the contrast involved. While physically it's probably going to be amazing because they know what you like, at the same time it's sad because you don't feel the same way about each other anymore. So when I did fall into that situation while working on the album, I was like "Well, this is the time to write that song."'

Indeed, the song's brutal, stormy message comes as a surprising contrast to the intense vibe of the music. Its moody atmosphere and air of dreamy eloquence came from a loop Salaam had originally created for Amy's favourite rapper, Nas. The rapper had abandoned it and so it became Amy's gain.

Played out to this loop, animal passions awaken two ex-lovers who – in spite of their nostalgic fumbles – are little more than 'two ships passing in the night'. Amy knows she will never welcome him into her family unit, conveying this with the slight that he'll never give her mother a lift, yet she finds herself entangled in yet another ill-fated sexual encounter with him. The 'river of no return' she speaks of is a metaphor for her unstoppable arousal. Yet while he hopes that their tryst spells reconciliation, to alpha-female Amy it is just another orgasm – she can 'separate sex from emotion.' Yet again she plays the role of the spiteful heartbreaker, although her ex might not be the only one feeling the pain.

Taking the reins into her own hands, Amy produced the song 'Take The Box' herself. Private pain becomes public heartbreak in another troubled number about her ex-boyfriend Chris. Following the break-up, Amy fills a box with all the beloved keepsakes her other half has given her. She discards her coveted Moschino bra, the T-shirt of his she used to sleep in and his most treasured gift to her of all – the Frank Sinatra CD he bought her for Christmas. 'When I say "Frank's in there and I don't care", that is literally a Frank Sinatra CD,' Amy blazed. 'He bought me *In The Wee Small Hours*… ironically, because it's one of the classic heartbreak albums of all time.'

After surrendering everything linked to him into one small box, 'I smashed up everything in my room. There was nail varnish down the walls.' Yet after her self-destructive fits of rage, the woman scorned sets about using her energy more wisely – 'I gave him the box, then I wrote the song – and I'm fine.'

Next on the album is 'October Song', the track which she was loathe to include. The canary she dedicates it to is an ideal companion for her as she identifies with its beautiful voice, innate fragility and graceful elegance. Although she claimed the bird died of natural causes, a weekend without food seems sure to have been a contributing factor. Either way, the peaceful send-off she penned to relieve her guilt is something Amy would rather have forgotten – but her management insisted that she included it.

'What Is It About Men', featuring no fewer than nine song-writers, speaks of Amy's painful past and her penchant for infidelity. Her dissatisfaction with her father's liaisons - 'all the shit he put my mother through' – leaves her smarting so much that she quickly abandoned the number from her live set list, branding it 'too personal'.

Maybe that was just as well for her embarrassed father. 'My dad said "You've got to stop talking about me – you're making me sound like a serial philanderer!"' Amy chortled to *Totally Jewish*. 'I never actually said that though.'

Yet she questions, seeing the pain her mother faced at the hands of an unfaithful husband, how she could repeat the pattern with her own illicit liaisons. She concludes that it must be her 'Freudian fate'.

Earl Chinna Smith channels the soulful, reflective vibe with a juicy, slightly reggae inspired beat. He both co-produced and played guitar on the track, leaving Amy to focus on her rich vocals – ones that are stretched powerfully by the vibe.

Meanwhile the dizzying 'Amy Amy Amy' focuses on light-hearted lust. The song is a shameless marijuana fuelled sonnet to the joys of sexual attraction. In a repressed work place environment, hormones run high and women like Amy are prone to fantasise. She hints that her feverish imagination runs further than the listener is allowed access to places so graphic that her lyrics cannot be used.

Conjuring up visions of X-rated rhymes, Amy proceeds to drown in a sea of hapless lust. However, her eventful time working at *WENN* is more about people watching and swaying past an admirer's desk in high heels than actually working. It is just the first part of a three song extravaganza tucked into one track.

Seconds later, Amy startles the listener by switching roles yet again – this time from a lust-crazed lady to a maternal Jewish mother, acting as an adviser to her brother in troubled times. Its understated reggae sounds accompany a compassionate vocal. She belittles the man in question's philosophy degree and expresses her resentment at carrying him even though he's bigger, before doling out the cruel to be kind advice that she can't help someone who won't help themselves. Tragically, years later these words could so easily have referred to Amy herself.

Finally, the energetic 'Mr Magic' pays tribute to Amy's departed uncles, conveying lyrically how much she misses them. Reminiscing on happier times in her musically themed childhood, she tells them earnestly that the songs sound better when they're around – in fact, they 'come naturally'.

There could scarcely be a punchier or more jazz influenced ending to keep the sounds of Amy ringing in her listeners' ears. Job done, the songstress departs with just one aim – to leave her audience hopelessly addicted.

After the recording, Amy left America – but not without delivering glowing words of praise for her producer Salaam Remi first. 'Salaam drew me out of myself musically,' Amy revealed to *Blues and Jazz* magazine. 'Because, while I'm a really wacky song-writer, he's exactly the same. He'll always strive for something different and I'd never met someone who can tap into an artist like he can – which, to me, is the mark of a great producer.' She added, 'With him, I feel like musically anything can be done – and I've never felt like that when working in England, where they don't want to listen to a girl who thinks she knows what she's talking about. Basically all they care about [in England] is listening to the record company.'

So the power struggles in the studio had ended on a positive note – and, what was more, Amy had been equally satisfied in the sessions with New Jersey based Commissioner Gordon. 'I love America,' she had reportedly sighed while on the east coast, before erasing the memories of the earlier strife with her co-writers – or, at least, until it came time to face the press.

As she jetted home to London, work began on the album's final touches. Backing singers and musicians were invited to enrich the sound. Layered with tenor saxophone, flugel horn, harp, piano, keyboards and even the humble art of the hand-clap, the album was quickly beginning to take shape.

It was now the mixing stage, overseen by Gary Noble and Steve Nowa. Steve was a renowned recording engineer who dominated the American music industry even in his early days – yet he knew as soon as he heard Amy that she would become 'my favourite artist'. At that time a mere assistant, he had begged Gary to let him loose on her music as a co-mixer, and he had agreed. Steve went on to become one of Florida's top mixers. 'Every five to ten minutes a song mixed by Steve Nowa is playing on a major Miami radio station,' his website boasts. Yet in a world of pop anthems from Ciara, P Diddy et al, Amy stood out and to him, today just as back then, she is still very much in favour.

After wiring the equipment, Steve then assisted in the mixing process. 'I helped add a vocal reverb and we tried unconventional compression settings on the vocals,' he told the author. ''Stronger Than Me' was the most fun song to mix because the track was bananas! The sounds were so live, so organic, yet they locked to a hip hop tempo.'

Echoing Amy's musical infatuation with her producer, he revealed that it was Salaam who had given Amy her vintage sound and that without him he believed it may never have fallen into place. 'Only Salaam could make a track like 'Stronger Than Me'. It takes a knowledge of gear, instruments and microphones that producers just don't have nowadays. Salaam's use of old school equipment gave Amy her throwback sound on original tracks. Most producers would have a very difficult time pulling that off without sampling.'

Despite that, Steve still credited Amy for being a real artist, the antithesis of a manufactured pop star. He explained: 'Every artist signed to a major label has thousands of songs submitted to them by professional songwriters with music made by major producers. They pick their favourite songs and have the intern print out the words at the printer. Then they read the words into the microphone and have the engineer draw their words in the computer to notes that are in key and they call it singing... it's a joke to me. Amy is the real thing. She performs her records. Whether it's in the vocal booth or on stage, she is a performer.'

He recalled the recording of his favourite song, 'You Sent Me Flying', when Amy had laid down the vocals perfectly after just one attempt. Whilst the average artist often needed three takes, with Amy, there had been no need to re-record. 'Her vocals used just one track,' Steve marvelled. 'Amazing. A performance like that makes me love my job, which in turn makes me love my life because it's sad to say but music IS my life.'

He believed that it was Amy's effortless ability that earned her the right to call the shots in the studio as often as she did, despite being a virgin artist without a single published album to her name. 'Amy was a little strong-minded in the studio, but it didn't seem to bother anyone because she's amazing and artists with that kind of talent get a pass on things like that,' Steve commented. 'I never witnessed her clash with Salaam though. Salaam is very smooth, he has worked with the biggest names imaginable, artists trust him and he knows how to harness their energy towards his goal of selling records. Their relationship was simple, it was Amy's first album, she was excited to be working with him, Salaam was making these amazing tracks and she was writing amazing songs and they complemented each other.'

Of course alongside the hard work, there was time to relax too. 'She was a sweetheart,' he recalled of their time together. 'She was very well spoken and she had a beautiful smile. We played a few games of pool and she was very competitive - she's actually a really great pool player. I'm definitely better, but I felt bad, so I let her win and pretended she was better than me, it was very cute. It made her very happy.'

Despite working with numerous respected artists, Amy was still her favourite and he knew exactly why. 'There isn't just one thing about Amy that makes her my favourite - she is the whole package. When you first get into the music business the job seems so exciting, so glamorous… that quickly fades and you realize it's tedious and it's extremely hard work. Yet when I get to work with someone as talented as Amy I remember why I got into the industry. She is captivating and hearing her voice come through the mixing board is an engineer's dream come true. Her voice has a tone from a time when you couldn't fake talent. She is cultured and she's edgy. Her personality shines through her tracks, you can actually get to know her by listening to her music. She's not trying or faking or putting on a show, she just is Amy Winehouse.'

Mixing over, the album - christened *Frank* in an ode to Amy's obsession with Sinatra - had completed its journey. In just a few short months it would be winging its way onto record store shelves.

Pressing play is like stepping back into time to the jazz cafes of 1940s America, yet a deluge of modern references also creep in – Gucci heels, Moschino bras and Outsidaz albums. Blending both new grooves and traditional blues, *Frank* would prove hard to be pigeon-holed.

Amy would play a heartbreaking, resoundingly beautiful loss of love song in the style of Billie Holiday, Ella Fitzgerald or Sade, and then accompany her brass band for a jaunty jazz number. Yet, in direct contrast to the smooth-voiced love songs, she aspired to be as straight-talking and controversial as Missy Elliott, as ballsy and fearless as L'il Kim. Like the latter, Amy was short in stature but compensated for her lack of height with attitude. A touch of hip-hop, a sprinkling of Salt and Pepa and the sounds of the streets were added to the mix with 'Fuck Me Pumps' and the playful yet self-despised 'Amy Amy Amy'.

The album's no-nonsense candour would later see it compared to TV show *Sex and The City*, but in Amy's case the script was not as predictable. The name *Frank* might have been an ode to Amy's Sinatra CD collection but it could just as easily have encapsulated the frankness of her no-holds-barred tunes. Here, through song, Amy can speak frankly to her father, her boyfriend, her best friend or even her producers, in a way that she could never articulate through words alone. Perhaps she couldn't express it, or perhaps she wouldn't dare. *Frank* becomes as intimate as listening in on a private conversation, one that becomes therapy for both its speakers and its listeners. One thing was for sure - Amy had made her mark with *Frank*.

After all those months locked in the studio, she was now ready to share her songs with the public. During the final stages of Amy's transatlantic channel hopping, she found the time to put on three shows at private members club the Cobden, which – in Kensal Rise – was just a stone's throw away from producer friend Major's studios. Proving that she was still a North London girl at heart, Amy threw herself wholeheartedly into these performances.

Exclusive yet accessible, the club charged a £1000 per year membership fee and was located in a charming Grade II listed building. Its Grand Hall boasted a Victorian stage and 30ft long bar, providing the type of decadent old world style cabaret surroundings that Amy would have relished. 'No other contemporary club in London can rival this room for sheer glamour and size,' the Cobden's website claimed. Sizable enough to wow performers with its grandeur, it was nonetheless intimate enough to dispel the stage fright normally associated with larger audiences.

For her first show on July 22nd 2003, Amy arrived with little more than an old Stratocaster guitar – no back-up band, no fancy clothes and not even a beehive to hide behind. Yet the moment she began to sing, the reason that the Cobden had chosen her became clear.

Back then Amy was petrified by the idea of playing live but once she had made it onto the stage, the adrenalin rush took over – one that Amy had passionately declared was 'better than sex'.

An onlooker recalled, 'Amy looked scared stiff at first and seemed reluctant to go out there. Her presentation was kind of clumsy, but once she got up there, something took over and no-one in that room could take their eyes off her. She said afterwards how she couldn't wait to do it again.'

She didn't have to wait long. Her next show at the Cobden was scheduled for August 11th – and this time she meant business, arriving with a full band to back her up on harmonies. Amy was no longer a one trick pony, but – as she later assured *The Independent* – 'at least a five trick pony!'

Amy was also scheduled to play the V festival, which offered alternate days in Chelmsford and Staffordshire on August 16th and 17th. However, she was intimidated by the larger audience. Ian Barter, her musical director, recalled: 'I remember playing at the V Festival with her in the jazz tent and as we were about to start the first track, 'Best Friends', she came over to me behind the keyboard and said "Ian, I am really too nervous to do this in front of a large crowd – what do I do?" I responded to her, "Just go to the mic and say "I am Amy Winehouse" and then I'll count us in for the first song. She did just that and then after the second song, she came over and said "I love this buzz from being on a large stage – I want to do this more!"'

The media proved to be as enthusiastic as Amy was. *Essex Uncovered* raved 'Crucially, Amy's musical debut revealed an utterly unique, genre-challenging artist who – bolstered by her performance this summer – is destined for even greater things in the future.'

Amy's next foray into playing live was for Mastermind Soundsystem on August 25th as part of Notting Hill Carnival. Hip-hop, R & B, soul and reggae were among the sounds that Mastermind was designed to celebrate and she was primed to fit in perfectly. Amy also appeared on the cover of Time Out's carnival edition – before she'd so much as released a single song. In retrospect, she was described as 'virtually unrecognisable in early rave tourist mode'.

Tragically, a man was fatally wounded during the carnival parade just yards from the Cobden club where she had performed days earlier. However, according to Mastermind, that didn't deter her from playing a 'blinding set'. Sean Paul had performed there just before he rose to fame with hit single 'Gimme the Light' and the then unknown Tinie Tempah debuted 'Pass Out' on the very same stage. There seemed to be no better place for a beginner hoping to launch a glittering career.

Promoter Lewis Benn recalled: 'We like to promote the best of British R & B. I got a phone call saying "Amy's gonna be the next big thing, you've got to get her." All the talk was about this diminutive white girl who was singing so sweet. Colour's not a barrier and she was so talented. When she arrived, she was very quiet and introverted, with a small entourage around her, but she was a pure professional. The crowd loved her.'

Her third and final show in the Cobden took place on September 1st 2003. Away from the 'suffocating' influence of her label, who struggled to deter her from her penchant for indulging in her fantasies of guitar ballads without a discernable chorus, Amy played freely – and an attentive audience was listening.

Thrillingly for Amy, a scattering of famous faces were in the crowd – and Annie Lennox was one of them. The ex-Eurhythmics singer had taken time out from recording her new album at nearby Mayfair Studios to visit. She told *The Times* 'She was like a woman in her thirties, with a whole seasoned delivery, not fazed by anything at all. I was in awe of her. I thought, "Wow, you have a special talent. God, you are 18. Where did that come from?"' Amy had been plucked from obscurity when she signed to Island, yet mere months later, established artists were raving about what she had to offer. It was very flattering for her. Yet the biggest excitement of all for Amy was the release of the forthcoming album. She and Island were officially on tenterhooks.

CHAPTER 5

Up to that point, the jazz scene in the UK had largely bypassed the charts. Among the few exceptions, standing alone in a so-called music desert, was new vocalist Norah Jones. She was beautiful, gracious, demure and inoffensive and had put her own mainstream spin on jazz. She was different enough to stand out, but conventional enough to be accepted by the record buying public. The sugar-coated young singer might have eased them in gently but were the masses prepared for her polar opposite, Amy?

The new addition on the scene was opinionated, outspoken, rough and ready and could prove a bitter pill to swallow for the uninitiated. The instantly likable Norah would be a safe bet to play to the grandparents whilst risqué Amy, on the other hand, was definitely an acquired taste.

How would the public react to her arrival on the music scene? They were about to find out as lead single 'Stronger than Me' stormed into the charts on October 6th 2003. It peaked at No. 71 in the UK, but despite its modest chart position, it had everyone talking.

'What It Is' had been chosen as a B-side, completing the double dose of recrimination directed at Amy's long suffering ex-boyfriend. Dark and contemplative, the song's music and vocal are spiked with danger, despair and venom. Here, Amy is the very person Sade warned us of in 'Smooth Operator' - neither for beginners, nor sensitive hearts - and that's only too clear as she serenades her victim in a voice laced with deep sarcasm 'Mr Ultra Sensitive, I'm sorry if I upset you.'

Her verbal jibes certainly did upset her ex-boyfriend. The speculation over his sexuality would mortify any red-blooded heterosexual, but

Mr Ultra Sensitive in particular didn't stand a chance. On account of these songs, the diminutive Amy, at just 5"2 inches tall, had a grown man fleeing his home. She confessed to *The Guardian:* 'He left his job and now lives in the North. There came a point when they couldn't hide the articles about the album from him anymore.'

Quickly cementing her reputation as a man-eater, Amy continued with a note of surprise that he 'hadn't appreciated' her efforts in dedicating her album to him. For Amy, *Frank* was a series of unconventional love songs, but to Chris, the shame was unbearable.

How did the single fare with the public - was it off limits for the beginners and sensitive hearts among them? Gary Mulholland of *The Observer* was instantly intrigued, dubbing her 'politically incorrect' and 'recklessly provocative'.

'For 30 years or so, the female singer-songwriter has been the biggest fan of New Man,' he wrote. 'Whether seated at piano or perched on stool with guitar, the sensitive songstress has presented pleas for a similarly sensitive male - touchy-feely, open, kind and loving. And... we liberal, reconstructed ex-student males have responded to the challenge, hoping to God that all this soft-voiced cuddliness presents our best chance of getting our dicks sucked.' His preconceptions were to be turned on their head when he first heard Amy. 'Then this Jewish teenager from North London comes along and tells us we're just a bunch of poofs... my world view is threatened by it,' he raged satirically. Reluctantly he added, 'Which means it's doing what pop ought to do.'

The track also delighted the staunchly feminist webzine *The F Word*, albeit for a very different reason. She earned her bra-burning credentials for the song's unconventional brand of feminism, with the reviewer reporting that she'd 'happily crooned along... in a hazy state of rapture all weekend'.

However Radio 3 felt differently, ranting: 'The immature, homophobic bitching of Amy Winehouse is a blunt, ineffectual weapon.' Amy was horrified to learn that his scathing comments about her had directly followed glowing praise for a band she hated, 'one hit wonder' Ms Dynamite.

Amy's unapologetic jibes, such as 'He's a big pussy' were - for Chris - tantamount to being dropped in a vat of acid. However to Amy, it was all harmless banter. She claimed: 'I don't hate men... the things I said were out of frustration more than anything else because I liked him so much and he liked me. But just because you have a connection with someone doesn't mean it's going to be smooth running - life isn't like that.'

The same was true of her debut single. Loved and hated in equal measure, there was growing concern among the gay population that Amy was homophobic. 'Homosexuality used to be classified as a mental disorder until the 1970s,' raged one anonymous blogger. 'People used to go to prison for it. We as gay people have fought for decades to reverse the way our society, employers, friends and even parents see us – for something we can't change. We wouldn't be able to change even if we wanted to – so, for Amy – who music lovers will look up to and try to emulate and who has a single in the charts – to sneer at someone for being or acting gay? That undoes decades of anti-discrimination campaigns! It's an invitation to the wider world for gay bashing!'

Yet Amy hadn't been openly hostile, unlike the rap group DMX, whose lyrics had openly advocated knifing or killing homosexuals. She might have been caustic, smouldering and withering about an ex she'd once loved – and perhaps even a little uninformed about how her open letter might have been interpreted – but was she really homophobic?

According to another blogger, she wasn't prejudiced in the slightest. 'I'm gay and I LOVE Amy Winehouse,' he countered. 'She's obviously picked up on the fact that some gay guys are effeminate and prefer girly gossip to a night at the football, but that's real life, surely.' Referring to an interview she'd taken part in earlier that year, he added 'Didn't Amy even say she liked to experiment with homosexuality herself after a few sambucas?' Good question.

The dust had barely settled on the homophobia debate when it was time for Amy to unveil her album. It was released on the same day as Jamie Cullum's, whom she would be supporting on tour that year. Jamie was already established in the business, with his third release, *Twenty something*, heralded by BBC Music was 'one of the most talked about jazz releases of the year'. Yet Cullum, who had worked his way up after self-financing his debut album in 1999, a mere 500-copy effort, had as yet failed to break the mainstream. Island was desperately hoping that its attempts to modernise Amy's sound would pay off and that she would break the mould and change the face of jazz in popular culture forever.

One thing was for sure - she was certainly standing out. 'Teenage female singers tend to fall into one of two categories: the pneumatic pouting sex bomb a la Britney and Christina Aguilera, or the attitude-laden, self-styled misfit image of Avril Lavigne or Amy Studt,' *Music OMH* wrote, hinting that both categories were manufactured for effect. 'Thankfully, 19 year old Amy Winehouse is as far removed from those two stereotypes as you could imagine.'

Indeed, refusing to let a Simon Cowell type figure 'swoop in' and control her image, personality and sound, Amy was quickly making a name for herself as the antithesis of the mass-produced star. She had no interest in embracing a media friendly image. Whether it was an ill-advised peroxide blonde due job or a beehive taller than the highest pair of skyscraper heels in her collection, she presented herself the way she wanted. She cared little for whether it was fashionable and even less for whether it portrayed the kind of sex appeal her managers would froth over. In fact, she pitied carefully crafted sex sirens as merely painted dolls, victims of their management's visions and devoid of their own self-expression.

There were no elocution lessons for someone like Amy, no fake 'natural' look that took three hours in hair and makeup to perfect and no hiding behind a veneer of polished perfection. She wanted to be on the outside exactly who she was on the inside – whether that was the good, the bad or the ugly.

What was more, her crossover attempts musically were making headlines too. She was pairing vintage jazz sounds with an ultra-modern twist and her velvety voice added a 'Heartbreak relief' potion. Meanwhile her attitude was pure rock 'n' roll – an intriguing combination.

Puzzlingly though, Amy lacked the rabid ambition of her contemporaries to get ahead – she seemed to see music as her therapy, or an indulgence for her to enjoy with herself, rather than a fast-track route to fame and fortune. She didn't see the need to consider her bank balance, or even her audiences. The sudden adulation almost embarrassed her. Yet there was plenty more to come.

Some of it was from BBC Music, when journalist Greg Boraman delivered the glowing praise: 'It is rare for such a young performer to debut with such assurance, confidence and to such instant acclaim, but North London sensation Amy Winehouse already has a reputation many more seasoned artists would swap their gold discs for.'

He hadn't been exaggerating either. As early as her first major public show at the Cobden, she'd had already established celebrities such as Annie Lennox raving about her. Back then, there had been no expensive production budget and no extensive brass band to hide behind. She'd attracted famous admirers in her rawest form. Her contemporaries in the studio had been equally impressed, lauding her self confidence, sense of direction, and her lack of nerves.

BBC Music also raised a question that was on many people's lips – her influences. Some claimed that she was a copy-cat version of jazz greats from yesteryear, yet Boraman seemed to think that not only was Amy fit to stand alongside these legends, but that her prowess might just exceed them. He claimed: 'Amy's influences Vaughan, Dinah Washington and the more contemporary like Badu et al) are obvious but not over-powering and Winehouse has enough attitude, talent and chutzpah to make any comparisons fleeting and pointless.'

MP3.com had equally positive words. 'Despite her boozy persona and loose-limbed delivery, Winehouse is an excellent vocalist,' the website claimed. 'What lifts her above Macy Gray is the fact that her music and her career hasn't been marketed within an inch of their life. Instead of Gray's stale studio accompaniments, Winehouse has talented musicians playing loose charts behind her with room for a few sales... instead of a series of vocal mellitluities programmed to digital perfection. The record doesn't have the feel of being meddled with and fussed over – and losing its soul in the process.' The review also praised her versatility, adding: 'A club version of 'Moody's Mood for Love' not only solidifies her jazz credentials but proves she can survive in the age of Massive Attack.'

However a few remarks would make uncomfortable reading matter for Amy. The review stated: 'With 'In My Bed', she even proves she can do a commercial R & B production' – exactly the style Amy had sought to avoid. Tussles with the record label meant that the album was straddling the intersection between R & B and jazz. To Amy this made it an unsatisfying no man's land, but according to various reviewers, the crossover attempt had worked. 'She is Billie Holiday, crossed with ball-busting rapper Eve,' claimed *Q* magazine.

Meanwhile on *Metacritic*, a website where users post their own reviews, Sami P stated: 'It demonstrates that vocal prowess and meaningful lyrics still have commercial credibility.' Another user, Aiden, wrote of *Frank*: 'This exposes the contemporary music industry for the fake that it is.' It seemed as though, according to these listeners, Amy was hitting the spot and succeeding in diverting the mainstream. They believed her music had soul and meaning, rather than being the work of a group of producers ruthlessly crafting the next chart hit and pairing it with a busty, beautiful, TV-friendly young woman as a mere money-making prop. Many believed that, in this context – taking into account the superficiality of the musical climate at that time – Amy was unique. Yet she had little time to process these words before she headed off to take the album on the road for the first time.

For a virgin performer like Amy, her first proper tour meant taking the role of support act - both on Jamie Cullum's UK tour and on the London leg of jazz bad boy Finley Quaye's tour. Like Amy, Jamie was a genre-defying artist who refused to be pigeon-holed, mixing old world jazz standards with songs by rock bands such as Jimi Hendrix, Radiohead and the Who. During the tour with Amy, he even surprised onlookers with a version of Pharrell's 'Frontin''.

During the tour with Jamie, Amy was joined by a modest three piece band. Ian Barter, her self-appointed Musical Director, played guitar, flute and keyboards, Dale Davis played bass and Stuart Anning took on the role of drummer. The gigs with Jamie would see Amy described as 'a true professional'. Yet she was harbouring a dark secret during those early shows – musical differences with her drummer were driving them apart. The feeling was mutual and, at the earliest opportunity, she and Ian began to hold auditions for his replacement.

All of the auditions had been prearranged with the exception of one. In a curious twist of fate, Amy had spent an evening at her local nightspot, the Torrington, to watch a band called KO, whose guitarist was a friend from her schooldays. The drummer of the group, Nathan Allen, instantly caught Amy's eye and she approached him in the bar after his performance to summon him to the auditions the next day.

Nathan didn't need to be asked twice. He joined ten other drummers at the Ritz studio in Putney the following afternoon. The atmosphere was intense, with the ten ambitious hopefuls packed into a tiny room waiting to be called while Amy and Ian checked out the talent in a second room next door. Fights were on the brink of breaking out as each had their eyes on the prize, but Nathan had an advantage – his speed. 'I got the material on the day when all the others had it given to them prior to that,' Nathan recalled. 'I had to play 'In My Bed' and 'Take The Box' and I think Amy was impressed by how quickly I picked it up.'

Unlike the other performers, Nathan hadn't had the luxury of time to learn the unknown material, but Amy soon made him feel at home – some might say, a little too much at home.

According to Ian Barter, Amy's rampant lust was causing some problems with objectivity. 'She had a lot of opinions and I didn't mind that [but] she would sometimes want to hire a drummer at the auditions because she fancied him as opposed to which one was best!' Ian told the author in reference to Nathan.

In fact, in the months to come, a casual sexual relationship formed, with Nathan staying with Amy on the artist bus after joining the band instead of the crew bus where the other musicians would travel.

Fortunately, however, Nathan was not just a convenient lust object for Amy, but a very competent percussionist and he was about to impress her again, as he had just five days to learn the six songs for her 30 minute support slot. 'Amy called me personally to ask if I wanted to do her next show,' Nathan told the author. 'I got the call on Saturday and the show was on Thursday.'

Back then an inexperienced sixth form college student from Thames Ditton, Nathan was thrown into the fast-paced world of showbiz in an instant, combining shows with Amy with studying for A-Levels in Music, Business Studies and Graphic Design. 'It was a bit surreal as I'd never been on tour before and I had to juggle that with college, doing a show with Amy one day and going back to college the next.'

Yet Amy was rapidly becoming a motherly figure to him. 'I was 18 at the time and she was like my mother, trying to look out for me and look after me. She cooked the best West Indian food and she tried to shield me from negative situations and from taking drugs,' he recalled. 'Her advice was just to be yourself. The industry is intense, no messing around, but Amy was never as cut-throat as the other artists. She likes to hang out with the band – some artists travel on a different bus but she was on the same one. She's a musician too so I think she could relate to me.' Thanks to sharing a bus with his new mentor, he was introduced to her musical favourites too – including R & B crooner Brandy, who was constantly on repeat while they were on tour.

Amy also shared her formula for success with Nathan, 'Imitate, Incorporate and Innovate'. 'She imitated when she was a child, she later incorporated both the old and the new sounds, and then she took a hybrid and made something new about it. By doing that, she innovated and inspired other people,' Nathan claimed.

He added: 'Working with Amy was the best situation I could have been in at that time. Had I played with a pop artist like Natasha Bedingfield, it wouldn't have been the same. Some people get star-struck, but Amy wasn't fazed by being famous – she knew what to expect.'

Their first show together, without the presence of the previous drummer, who Amy felt – according to Nathan – 'wasn't playing her stuff too well', was supporting Finley Quaye at the Shepherds Bush Empire on November 13th 2003. The show saw her heralded by *Music OMH* as a 'promising girl with a powerful voice'. The website claimed that although she came across as 'harsh sounding' on the big numbers and the set was on occasion a little clumsy, 'at just 20 she has loads of time to polish her live performance'.

Supporting her more experienced contemporaries was all very well but Amy soon longed for the spotlight, and to run her own show. Fortunately, she didn't have to wait long. One of Amy's first solo shows was on the tiny Virgin Megastore stage at London's Oxford Circus. The cramped shop, which saw guests jostle with each other to fight their way through the cramped CD racks, was not an ideal location for a low-key jazz show. However, there was a method in the madness as if they enjoyed the performance, onlookers couldn't be in a more convenient place to pick up a copy of the new album.

There to showcase 'Best Friends' and first single 'Stronger than Me', Amy had the awkward demeanour yet boundless enthusiasm of a nine year old child. Dressed in an oversized jumper, her long hair carelessly strewn across her shoulders, she portrayed all the innocence of a first time performer, with the beehive hair do that would become her trademark as yet nowhere to be seen.

Gary Mulholland interviewed her following the show and recalled, 'She is still wearing the tight black and white woollen mini dress that she performed in earlier this evening and, when she takes a toilet break, she unleashes a butt-swinging Jessica Rabbit walk that makes every man in the place turn round and leer. She appears to have no idea of the reaction she provokes.' The new unconventional sex symbol of the time was making waves already, ahead of her first solo tour.

On December 5th 2003, on the same day that Jamie Cullum took to the Virgin Megastore stage, Amy would move onto London's Bush Hall – and her biggest headline performance yet.

Formerly the home to a wealthy publisher and his mistress, Bush Hall had been transformed into a concert venue in 2000. Since then, it had been primarily used for new artists just starting out on the touring circuit, or for established artists showcasing a new album to a small number of die-hard fans. For Amy, it was dual purpose. She would join the realms of REM, Courtney Love and the Scissor Sisters to headline on that December night.

She strode on stage with a rock chick look not dissimilar to Courtney's, with an aquamarine coloured guitar, leopard print leggings and alarmingly high heels. There were audible gaps from audience members when Amy belted out 'There is No Greater Love', while the feisty 'In My Bed' prompted *The Guardian* to muse: 'So angry, so young; generally it takes a lifetime to accrue such a rich vein of resentment.'

Yet she achieved mixed reviews for the performance at the 350-capacity venue. Perhaps her penchant for selecting cute, rather than creative, band members had caught up with her as *Guardian* music critic Caroline Sullivan recalled: 'Her first substantial London headline show pinged around confusedly for a while – Winehouse and her brass section jostled for space on the pocket-sized stage and when at one point they wandered off, she hissed "Come on!"'

Things picked up towards the end though. 'The gusty cheers eventually punctuated her prickly shell and after a few numbers she progressed to cockney pleasantries ("I'm really snotty tonight" accompanied by a resounding snort),' she added. Amy might have been nervous singing to thousands of people at the V festival, but she was shamelessly unsophisticated when it came to her own live shows. And there was more candour to follow.

19 had expected their new singer to toe the line in the studio, yet what they hadn't bargained for was the moment that Amy opened her mouth in public. Spurred on by a flurry of media attention, she spent the early part of 2004 verbally annihilating almost every one of her opponents on the modern music scene.

Girls Aloud were among those to meet with Amy's disapproval. Not one for a diplomatic shrug of the shoulders, she stormed to webzine *Pop Justice,* 'I think 'Love Machine' is a fucking brilliant name for a song. Well done, girls! Well, they didn't have to think of it themselves, but well done for being there when you were being told what the song was being called... I can't even hear that shit, to be honest. It won't even go in my ears.'

Amy openly criticised ex-classmate Rachel Stevens, dismissing her four number 1 singles with S Club 7 with the words: 'I watch her singing and think "Fucking hell!" but at least she didn't write that piece of shit.' Coldplay, who had sold five million albums, were not immune from Amy's executioner's block either. She laughed: 'I bet if [singer Chris Martin] heard his stuff, he'd be like "Who is that wanker?"'

In an interview with Simon Amstell, Amy spotted a poster of Dido out of the window of the taxi the two were in and - in front of the cameras - let rip. Later, she confided, 'Dido makes me want to vomit.'

Amy had once listened to Madonna on a near daily basis, but now she was taking no prisoners. 'She can't shock any more,' Amy cackled. 'She's too old. She should just get a nice band, just stand in front of them and fucking sing.'

As for Ashanti, Amy groaned: 'I categorically couldn't be like her, singing "Baby, baby" 20 times.' Amy was also openly contemptuous of the acts she shared a management company with. The fact that Victoria Beckham was a former member of the Spice Girls, who had earned her management millions, meant little to Amy as she blazed: 'Victoria was not put on this earth to sing. Posh Spice needs to give up. So what if [husband David] fucks 20 other women? She can never leave him because she'd just be forgotten about. Bang. No-one cares.'

Hilariously, oblivious to the snubs, Victoria later gushed about how Amy was one of her favourite performers. She gushed that she 'just loves' her music, and praised for her being 'unique and original' and an 'amazing' singer. Obviously Victoria had not read her press.

With all the subtlety of a circus performer, Amy also let rip about J-Lo. The American starlet had approached her long-time friend Juliette Ashby, inviting her to pitch some songs for her to use on a forthcoming album. 'They told [Juliette] not to sing too good... they were like "You need to tone it down" and she was like "Oh, you mean really basic!"' she guffawed.

J-Lo seemed to agree with Amy's criticism when she told *News of the World* that she disapproved of *American Idol* contestants covering her songs, implying that they were not vocally ambitious enough. 'It's cute, super entertaining and flattering but no... we're trying to mentor them to the next step,' she said.

If this seemed an astonishing admission of weakness, it was nothing compared to Amy's level of candour. By this time, the press was open mouthed. Amy was letting loose the sort of sensational banter normally reserved for private conversations to national newspapers. With scant regards for the consequences, she continued to make a mockery of the UK's much loved pop scene. 'Every lyric comes from me, so I'm lucky I can explain myself,' she told *The Times*. 'With Britney, when they say "What do you mean by this, Britney?", she says "Wait a minute, I'll call the song-writer."'

She later added of the singer, who had sold over 40 million albums at the time of her comments, 'I wish her luck with her marriage as I hope it stops her going into the studio.'

When Amy's second single, 'Take the Box', achieved a meagre No. 57 chart position, Amy's frankness shifted to her record label. Whilst several reviewers praised that *Frank* had not been aggressively over-promoted, Amy was furious that the single - featuring a cover of Thelonious Monk's 'Round Midnight' and a live version of 'Stronger Than Me' - had not received more attention.

Eroding the fraught relationship with her record company even further, she claimed: 'The marketing was fucked, the promotion was terrible. Everything was a shambles. It's frustrating because you work with so many idiots, but they're nice idiots. So you can't be like "You're an idiot."' She added: 'I hate them fuckers. I've not seen anyone from the record company since the album came out and I know why... they're scared of me. They know I have no respect for them whatsoever.'

Even worse, Amy then claimed that she had never heard the album from start to finish, as she found the recordings mortifying and that she didn't so much as own a copy in her house. What was more, she also openly admitted to being bitter.

Aside from production issues, Amy's biggest bug bear was marketing. That said, her own attempts at self-promotion had not been much better. 'Listen to this,' she had mumbled with a lack-lustrous, barely coherent, air, into the microphone at Brighton's Concorde, failing to enlighten her audience as to the name of the song.

Interviews had also been difficult for Amy, who disliked discussing herself. 'It doesn't come naturally talking about myself,' she claimed. 'No offence but I could be at my nan's house right now, or... waiting at home for the plumber to come and fix the washing machine.' Her candour was ill-advised by the beloved grandmother she spoke of, who told her: 'Amy, you're a nice girl but people don't know you're nice. They pick up *The Mirror* and think you're a little bitch.'

Fortunately for Amy, she had her very own marketing manager in the making - her father Mitch. He even spoke of her free of charge. After clamouring that his debut in 'What Is It About Men' had made him famous, a dubious accolade due to how it portrayed him but one he wore as a badge of pride nonetheless - he returned the favour. He would relentlessly play her album to tourists who caught a ride in his cab, or boast 'That's my daughter' if he happened to drive past a poster with her name on it.

However, soon Amy would barely need promoting at all. Her luck would soon change as she caught the eye of the organisers of the UK's biggest music ceremony – the Brit Awards. She had been nominated for two categories that year. Firstly, she would compete with her friend Jamelia, an urban artist with an R & B flavour, Annie Lennox, who had caught her first show at the Torrington, Dido and the 'appalling' Sophie Ellis Bextor for the coveted award of Best British Female. She was also up against Dizzee Rascal, Misteeq, Lemar and Big Brovaz – an unlikely candidate amongst the hip-hop hopefuls – for the prize of Best Urban Act.

Nominated alongside people like Annie Lennox, who had been in the business for years when she watched one of Amy's earliest performances – might have been a thrill for the average pop artist. Yet Amy was thoroughly unimpressed. She told *Music OMH*: 'That's cool. Whatever. I don't care about that', before adding 'I'm not the kind of person that would ever have gone if I wasn't nominated.' When asked who she thought would win on the night, Amy instantly responded, 'Dido – even though she's rubbish.'

Unfortunately her prediction was proved correct, with Dido beating her to the title of Best British Female and Lemar picking up the gong for Best Urban Act. Perhaps it was lack of confidence that had inspired Amy's lukewarm reaction to her nominations, or perhaps she was genuinely disinterested in mainstream events. Paradoxically, maybe it was even a statement of arrogance, showing that she felt superior to her pop counterparts. Whatever the reason, her nominations caused a flurry of publicity – something that an angry young Amy had started to hanker after.

Yet the Brits had a nasty surprise in store for her. Her tour-mate Jamie Cullum was making a live appearance with one of her most hated rivals – Katie Melua. The two would be performing a cover version of the Cure's 'Lovecats' together. Just a year younger than Amy, the angel-faced singer had escaped political tension in her homeland of Georgia and made the UK her permanent home. Whilst here, she had earned a recording contract and her debut effort, *Call Off The Search*, had rapidly sold over a million albums. Whilst some reviewers claimed that she was a 'nearly Norah' and that she offered 'polite pop' instead of sultry jazz, her record sales were speaking for themselves and Amy, who at that time had sold just 200,000 copies of *Frank*, was not amused. 'I'm bitter because I haven't sold as many albums,' she claimed, perhaps sarcastically. Whether it was an ironic comment or just part of her trademark honesty, it was to be the preface to a series of slurs about her arch rival.

The unsuspecting Katie had, just days earlier, claimed *'Pop Idol* and *Fame Academy* have really highlighted to the mainstream public how much music is manufactured. I think people wanted something different, something with melody and interesting lyrics by artists who are musicians. People like me and Jamie Cullum and Norah Jones and Amy Winehouse...'

Yet Amy, unimpressed by her compliments, had raged: 'I'm a songwriter but she has her songs written for her. She must think it's her fucking lucky day, being compared to me and Jamie... it's not like she's singing old songs like Jamie, she's singing shit new songs that her manager wrote for her.'

Appearing on the BBC show *Never Mind the Buzzcocks*, Amy again made her feelings for the singer only too clear. When presenter and peacemaker Simon Amstell asked Amy, 'Why don't you do something nice with Katie Melua?', she responded, 'I'd rather have cat aids, thank you.'

When pressed for a response, Katie told the *Music OMH* website: 'Music is so much about opinion, and she is completely entitled to her opinion. I think it's hilarious actually. You know, it's very funny to have the courage to say that in the music industry, although I don't know if it's foolish or if it's good on her part. But obviously I have to defend myself. She's absolutely right, the album is not about me as a writer, it's about me as a performer. I met up with [songwriter] Mike and he had these great songs. She might think his songs are shit - I think they're fucking brilliant.' She added: 'And he didn't write all the album. There are... two songs of my own and they weren't songs that I co-wrote with some producer, they're songs that I wrote myself about me.'

She told another reviewer: 'I don't know why she'd say these things about me... her voice is stunning.' Yet Amy, who claimed that she'd never heard her rival's music, insisted that it was 'shit'. The debate continued, with the *Montreal Gazette* coming out in favour of Amy. Despite Amy's music not yet being available across the pond, the newspaper made some unfavourable comparisons with her following Katie's performance at the local Jazz festival. The headline was: 'Katie Melua - Amy Winehouse, she's not'. The reviewer went on to claim 'At least [Amy] has personal-ity. Though I suppose Katie Melua has personality too. It's just bubbly, innocent and seriously lacking in edge... her performance was squeaky clean, which is a problem when singing the blues... As for the mid-show reggae number, don't get me started. Somebody get the girl a drink.'

This was a victory for Amy, although online responses to the article revealed mixed opinions. A blogger by the name of Nathan remarked '[People] see the life of Amy Winehouse as being more attractive because basically she's a slut. They think Katie Melua is boring because she doesn't drink or take drugs – a sure sign that our society is getting more and more depraved every day.'

Another named Ren concurred: 'Who says you have to be like Amy Winehouse to have personality or edge? Not me!... Who says you can't be squeaky clean when singing the blues? The world needs more Katies and less Winehouses.' Yet a third blogger, Missy, added to the debate and offered support for Amy, saying, 'Sorry to Katie Melua fans, but I do know a good brand of ear-plugs I can recommend. I'd also suggest super-gluing them in.'

The controversy was becoming too much for Katie, particularly when the two met in person and Amy allegedly proved polite. 'We'd never met when she made that comment, but we did afterwards and she was really nice to me. All I would say is if you're going to be mean, do it to my face,' she told the *Daily Mail*. In the same interview, she finally exploded, claim-ing that Amy's risqué image and behaviour was a 'bad influence' on fans. 'It makes me angry that people like Amy Winehouse... are glamorised for their behaviour,' she added.

Courtesy of the ongoing war of words, some might have felt that Katie was becoming more famous through association to Amy than via her own music. Desperate to change this, Katie had hoped for a positive response when she headlined the Shepherds Bush Empire in west London, one that Amy had headlined shortly before.

However BBC Music was almost as scathing as Amy. 'Anyone expecting a thrilling night... was either lost or deluded,' the review claimed. 'The most exciting thing that happened during Melua's 90 minute set was the forced removal of a candle she had lit in memory of her idol, Eva Cassidy.' Talking of her songs, the website sneered 'An up-tempo rendition of 'Lovecats' brought back memories of her disastrous duet with Jamie Cullum... mercifully we were spared a repeat performance, with Melua informing us sadly: "Jamie has to be with his mum tonight."'

The one politically incorrect side of her stage show was a song that revealed the controversial lyric: 'If a black man is racist, is it okay?' The frankness of this statement might have matched Amy's candour, yet instead of sending shockwaves through the media, BBC Music condemned the song as 'hilariously naive'.

It seemed as though Amy, whose fame was rapidly growing, had won that round. Yet, undeterred from being outspoken, she merely shifted her attention to the sexy side of popular culture. Christina Aguilera had stormed to instant success after the single 'Dirrty' was released, featuring a scantily clad Christina writhing provocatively with both men and women in a boxing ring. Amy's opinion? 'She's a talented girl - but you couldn't really see it until she was wearing those chaps with her ninny hanging out,' she told *The Times*. Ouch.

Amy also had a put-down for glamour model Jordan - 'She's like our Pammy [Pamela Anderson] except Pammy is stunning and she's a poor man's Pammy.' It was perhaps an indication of Amy's musical notoriety that a respected broadsheet newspaper was taking her comments seriously enough to print them. Amy had a final dose of ammunition for *The Times* - 'I don't say things because I'm bitter. I say things everyone else is thinking but no-one dares to say.' This young singer had certainly earned the title *Frank*.

CHAPTER 6

Where next for a singer who wasn't afraid to giggle coquettishly in front of a live audience before cursing 'Oops! That wasn't very eloquent'? Fittingly, Amy's next show was at an understated, unpretentious Soho branch of Pizza Express. The jazz club there combined the simple pleasures of cut-price food with a sophisticated jazz scene. It was a small concert and one which focused on fun rather than financial reward, but it would introduce her tunes to a wider audience. This fitted in with Amy's ambitions perfectly.

Her manager Nick Godwin told *The Times:* 'She had that old jazz notion that you turned up somewhere, played a set for a few drinks in front of some friends and then went home.'

Perhaps this notion, combined with its casual location, was just as well as Amy's restaurant decorum was not for the faint-hearted. 'It's not just children we object to in restaurants, but anyone who draws overt attention to themselves,' Nick Duerden wrote in *The Independent* of her experience of Amy that day. 'I once interviewed Amy Winehouse in a Pizza Express. The moment she stood up, swore, grabbed at her chest and hollered "I've got my boobs back!", a great many customers complained.'

This wasn't the only awkward incident. A journalist in Montreal interviewed her in an upmarket restaurant following her performance at the Jazz festival. A waiter restrained her from stretching out over several seats while she enjoyed her meal, prompting the response of: 'You ever just want to go to McDonalds?'

Her table manners were about as tactful as her conversations with the press, but none of that mattered as she prepared to play her show at Pizza Express. It would be a two-night extravaganza that just a few years later might have made headline news in every national tabloid, but these shows – performed on March 8th and 9th – were very understated.

The Brad Webb trio was Amy's backing band for the night as she joined her father Mitch for a duet on the Frank Sinatra version of 1930s jazz classic 'You Go To My Head'. That night, roles reversed and Amy was the proud parent, boasting to *The Independent*: 'My dad's great – he's like the karaoke Sinatra. He could be a lounge act – he's that good!'

Her praise was not lost on Mitch, whose airs and graces – like his daughter's – were also in short supply. 'With all the casual menace of an Eastenders villain, he paused to enquire of the fresh-faced piano player: "Was that the bridge, or were you just doodling about as usual?"' *The Telegraph* reported. Perhaps Amy's candour had a genetic basis.

Amy also performed the track 'What A Difference A Day Makes' by Dinah Washington, to the awe of a keen audience. Capturing the mood of that evening, Simon Price of *The Independent* marvelled: 'She exudes an effortlessness which suggests hard work was never her style. For a stage school kid, she's also remarkably unaffected and natural. A dark beauty with an equine face, she alternates between grinning like a child and tossing her hair like a flamenco dancer. Her voice is extraordinary, a languidly sexual instrument, so potent that she only needs to be in the general vicinity of the mic (even a casual, shut-lipped "mmm" goes right through you).'

After a thoroughly unpretentious concert, an equally unpretentious girl – the one with a hole in her living room ceiling, and the one who'd turned down work as a showbiz journalist to be one of the minions who made tea at the reception desk – just as Nick Godwin had predicted, went to bed.

Amy's next major appearance was on the Jonathan Ross show on March 19th 2004, where she declared: 'I didn't wanna write about love, but then I went and did it anyway.' Her next single was a prime example of that. A double A-side winged its way to the charts on April 5th featuring 'In My Bed' and 'You Sent Me Flying'. Also included was the song 'Best Friends' which, prior to that, had never been officially recorded. The release reached a meagre No. 60 in the charts, which came as a disappointment to Amy. Little did she know that in a few years time the single would have sold out and would be changing hands on Amazon for more than £100 per copy.

Yet, despite releasing an album almost six months earlier, she had never embarked on a full scale headline tour – could that explain her lukewarm reception in the charts? If so, her luck was about to change.

No longer a London sensation, the melodies of *Frank* were about to hit every major city in Britain, beginning in Glasgow on April 21st at the Cottier Theatre. However *The Scotsman* described her sell-out show as 'tedious'. Sharing Amy's embarrassment over the inclusion of early number 'October Song' on the set-list, it added acerbically: 'As for candid lyrical revelations, the audience lapped up the one about her dead canary.' Even more excruciatingly for Amy, the newspaper compared her to the TV show she hated the most, denouncing her as 'just another competent *Pop Idol* wannabe, mistaking verbal acrobatics for sophisticated soulful expression'.

However, the words came in direct contrast to those of the website *MP3.com*, which raved: 'Winehouse is an excellent vocalist, possessing both power and subtlety – the latter increasingly rare amongst contemporary female vocalists.'

Smarting from the bad review in Glasgow, Amy then moved on to Northumbria University, where she was forced to laugh off an embarrassing incident that saw her stumbling down the steps at the side of the stage and falling flat on her face.

Things didn't get much better at the Manchester Academy on April 24th. A painful review by the *Manchester Evening News* summarised: 'Amy Winehouse has been eulogised by the press and public alike and one would expect a show to justify the hype, but she was found desperately wanting when it came to delivering the goods last Saturday night. Opening with album stand-out Know You Now, she sauntered on stage looking vague to say the least... she sorely missed backing vocalists with all the beautiful harmonies dropped in place of bland horn arrangements. [Her voice is] an extraordinary instrument but it went to waste too many times.'

It added 'Complete with her atrocious diction and phrasing, her band fared little better... her bassist looked like he was about to cry at any moment and there was an embarrassing lack of cohesion and communication to their playing. Encoring with an awful remix of Take the Box and the gimmicky but annoying Fuck Me Pumps, her show weighed in at an emaciated one hour. Ultimately though it was her attitude that was the biggest let down, almost insulting the crowd at times with her lackadaisical demeanour. She may have one of the most distinctive voices around, but talent does not a good show, nor an artist for that matter, make.'

It seemed that reviewers either loved Amy or hated her, but did the bad press faze her? Not one bit. 'It's not important to me to make other people at ease – I am difficult, but that's because I really don't give a fuck,' she told *Blender* magazine haughtily. She defiantly celebrated the 'vagueness' a reviewer had accused her of, claiming: 'To play and sing live, for me, is just like going on auto-pilot. I'm not there to be like "Hi everyone, if you don't have my album, go and get it!" It really is just a case of wanting to please the crowd by giving the songs their just due.'

The songs were Amy's first love – they were what mattered to her when she got up on the stage. And as much as she wanted the world to hear her music, her audiences could at times be an almost unwelcome distraction. Despite mixed reactions to her live show, she had sold out every venue she had played. She was also having a lot of fun between shows on her tour. 'Amy was addicted to pool. She would register to play pool at pubs in every single city we went to,' Ian Barter recalled.

Amy was then invited to take part in a tribute concert to celebrate the late Billie Holiday – something that Amy was honoured to be involved in. Questioned merely a week before the concert, Amy was still unsure about which of the legendary singer's tracks she would choose to cover. 'I love singing 'Autumn in New York', she mused 'and that song 'The Man I Love.''

Amy's sell-out tour concluded with a double-nighter at the Shepherds Bush Empire on May 3rd and 4th. She started feverishly networking at the aftershow party, which saw one of her favourite artists, Mos Def, in attendance. John the White Rapper, who was also a special guest at the party, recalled 'I was looking around and people like Mos Def were there and it was like "Our idols are here checking you out! I wash your plates! How cool is that?" I get more excited than Amy about her career.'

She and Mos Def would cross paths again just days later as the two were scheduled to appear at the Prince's Trust Urban Music Festival on May 8th. The two would share the bill with highly acclaimed artists such as Alicia Keys, Beyonce, Dizzee Rascal, The Streets and Jay Z. Proceeds from the concert, including Amy's short set, would be spent on supporting troubled young people with financial problems and helping them to get back on their feet. As Amy's friend John had suffered enormously in his early life, the charity was close to her heart – and being part of it meant more to her than any review in the media.

To her surprise, Amy was then nominated for another award – this time at the swish Ivor Novello ceremony, which took place at London's Grosvenor House Hotel on May 28th. Amy's opinions about the competition were as frank as ever. Speaking of her rival Dizzee Rascal, she squealed: 'He's beautiful – he looks like a cat!' Meanwhile Sting, who was also present, received even more generous praise. 'I would fuck him,' Amy smirked. In reference to his self-confessed penchant for tantric sex, she cheekily added, 'I don't know about ten hours though!'

On the night, Amy drove off all competition to claim the gong for Best Contemporary Song, courtesy of 'Stronger than Me'. Wearing a zebra print boob tube dress with roses emblazoned on it, Amy took to the stage, clutching her award possessively before bashfully saying, 'I have to write honestly about things which happen to me and I hope people can relate to that.'

Confessing that the Ivor Novello awards meant much more to her than a Brit nomination, she added later, 'I don't want to be best female. The Ivor Novellos are for song-writers and that's what I am.' Just a few days later, album sales had soared and Frank had reached an impressive number 13 in the album chart.

Amy was keeping it real, but the nominations simply kept coming. While she was enjoying the summer festivals, she heard that she'd been nominated for Best Album at the Mercury Music Awards. She'd barely processed that information before she found herself performing to her biggest audience yet on the Jazz Stage at Glastonbury Festival on June 27th. Bizarrely, reviewers at the event wrote her off as 'parent friendly', a reputation that would prove to be extremely short-lived. She also appeared at T in the Park on July 10th and returned to the V festival on August 19th, where she would party with her friend Jamelia before taking to the JJB Puma stage.

This performance was tailed by a humiliating surprise at the BBC Jazz Awards, an annual event in support of the UK's top jazz sensations. The event was to be held on July 29th at the Hammersmith Palais. Despite her high-profile success at the Ivor Novellos and the nearly nailed nomination at the Brits, the Jazz Awards had more street cred for a performer who prided herself on shunning the mainstream pop industry. However, she was to be sorely disappointed when she learnt that organisers had omitted her from the program altogether.

Both she and Katie Melua, whom she could hardly bear to share a room with, had been invited to present awards to others at the event, but neither would be shortlisted themselves. In fact, insiders revealed their presence was just to boost ratings. This news brought a stunned silence to the debate over which of the two were real artists – in the eyes of the Jazz Awards, the answer was neither of them.

When Amy arrived at the ceremony to present the song for Best Instrumentalist to little known artist Soweto Kinch, she was already not in the best of moods – in fact, she was furious. First of all, she caused a stir when she and Katie refused to play nice for the cameras, declining to have their photograph taken together. Concerned organisers were forced to seat the pair two tables away from each other in fear of a cat-fight between the two stealing the limelight.

On the day, however, Amy was content in the end with a low-level snub. 'I pride myself on being different,' she asserted. 'Jazz is all about pushing the boundaries and experimenting. I have never listened to Katie Melua's music but it's all written for her and it's shit. I have been compared to her but I'm nothing like her.' It might have sounded caustic, but – in comparison to her previous attacks – her words seemed almost diplomatic.

It wasn't just Amy and Katie who would leave empty-handed – Norah Jones, Jamie Cullum and Joss Stone – all lauded as serious contenders in the popular press – had also been sidelined. Why had they been snubbed? A source at the ceremony revealed: 'The jazz establishment has refused to accept them. It is absolutely ridiculous but they feel they are too mainstream, young and inexperienced to be taken seriously. They classify them as pop stars. They are here only to present awards and raise the profile of jazz.'

It felt as though she'd been plucked from her pedestal of mainstream notoriety to be used as a free of charge advertising billboard – and all for an industry event at which promoters felt she didn't even belong.

For Amy, it felt like a frustrating case of mistaken identity, but she was forced to grin and bear it. However she did triumph in the press when the arts division of the British Council produced a pamphlet about the event. In it, Katie was criticised with the words:'Her jazz pedigree and content is dubious', while it asserted that Amy's music 'stands out for its raw message that is missing from the jazz lite flavours of the mainstream.'

Determined to try harder to steal the hearts of the jazz world, or at least evade any snobbery, Amy released the controversial 'Fuck Me Pumps'. A double A-side single, it shared the spotlight with 'Help Yourself' and benefitted from an added track – a live version of 'There is No Greater Love'.

Released on August 23rd, it sank to a new low, peaking at just No. 65 in the UK charts. Only her first single, 'Stronger Than Me', had performed worse. There was more bad news in store when Amy failed to win over the public vote at the Mercury Music Awards. After a stormy performance of 'Take the Box', she sat in the wings and watched Franz Ferdinand claim the glory. The Glaswegian group walked away with a cheque for £20,000 after triumphing with their self-titled first album.

There were better tides ahead, however – on September 30th, Amy arrived at the sumptuous Royal Albert Hall to participate in the MOBO Awards, renowned for their role in 'honouring the best in black music'. The letters MOBO stood for Music of Black Origin and it might have seemed an unusual ceremony for the fair-skinned Caucasian singer to be attending. However, Amy lived for black music and, had one closed their eyes, her vocal tone could easily have been mistaken for that of an African-American soul singer. Amy had near-miss nominations for both Best Jazz Act and Best UK Act. Although she lost out on both counts, the former went to her friend Jamie Cullum, which helped to soften the blow.

It was now time for Amy to embark on a second British tour aimed at promoting her fifth single. Whilst she had not yet attained a spot in the elusive top 40, a healthy turn-out at the new shows proved her continuing relevance on the jazz scene. This time, Amy would be taking to the streets once more with friend and sometime lover Tyler James. The arrangement was one that Amy had allegedly chuckled would earn her 'sex on tap'. Tyler was keen to speak of the convenience of this arrangement too, although a little less obviously. 'Because she's my friend, I know her band really well and she knows my band really well. A guy in my band was one of the first people to teach Amy to play the guitar, so we get to have a really good laugh, like going away with your mates on holiday. We get to go on stage every night, have a wicked time and then go out with our friends.'

The tour was just as memorable for Amy's young producer friend Jack Freegard. 'I was lucky enough to tag along,' he told the author. 'One memorable gig was at the Concorde 2 in Brighton. Me, Tyler, Juliette Ashby, Nick Shymansky and a whole bunch of people were there. The performance was first class. We spent the whole rest of the night clubbing and the next day a few of us stayed behind and spent the day in Brighton. It is a legendary night in our friendship circle.'

Not only was the post-show entertainment legendary, but the shows themselves were beginning to earn Amy a generous helping of praise. Far from the negative press she had endured up to that point, *The Mirror* marvelled: 'Madonna may, or may not, mime but Amy has a voice of such intensity as to make Madge look like a karaoke singer.'

The praise for that night's show was also demonstrated on the website *Real Brighton*. 'It's obvious that despite her soft, raspy voice, this is not a woman to be messed with,' wrote Daniel Reagan. 'Amy could almost be mistaken for a sassy jazz singer of the forties, cigarette in hand with the lights down low, and a crowd of swinging punters gazing into her experienced eyes.'

Humorously he concluded, 'The fantasy ends abruptly when introduced to Amy's speaking voice, an incongruence that is summed up in the sardonic analogy of The Streets singing opera.' The analogy worked – few could inmagine the rapper Mike Skinner taking on the vocal intensity of an opera singer – and even fewer could imagine that this velvety voiced jazz singer would have anything in common with a Cockney accent.

Yet this singer was full of paradoxes. At the show she wore a blood red Adidas dress, one that was said to elicit sighs of lust and jealousy across the tightly-packed 400 capacity hall. The front row was close enough for punters to see the miniscule tattoo of a lightening bolt on their idol's hand as she clutched the microphone. Notably, this show did not attract a single negative review.

Strengthened by the praise of the media, Amy hit Liverpool, Sheffield, Nottingham, Birmingham and Bristol to name but a few cities, culminating in a show at Brixton Academy, south London on November 29th. In this buzzing predominantly African and Afro-Caribbean area, Amy would compete for attention with street hustlers, ticket touts and locals selling marijuana. Yet, in spite of the chaos, according to reviewer Christina Jenson, all would be forgotten the moment the long awaited singer took to the stage. 'It's not surprising that this singer has a MOBO nomination under her belt,' she blogged. 'Close your eyes and be transported to another world – one where the smoothest grooves of the most influential black artists flow out of supper clubs. This era was glamour at its best, without the need for skyscraper heels and attention seeking gimmicks. Amy like so many greats before her, is at her best when stripped down.' As an afterthought she added 'Escapism at its best, the listener forgets their gritty urban location the moment the first notes ring out on 'I Heard Love is Blind'.'

The enthusiasm of punters like this one was echoed by Amy's record sales. By the time of the MOBO Awards, Amy had sold 200,000 copies of *Frank* – a number that would eventually increase to almost a million, earning it a status in the UK of triple platinum.

While it peaked at No. 14 in the UK charts, it surpassed this record in Austria, France, Germany, Poland, Portugal and Spain where it achieved the No. 1 spot. The album had gone gold in seven countries and platinum in three. Amy was euphoric.

Another victory for Amy, albeit a less serious one, was that Katie Melua had backed down. In a confession about her music, she admitted, 'There were things that I thought were so great at the time, but when I look back, it was just a pile of crap.' Amy allowed herself a smug smile of satisfaction – it was the ideal note on which to end her UK tour.

For Amy, the end of the tour would mean returning to the anonymity of her modest two bedroom flat. A million miles away from the chaos of the past year, it more closely resembled an untidy student digs than an award-winning songwriter's pad. An interviewer from *Scotland on Sunday* had gawped in horror on introduction to the place, noting the 'empty cans of Stella littering the garden' before committing to writing that the flat itself 'looked like a crime scene'. Fine art was absent, shunned in favour of a football at the corner of the living room, whilst a gaping hole in the ceiling had – after all those months – still not been repaired.

The contrast between the flat and Amy's image as a glamorous, up and coming artist reflected just how much had changed for her that year. That said, she couldn't bask in the glory for too long, as personal pain and grief were her primary inspirations. 'I'm going to take time off and live a normal life so that things can happen to me again that aren't all good. Otherwise, I'll have nothing to write about on the next album,' she laughed.

Yet before she took a rest, she had one more personal appearance to make. She had been invited on to the national TV show *Later with Jools Holland*, which aired on November 31st. She would use the opportunity to talk animatedly about her album. However, the highlight of the show was a demure Amy, the picture of innocence, clad in a white school-girl style blouse, singing the Dinah Washington classic 'Teach Me Tonight'. Portraying the role of a virginal young woman willing to be introduced to 'the ABC' of sex by her first lover, Amy channelled that Lolita-like seductress role surprisingly well. There was a stunned pause after the final note rang out before the hall filled with the sound of rapturous applause.

Yet it seemed some were taking her role-play a little too seriously. She was accused of being a middle class bore who was faking rebellion in the interest of self-promotion. Instead of denying their claims, Amy hit back with: 'Yes, I'm a good girl. I haven't smoked crack. You can get a lot worse, I'm sure.'

Tragically for Amy, things *were* about to get a lot worse – but the full force of this irony would only be discovered later.

CHAPTER 7

To the untrained eye, Amy was now a blissfully untroubled star in the wake of success but typically, Amy being Amy, conflict was never too far away. She had plunged from a fast-paced schedule of adoring fans and sell-out concerts to near obscurity in a matter of days and the devil had found destruction for idle hands. With little to fill her days with other than smoking weed, drinking beer and playing pool, Amy idled away much of her time in local pubs. 'I used to be there before the pub opened,' she told *Blender* magazine, 'banging on the door.'

The three months her management had allocated to her for a break came and went, yet Amy continued her self-destructive pattern of binge drinking. She would arrive early and down potent cocktails until the sun came up, while her writer's block showed no sign of subsiding.

Lonely and forlorn, the songstress began to look around her for fresh inspiration. Without the emotional pain that had triggered most of the songs on her first album, Amy felt strangely empty - and the masochistic desire she harboured to 'fuck up' in order to become creative again would soon become a grim reality.

One evening, a chance encounter with a man named Blake Fielder Civil would send shockwaves through her system and change her life as she knew it forever. Blake, the figure that would become so important in her life, was a talented grammar school drop out who had once aspired to be a journalist but had since given up on his dream. Refusing to complete A-Levels despite his intellect, he was soon seduced by the bright lights of London and - together with a friend - had left his home in rural

Lincolnshire for the city. Once there, the lure of the drug scene would prove irresistible.

His life up to that point had resembled that of Howard Marks in the 2010 film *Mr Nice*. Based on a true story, the film follows an intelligent young man with an offer of a place at Oxford University who gives up his future for a taste of danger, going on to become a notorious drugs baron.

Career-wise, Blake had initially been interested in hair-dressing. Back then, however, even a senior hair-dresser barely scraped £200 per week, while a trainee commonly earned less than the minimum wage. With this meagre salary, every day would be a fight for survival, barely allowing Blake to support himself, let alone his new found drug habit.

Fortunately, his mother Georgette had recently opened a hair-dressing salon in the capital and she was able to provide a more generous allowance, in return for his help there. Some might have denounced hairdressing as an overly feminine career choice, but Blake was a creative, unconventional 'New Man' type at that time, who wasn't swayed much by the ridicule. He supplemented his mother's handouts with part-time work as a gopher on music video sets, where he was responsible for hair and makeup. However, much to the horror of his mother, he continued to be a regular on the drug scene and it wasn't long before he succumbed to its easily available nose candy.

'We were horrified at the thought [he could be taking cocaine] and confronted him at once and he didn't deny it. He told me "It's normal, mum. Everyone takes a bit of cocaine." And the evidence of what he was saying was staring us in the face. He was more verbally aggressive, edgy and tense.'

As his involvement with drugs increased, his personal appearance and commitment to hygiene began to suffer. 'Looking at him now, all dishevelled and unkempt, it's hard to believe that [before] he wouldn't leave the house without showering, doing his hair and putting on after-shave,' Georgette ruefully recalled of her then image-conscious son.

After a brief period of being homeless, the entrepreneurial young man was, according to reports, selling cocaine on the party scene at weekends to stay afloat. His other vice was gambling, and it was a lucky bet which he was celebrating the night he met Amy. To her, their first meeting was a passionate, love at first sight encounter but Blake described it a little less poetically. 'We met at a pub called the Good Mixer in Camden,' he told the *Daily Mail*. 'I'd just had a good win at the bookies so I went to the pub to celebrate, opened the door and Amy was the first person I saw and that was it.' He added 'The drinks were on me for the first and last time. And from that night onwards, we began our torturous love affair.'

Amy was besotted and within a month had tattooed his name across her chest, inside a pocket just above her heart. Unfortunately for her, Blake already had a girlfriend by the name of Chloe, who worked as a journalist for a magazine. Amy would later describe Chloe as 'someone he was involved with a little too close to home'.

Blake was not an obvious choice for Amy. His rugged look was very different from the clean-cut boy band image she had usually found appealing and sought out in exes such as Tyler James. However, perhaps Blake was the very man she described in 'Someone to Watch Over Me', where she crooned: 'He might not be what other girls would think of as handsome, but to my heart he'll hold the key'.

On the other hand, Blake did tick a few boxes on Amy's list. 'If I'm checking out a man, I'll normally go for someone who is at least 5"9, with dark hair, dark eyes and loads of tattoos,' she told *The Observer*. In this case, her lover fitted the bill on all counts. Yet more importantly, the two had an instant chemistry. They would visit Blake's mother's salon, where Amy – seemingly oblivious to her reputation as an award-winning singer – would muck in and help out with the customers. The pair would also frequent the Hawley Arms pub, where Amy would get behind the bar and serve drinks to her friends. Wrapped up in her passionate love affair, it was almost as though she had forgotten that she was famous.

She was deliriously happy, but that wasn't to last long. Some of Amy's friends, including childhood buddy Juliette, were suspicious and disapproved of Blake. They saw him as an unemployable waster with a penchant for hard drugs and an out of control gambling problem, yet none of this deterred Amy, who was besotted.

With him, she found a feminine side she hadn't been aware of before. No longer the hard-hearted Amy of old, she longed to play the role of adoring wife – cooking meals for him and declaring her ever-lasting love. 'It was Blake who kick-started my domestic instinct,' she told *The Guardian*. 'I immediately saw he was someone who hadn't been treated right, so I practically put him in my bag and said "Right, you're coming with me!"'

Yet despite it all, their love affair crumbled and Blake returned to girlfriend Chloe. Amy recalled to Channel 4: 'I think we did the worst possible things two people could do to each other who were in love. We were also very young and we weren't prepared for the way we felt about each other. It was too much too young really and it was too intense. It just burnt out.'

As the destructive flame of addiction swept its way through her love life, Amy returned to music. She drowned her sorrows by playing a set at farm-based Cornbury festival, an annual music event located in the Oxfordshire countryside. Described on its website as 'a country fair with a rock and roll twist', 'a farmer's market with a dance-floor' and 'an eclectic and eccentric musical carnival... with a classic contemporary soundtrack', it was different from anywhere that Amy had played to date. What was more, it got her thinking about music again and reminded her of the rush she felt while performing. It was just what she needed to give her the confidence to start jamming again.

'I didn't want to just wake up drinking and crying and listening to the Shangri-La's and go to sleep and wake up drinking and listening to the Shangri-La's... so I turned the pain into songs. That's how I got through it,' she revealed.

Amy was inspired by the soundtracks to her meetings with Blake – mainly girl groups from the 1960s that she would hear on the pub jukebox. These artists, like the Shangri-La's, were the antithesis of Amy's hard-hitting feminist rages on *Frank*. Her new obsession reflected just how much she had changed her mindset. She concurred 'I was a defensive and insecure person. [On *Frank*] when I sang about men, it was all like "Fuck you, who do you think you are?" The new album is more like "I will fight for you", "I would do anything for you" or "It's such a shame we couldn't make it work." I feel I'm not so teenage about relationships anymore.'

A friend of Amy's recalled of her special relationship with the Shangri-La's: 'Their theme of heartbreak and loss of love, of prostrating yourself on the pavement for the one you cared about, really fitted into the way Amy was feeling.

Bruised from the brutal ending of her relationship, how exactly was Amy feeling? 'I was so mixed up in the head, I had literally hit… not rock bottom – I hate to use such a phrase, since I'm sure I will sink lower at some point,' Amy told *Entertainment Weekly* despairingly, 'but I was clinically depressed.'

Her attitude might have seemed perverse. Amy had been blessed with natural, effortless talent and was achieving unimaginable notoriety for her music, appearing as the star of many a prestigious award ceremony – but none of that was enough. She'd started singing in the first place to exorcise her demons and express her pain – and no amount of fame and fortune achieved by that was going to cure her. She'd never sought adulation and a glittering trophy – or even a few dozen – wasn't going to be sufficient to cure the heartache. If what she said was to be believed, she needed only the love of a good man. Now, without Blake around, she wasn't content with leaving it at singing when she felt sad.

Amy had also been smoking non-stop and indulging in junk food binges to mask the pain. In a bid to get herself healthy and undo the damage, she signed up to her local gym, where another addiction began. Exercise released pain-killing, mood-boosting endorphins and Amy would soon become a fan of the rush. 'She has the physiology of an Olympic athlete,' Mitch later said of his daughter admiringly. 'A doctor who saw me… said "She could go into the Olympics, she's that fit."'

Amy's ambitions were a little more clear-cut. 'I got into the gym because there are all these sweaty men around to gear me up and get my adrenalin going,' she told *The Guardian*.

However, there was a sinister side to her new fitness regime. Amy had started a new diet, which involved chewing her food to get a taste of it before spitting it out. She became worryingly thin and ever more unhappy. It seemed that all the fame and success in the world couldn't heal Amy's troubled heart.

Things came to a head during a late night drinking session with ex-lover and close friend Tyler James. Smarting from the pain of losing Blake, am insecure Amy had started staying at his house overnight for company. She would drink from the moment she woke up in an attempt to block out her heartache and took refuge on his sofa, crying, drinking copiously and refusing to eat. At a loss for what to do, Tyler called Amy's parents. 'I got myself into a really dark place,' Amy told the *Album Chart Show*. 'My friend phoned up my dad and said "We can't do anything with her, she's drinking as soon as she wakes up, she won't talk to anyone — she's mad."'

Mitch immediately went to Tyler's house. 'My dad started crying,' Amy continued, 'because he's really soppy and I hate to see my dad cry so I was like "I'll do anything you want."' Seeing his daughter's pale, skeletal figure crouched on Tyler's sofa, a fraction of her former self, broke his heart. Taking a look at her tear-stained face, he knew what he wanted her to do — stay at his place and let him nurse her back to health. She agreed, but it then emerged that the problems were far worse than he'd first thought.

Once a voluptuous size 14, Amy had now shrunk to a size 6, her frame tiny enough to shame the world-renowned slimmer and Hollywood socialite Nicole Richie. After alcohol-fuelled nights out, Amy would eat huge bowls of pasta and then nibble on nothing more than salad the next day to cancel it out. All the while she was continuing to exercise voraciously.

'The thing is, if you're an addict, you don't get over it — you're just in remission,' she claimed. 'So I won't sit there and go "No, I don't have a problem with food anymore." I do forget to eat a lot and I do have days where I think "You can't eat that because you ate… yesterday."' She added that she believed her unhealthy relationship with food and body image was symptomatic of being female and something that all women struggled with to a certain degree.

As alarming as it sounded, perhaps Amy wasn't far wrong. By some researchers' estimates, up to 80% of women in the UK suffer disordered eating, while around 20% will develop anorexia or bulimia at some time in their lives.

What was more, one study published in *Time* magazine revealed that 99% of nine-year-old girls owned at least one Barbie doll. Yet even an innocuous Barbie came with feminist politics as the study also showed that a woman who proportionately matched the doll's dimensions would be 6ft tall with a 31" bust, a 21" inch waist and 39" hips. She would only have room for half a liver, would be forced to crawl on all fours due to her unsupportable frame and would quickly die of malnutrition. Yet many youngsters longed to look just like their doll companion – styling their hair like her and seeing her as a role model. For some girls, then, chasing plastic perfection came with a death sentence – and Amy, who had already started self-harming and experiencing feelings of worthlessness by age nine, was particularly vulnerable.

Like many women, Amy had also grown up during an era when the media was saturated with images of a size zero ideal – something unhealthy and, for most, unattainable. Her appetite for fashion magazines as a teenager would have put her directly in the firing line for further insecurities.

Despite many men finding Kate Moss – who had a personal motto of 'Nothing tastes as good as skinny feels' – too thin and androgynous to be sexy, women who admired her fashion sense continued to emulate her. That would be a losing battle – statistics show that a catwalk model is on average 23% slimmer than the average young woman and that less than 5% of women can attain the figure of a model. Was reading *Vogue*, packed with page after page of self-proclaimed 'super-waifs' slowly but surely eroding Amy's self-confidence? Was it altering her perception of what was normal, realistic and desirable?

Studies from Iran suggest that the proliferation of thin models in the western media is responsible for the prevalence of eating disorders. The studies show that, in a country where western TV and magazines were once censored and have never been anything less than tightly controlled and where women are discouraged from wearing form-fitting clothes, eating disorders were almost non-existent.

In stark contrast, Western women glorified and idealised supermodels because they were fashionable, famous, wealthy and enjoyed the glamour of near-permanent full-face makeup and high-profile coverage in glossy magazines. For young people at a time when they are still forming their identity and sense of self, the lure of this 'uber-glam' image can be irresistible and near impossible not to crave for themselves.

For obvious reasons, being in the public eye has a well-documented tendency to accentuate these problems. By 21, Amy had gone from reading glossy magazines to being in them – and, with such a rapid transition from anonymous child to world-famous young adult, she neither felt prepared nor that she looked the part.

Some say anorexia and bulimia have a genetic basis, with research isolating specific chromosomes believed to be associated with the onset of the disorders. Some suggest sufferers are trying to cling to a pre-pubescent child-like body to escape from responsibilities of adult life. Others blame parental behaviours and attitudes. However an all-prevailing theme that runs through every hotly-debated theory is a lack of self-esteem – and, by all accounts, Amy's was at an all-time low.

It wasn't just her eating that was suffering, either. It was at around this time that Amy confessed to smoking two ounces of weed per week, blowing £200 in the process. Tyler had become so concerned about her habitual drug use that he spoke to *Grazia* magazine about it. 'She started using more weed than anyone I know, and everyone tried to stop her and look out for her, but you can't tell Amy what to do. A little becomes a lot with Amy and that's the slippery slope. [She] will do whatever she wants.'

Amy had by now returned to Southgate with her anxious father. A daddy's girl at heart, if the words of her largest tattoo were anything to go by, would Mitch – if no-one else – be successful in curbing her wicked ways?

He and Nick Godwin had managed to persuade a reluctant Amy to confront her fears head-on and attend an interview with a drugs counsellor at the Priory clinic in Southgate. 'My managers took me [to rehab],' Amy told the *Album Chart Show* 'and this guy said "Why do you think you're here?" I said, "I do drink a lot. I think it's symptomatic of my depression – I'm a manic depressive. I'm not an alcoholic" – which sounds like an alcoholic in denial. He goes, "Will you fill in this form?" I went, "How long does it take?" He said, "About half an hour", so I said, "I don't wanna waste your time." Meanwhile my managers were in the pub down the road having Sunday roast – it's a joke.' She added: 'I just thought, do they have a gym there? Who's gonna feed my cats?'

That concluded Amy's first experience with rehab. The answer from an indignant Amy was a resounding 'No'. 'My manager wanted me to go, but my dad thought differently and I respected his opinion more,' she recalled. However the experience had shocked Amy into picking up the pieces – something she knew she'd need to do to prove she didn't need institutionalising - and getting started on writing some new material.

Now that it was time to start recording again, Amy's attentions turned to her management and she was desperate to break free. She hadn't wanted her sound to be geared towards a gap in the market or the latest trend, but to decide for herself where her music was headed. Moreover, she might have held a grudge about a blood-curdling media reference that described her as a 'slightly edgier Dido'. To Amy, this was tantamount to telling a devoted parent that a paedophile has just taken possession of their child. The response would be one of fist-shaking fury.

As it turned out, Dido wasn't too happy about the comparison either. However, she was a little more polite about it. She ranted to *Celebs on Sunday*: 'It really makes me mad that people keep comparing me to Amy Winehouse. It's just labelling me as something else without any respect for the struggle and the determination, the focus or artistic vision I have.' She added: 'I think it's strange and disheartening to be constantly told who I look like or who I sound like. I just want to be me.'

That was one thing she and Amy would agree on. In fact, Amy was already terrified of the next embarrassing comparison that 19's influence on her might inspire. She simply felt that with her current management's presence she wouldn't be able to make the album that she wanted to produce. In a further snub, she had told the press that Fuller – public enemy number one in Amy's eyes – had merely funded her managers, Nick Godwin and Nick Shymanksy, instead of playing an active role. What was more, she wasn't happy with the direction her two mentors were taking her in either.

Jack Freegard told the author: 'Amy and Nick [Shymansky] had a turbulent relationship. Nick is a real music guy – he's not one of those A & Rs who just works in the industry for superficial reasons – a lot of A & R s do. He really loves music, has a great ear and a great sense of direction when it comes to a project. Amy and Nick were like siblings – they loved each other but this was also, I think, the reason for a lot of arguing. You couldn't be around the two for five minutes without them disagreeing over something, musical or not. I think this is what eventually led to them parting ways.'

Amy concurred. 'As soon as my contract was up, I ran away,' she told the Sunday Tribune with barely disguised glee. Up to that point, 19 had been accustomed to dealing with malleable artists, who were happy to take instruction from producers, stylists and mentors – and Amy would never have fitted that description. What 19 had seen in her was raw talent and ambition which – as such – could not be tamed.

The very things they had adored about her had been the same things they were starting to abhor. Amy was not a squeaky clean artist - dignified silences and diplomatic shrugs of the shoulders were simply not her style. If she didn't like one of her contemporaries, she would let rip, offering an unforgiving character analysis of all their worst traits – with little regard for whether they shared her management company or not. Some artists, faced with a question on a rival performer they detested, might diplomatically reply that they preferred a different vocal style. For Amy, on the other hand, the answer was simple – 'They're shit.'

It made for car-crash viewing. Unlike those who tried desperately to win favour and to please their audiences by being polite, gracious and charming, Amy wasn't interested in playing that game. She couldn't have cared less whether her CD sales were four or four million, and even less whether the artists she delivered put-downs to were succeeding. All she was interested in was producing something she could be proud of – and, to the disapproving eyes of 19 Management, that attitude could mean career suicide. It was time to put an end to the power struggles once and for all, and for Amy and 19 to part ways for good.

Relieving herself of all contractual obligations, Amy was now a free woman – but not for much longer. Enter Raye Cosbert, a promoter who had been on the music scene for decades. When Amy had first met him in 2003, he had been able to boast 14 years of music industry experience, having promoted Blur, Robbie Williams and Public Enemy to name a few. He had also been promoting Amy's shows on behalf of Metropolis Music, so the progression from promoter to manager seemed a natural one. Sporting long dreads and a knowing smile, Raye brought with him a wealth of knowledge and experience. The deal was sealed over a few beers in a Camden pub – he would become Amy's new manager.

Now there was just the question of who would produce her second album. The Miami based Salaam Remi, a favourite of Amy's from the first time round, was up for the challenge. Raye had also arranged a meeting with an up and coming figure on the American music scene, Mark Ronson. His only previous experience of Amy had been providing humble handclaps for *Frank*, long after her vocals had been recorded and she had headed back to London, and – having heard a lot about her - he was unsure what to expect.

Born to an English socialite mother and an American businessman father, Mark had been in turn a band member, a DJ and a producer but had remained largely unknown on the music scene at the time he met Amy. In fact, it wasn't until he was invited to DJ at the high profile celebrity wedding of actor Tom Cruise and actress lover Katie Holmes in 2006 that Mark began his own meteoric rise to fame. He went to produce albums for Lily Allen and Christina Aguilera and to pen his own album, *Version,* featuring cover songs by celebrity guest vocalists.

Amy was not keen on the celebrity circuit but agreed to give him a try. Initially typecasting Mark, perhaps unfairly, as 'a white guy who tried too hard', Amy found that in person they bonded over their shared Jewish background. Mark had regularly performed at bar mitzvahs early on in his career and was delighted to be nurtured by maternal Amy who made 'beef casseroles… lovely Jewish mother food'. More importantly however, the two shared an ambition to incorporate Amy's obsession with 60s music onto her finished album. Determined to give it a Motown feel, the pair set to work. The decision to do so together had ultimately not been a difficult one.

Amy's nature and forwardness might have infuriated some of the people she had worked with, but to Mark it was a welcome change. If she didn't like a beat he offered to her, she'd let him know straight away. 'Amy would just go, "Nah, it's shit," he claimed. '[If I offered to rework it], she'd say, "Nah, don't bother, it's shit." That's really helpful because you can waste time taking an idea that you didn't like in the first place and making it vaguely better.'

Not only did he like her dominant stance, but he was also very pleased with the musical avenue she was taking. 'Amy is bringing a rebellious rock and roll spirit back to popular music,' he enthused. 'These groups from the 60s like the Shangri-Las had that kind of attitude. Young girls from Queen's [a district of New York] in motorcycle jackets. Amy looks fucking cool and she's brutally honest in her songs. It's been so long since anyone in the pop world has come out and admitted their flaws, because everyone's trying so hard to project perfection. But Amy will say "Yeah, I got drunk and fell down – so what?" She's not into self-infatuation and she doesn't choose fame. She's that good, she doesn't have to.'

Amy was certainly honest and had spent the past three years in the school of rebellion, due to her former management. Mark's words were strong and supportive and Salaam was equally forward about singing her praises. An instinctive producer who worked closely with ProTools to see music in terms of textures and colours, rather than mere beats, he too was working to take her sound to the next level. Like Mark, he let Amy take the lead role, telling *Remix* magazine that 'what pulls the album together is Amy's confidence.' It had been a relief for Amy to have won back some of her missing confidence and to realise she was capable of writing again after spending so long locked in depression.

Dividing her time between New York with Mark and Miami with Salaam, Amy was enthusiastic about the idea of taking the album on the road again. With the exception of a charity show for Holocaust survivors on November 19th 2005, where she had performed a paltry three songs, and the festival in Oxfordshire earlier that year, Amy had not played live for over a year.

She was also looking forward to telling every aspect of her love story with Blake, hoping to exorcise the pain through self-expression. 'I realised that the Shangri-Las have pretty much got a song for every stage of a relationship – when you see a boy and you don't even know his name, when you start falling for him, when you start going out with him – and then when you're in love with him. And then when he fucking chucks you and you want to kill yourself,' she recalled. Like the Shangri-Las, Amy would bring that theme of a love and heartbreak album – the sweet and the sour – into the new millennium.

Yet before she could turn her attention to the stage, the album needed to be perfected and completed. One of the first songs to emerge from the studio sessions was 'Rehab'. The tune was a candid account of the 'revolving door experience' that marked Amy's first encounter with professional help. Parodying that time, Amy sang the simple hook 'They tried to make me go to rehab… I said no, no, no'.

She recalled: 'Me and Mark Ronson were just walking down the street in Soho and I sang the hook… I sang it as a joke. Mark started laughing, saying, "That's so funny, Amy. Whose song is that?" I told him, "I just wrote it off the top of my head", and he said, "It would be so cool if you had a whole song about rehab." I said ,"Well, I could write it right now!"'

The pair made a mad dash for the studio while they were still inspired – and, half an hour later, 'Rehab' was born. 'It was about what my old management wanted me to do,' Amy continued with a sarcastic snort of derision. This was to set the theme for the song – an account of personal pain turned on its head to become a tongue in cheek parody of rehab culture.

Upbeat and defiant, it details Amy's refusal to be admitted to a clinic. With steely determination, she uses her father's approval of her lifestyle as a defence. The verse 'I'd rather be at home with Ray' has the intimacy of a romantic clinch, but the listener soon discovers she is referring to her beloved Ray Charles albums – for it is music that provides Amy with real therapy. Also name-checking Donny Hathaway, she resolves to shun rehab and pour out her pain lyrically instead, relying on the friends in her record collection to get her through. Ultimately a middle finger salute to the horror of a ten week stint in rehab, it is the soundtrack to survival – a celebration of a natural remedy.

The next song, 'You Know I'm No Good', is a velvety-voiced confession of what Amy sees as her secret life as an infidel. She later claimed live on TV that her top tips for successful romance were to 'lie, cheat and steal' and this song introduces all three in gory detail. 'I don't have many morals,' she explained of the song later. 'My boyfriend is going "You cheated on me" and I go, "Well, I told you I was a good for nothing."' The bluesy number chronicles Amy's tears on the kitchen floor with the intense rise and fall of the brass section as an accompaniment.

In third song 'Me and Mr Jones', the object of Amy's affection is again a musical icon instead of a lover, but the passion runs equally deep. 'What kind of fuckery is this?' she exclaims indignantly, berating an ex-boyfriend who causes her to miss not only the Slick Rick gig, but a concert with favourite rapper Nas Jones as well. Harshly questioning whether he can make it up to her, she makes it entirely clear where her priorities lie. In an unmistakable nod to Nas, she sings 'Mr Destiny, 9 and 14'. September 14th is the birthday the two share, while Destiny is the name of the daughter Nas fathered with then girlfriend Carmen. Nothing comes between Amy and her infatuation with her favourite music – and least of all rehab.

'Just Friends' is an ode to Amy's ill-fated relationship with Blake and the snatched telephone calls and five minute meetings the two shared while he officially belonged to another woman. 'The guilt will kill you, if she don't first,' Amy advises, lamenting the impossibility of just enjoying each other's company, romantic complications aside.

'Back to Black', featuring an intense, throbbing bass line and a nod to the classic Supremes tune 'Baby Love', is another nod to part time boyfriend Blake. Looking back at the man who inspired the song, Amy recalled 'I had never felt the way I feel about him about anyone in my life. [Writing the song] was very cathartic, because I felt terrible. I thought we'd never see each other again. He laughs about it now… "What do you mean, you thought we'd never see each other again? We love each other. We've always loved each other." But I don't think it's funny. I wanted to die.'

The song dates back to the darkest of these moments, when Amy even tattooed a new boyfriend's initial on her ring finger in a desperate attempt to free herself from the agony of her lost love, but all in vain. She whispers a reminder to herself that they only said goodbye with words, hinting that the memories of her lover will scar her, both for better and for worse, regardless of the passage of time. The funereal atmosphere was inspired by the theme of 'Dressed in Black' by the Shangri-Las. 'I like old sixties heartbreak songs, girl group comfort music, songs you can sing into a bottle of whisky,' she recalled later. Deeply saddening but with a strangely uplifting beat, this Diana Ross tinged sonnet of despair mirrored their 60s feel.

Likewise, 'Love is a Losing Game' is the soundtrack to impossible love. The affair Amy speaks of is like heroin to her – potent, addictive and sadly, no less deadly. It is an attachment so strong that complications are almost an inevitable side effect. According to one blogger, the song 'has all the ingredients of a classic Winehouse track, but the depth and intensity here is thoroughly unparalleled.' Every part of the song is infused with memories of her brief romance with Blake, from the 'final frame' of their Camden pub pool sessions to the 'gambling man' – a reference to his obsession with betting shops. Saying her last goodbyes to the man she fears has left her sight forever, the song echoes the desperation of Etta James when she pledges she'd sooner go blind than see her lover walk away.

'Tears Dry On Their Own' is surprisingly buoyant in comparison. Featuring a sample of the classic tune 'Ain't No Mountain High Enough', the trumpet plays out Amy's fate as the perpetual other woman. She laments that she should be her own best friend, instead of resorting to 'stupid men'. Yet – unable to take her own advice – she typecasts herself as the other woman, no matter where she goes.

'Wake Up Alone' sees Amy transform from an angry young lover to a vulnerable girl barely past the rites of puberty – one who can't bear to be left alone. To the distant throbbing rhythms of the Dap Kings band, Amy confesses her innermost secrets, her plight of being starved of her lover's touch. The secrets are ones that she can hide from others, but not from herself. The voyeur to private pain, the listener learns she is consumed by dreams of her lover, awakening in the cold moonlight only to find that, again, she is alone.

In 'Some Unholy War', Amy plays the part of a feverish partisan who has lost all sight of her cause. Yet she stands by her man with drunken devotion and an all-consuming infatuation it would seem senseless to fight. She is armed with the ultimate weapon of war – her guitar case – and it is the instrument within that she hopes will win the war and heal her heart. Armed with a generous helping of 'drunken pride', she will fight against all odds for the man she loves. This track features a triple helping of guitar – from Amy, Salaam and the musician Vincent Henry.

'He Can Only Hold Her' describes Amy's senseless clinches with one man while her heart is taken by another. Knowing this replacement can never live up to her ex's glory, and despairingly wondering if any man ever will, she laments that her heart has been stolen. The listener is enveloped in Motown style beats that mirror her addiction. This sonnet caused controversy as co-writer P*Nut was un-credited on the original album. As he had also worked on material with Dido, jokes circulated that Amy had omitted from the final product to spare her blushes.

Despite the controversy, Neal Sugarman of the Dap Kings saw this song as his favourite one. 'It always felt great to me and maybe the closest to the Dap Kings kind of sound,' he told the author. 'The process was very much like when we record Sharon's records – very open micing and trying to make the music groove as much as possible.' He added: 'It would be cool to hear her do a Sharon Jones and the Dap Kings cover – maybe 'Game Gets Old' or '100 Days 100 Nights'.'

The final track, 'Addicted', is on a slightly more frivolous note. Berating a man who steals her weed, she optimistically crowns herself 'tighter than airport security team'. The sentiment evokes images of Amy's flat complete with sniffer dogs and X-ray enforcements, and returns a smile to the listener's face, who – given the intensity of the preceding songs – might otherwise have ended the album crying into their coffee.

Meanwhile drummer Nathan assured that Amy was not as stingy as she might have seemed. 'She would always share it,' he revealed. 'She just didn't like people to sponge.'

A selection of musicians had also taken to the studio to complement the vocal. Jamie Talbot, a saxophonist for the sessions at Metropolis Studios in Chiswick, recalled: 'The songs had a 60s feel and theme. Amy's voice suited this perfectly, even though she doesn't try to imitate the singers of that time. Listening to the ballad style of 'Love is a Losing Game', I'm reminded of the Bacharach songs sung by Dusty Springfield, Gloria Gaynor and Dionne Warwick and would love to hear Amy singing a cover version of something like 'A House Is Not A Home', or 'Walk On By'.'

Jamie had been responsible for adding tenor sax to 'Rehab', 'Back to Black' and finally 'Love is a Losing Game'. Another group who would play a huge role in the sound of the album were the Dap Kings. Mark Ronson had been trying desperately to create an old-school sound on the album using keyboards and drum machines. 'We were using every computer trick in the world to make it sound old,' he recalled, 'but it was just so ridiculous.' Enter the Dap Kings, who quickly became key players in the sought after 60s sound. 'The first day the Dap Kings joined, it just sounded a million times better,' Mark enthused.

The enthusiasm was mutual. Neal Sugarman told the author: 'The writing relationship with Amy was great. She always wanted the Dap Kings to feel involved and she was not like other pop musicians we have worked with. She wanted to be involved musically and challenged.' Amy's active, at times domineering, role in the studio was a refreshing change for the group, who wanted her to be pro-active in designing their sound. 'She really liked everything we did,' he continued. 'We for sure arranged that music and wrote great lines to her songs.'

With the Dap Kings groove now firmly part of her sound, Amy was ready to test her new songs on the road and get back to what she loved the most – performing.

A series of three teaser gigs saw Amy travel across the country to make her comeback. The first, at the Bristol Fleece on September 10th, saw Amy's voice described as a one woman production of *Little Britain*, with 'the garbled haste of Vicky Pollard, the camp bark of Marjorie Davies and the slightly unhinged gusto of that woman Matt Lucas plays who's always screeching "E's gawwwgeous!"' Referring to her weight loss, *The Telegraph* continued 'It's impossible that a frame so spindly should house a singing voice so colossal.'

Amy went on to showcase the new album at the Brighton Concorde on September 11th and finally the Bloomsbury Ballroom on September 12th. *The Evening Standard* was a little sceptical about her comeback, commenting, 'London has already taken one pop loudmouth to its heart this year in the garish shape of Lily Allen. Have we got the tolerance for another cavernous gob?' Gracing the same stage as Martha Reeves before her, Amy meant business and as the evening proceeded it emerged that she was still a formidable force to be reckoned with.

'She was so small, you could rest your drink on her, if you dared,' the newspaper teased. '[However] on stage, surrounded by tall male musicians, she still looked like the one with whom it would be most unwise to pick a fight.'

'With huge menacing swooshes of mascara around her eyes, a speaking voice that was more of a growl and a selection of lyrics so bitter they stung, she ruled the room,' the review continued. 'The wider public will find it hard to ignore her this time.'

Yet it was the tune 'Rehab' that really had the reviewers swooning. *The Evening Standard* added of the track: 'It was tremendous, a gospel stomp packed with handclaps and frisky horns and the killer chorus "Tried to make me go to rehab, I say no, no, no." This is surely her first major hit in waiting.'

Exactly as the newspaper had predicted, Amy was to take the world by storm with the very same song a mere few weeks later.

CHAPTER 8

In an era characterised by celebrity excess, with Kate Moss, Jade Goody and Robbie Williams all splashed luridly across the tabloids for their indiscretions, 'Rehab' had come at just the right time. A witty, pithy and deeply ironic take on the drug culture that surrounded the modern music scene, it rivalled 'Fuck Me Pumps' for its parody of nightclub culture. Yet, unlike its predecessor, which had miserably flanked the No. 68 spot, 'Rehab' was about to climb a lot higher in the charts.

By this point, staggering out of nightclubs surreptitiously scratching one's septum seemed to be inextricably linked with the public's image of celebrity. The song came at a time when rehab and all the poisons that led to it were both frowned upon and in fashion all at the same time.

Britney Spears, shunning her innocent image of yesteryear, had allegedly begun to abuse narcotics – shaving her head as rebellion against a hair strand test – and had dissolved into public floods of tears after being questioned about her inadequate parenting. Model Kate Moss, dubbed Cocaine Kate in the tabloids, had a brief flirtation with rehab to save her lucrative modelling contracts after an edgy cocaine-fuelled affair with shambolic musician Pete Doherty. It was later remarked that Kate's penchant for Class A substances had made her more famous than ever before, leading to the belief that society had allowed her to cash in on her notoriety. Not only that, but Kate's face had adorned modelling shoots of the 1990s in an era widely characterised by the media as one of 'heroin chic'. Had rehab become the new trend again?

Meanwhile Robbie Williams joined a string of high profile celebrities to be admitted to rehab, suffering from exhaustion, the perils of fast-paced living and, of course, drug addiction. Amy's rendition of 'Rehab' might have been a heartbroken account of her own personal troubles – and potentially a public humiliation – but it instead came across as a poignant anthem for 21st century excess.

Not only that, but it was a signature tune of defiance to Amy's long-suffering stint with 19 management. Soon enough they'd no longer be cramping each other's style, but as a parting shot she wanted to show them who was boss. Not only did the diva refuse to play along with their requests to dip a toe into the pop world, believing her fate lay with jazz and soul numbers, but she refused to take their advice about rehab as well.

'If my daddy thinks I'm fine,' Amy sang resolutely, leaving no room for negotiation. 'I trusted him over my management,' she would later explain.

'Rehab' shot to the top of the digital download charts a week before its release, peaking at No. 19. The following week, when it officially hit the shops, it reached No. 7. T-shirts emblazoned with 'Rehab? No, No, No' beside Amy's face became the ultimate must-have item for everyone from fashionistas to the likes of Miss Liverpool, who was snapped in the shirt the day after she was crowned. Rehab had officially become a part of pop culture. But what was Amy's personal view on going to a clinic and seeking help? 'I'm not against it for those who need it, but a lot of those programs are just for people who want to be babied,' she scoffed.

However, just a few weeks before the release of the single, Amy was to show the general public exactly why she had needed that intervention. On October 19th, she appeared on *The Sharon Osbourne Show*. According to newspaper reports, she had repeatedly begged her minders backstage to supply her with vodka, heckling them when they offered a mere glass instead of the entire bottle. 'She repeatedly asks a producer to get her the vodka,' *The Times* recalled of their backstage encounter with her. 'Finally he caves in and asks if she just wants a glass. "Are you having a laugh? Yeah, I just want a shot," she deadpans. "No, I want a bottle," she confirms like a dipsomaniac Veruca Salt.'

Amy's voracious appetite for alcohol was matched on that occasion by the show's host, who was celebrating her 54th birthday at the time. Horrified onlookers saw a shame-faced Sharon giggle helplessly throughout the interview, claiming: 'Oh fuck, I made a mistake!' and 'I'm so sorry I'm pissed but it's my birthday!'

She was involved in a similar scandal at the Brit Awards two years later when co-presenting the gong for Best British Album with equally drunken comedian Vic Reeves. Grabbing the award from his hands, she screamed: 'Shut up, you're pissed! Piss off, you bastard,' before taking control of the stage.

Yet Sharon celebrated her opinionated nature, telling the *Daily Mail:* 'Very few people in the public eye are actually willing to offer an opinion on anything. Everything is always wonderful. You can ask them what they think of anyone – Britney Spears, Amy Winehouse or Genghis Khan and they'll say "I love them. Oh God, I really love them." Of course they can't actually stand the sight of the person they're talking about but never in a million years would they admit it. I'm not like that.'

Her rare predilection for being shamelessly outspoken and controversial in the press was something she and Amy shared with each other. Yet newspaper reports indicated that there was no love lost between them. In spite of Sharon's own alcohol issues and those of husband Ozzy – whose battles with drug addiction had been well documented in the press for decades – she declared that Amy and friends were 'a bad influence' on her daughter Kelly.

Amy would give her comments ammunition with a shockingly self-destructive performance on *The Charlotte Church Show* on October 13th. Like Amy, host Charlotte was a good girl gone bad. She had begun her career as a teenage musical prodigy, achieving rave reviews for her gospel inspired tunes on the album *Voice of An Angel*. Yet Charlotte also had a penchant for strong alcohol and bad boys, publicly making her way through a string of troubled and volatile relationships. Despite Charlotte's devilish side, it was Amy who was in trouble on the day of the show.

The two had been scheduled to perform a duet, covering Michael Jackson's 'Beat It'. Unfortunately it was a show-stopper for all the wrong reasons. According to *The Observer*, it was 'an indelicate choice of cover version – Winehouse had allegedly punched a fan, then her boyfriend in another boozy altercation'. Aside from that, Amy had barely recovered from a liquid lunch in the green room and a copious supply of vodka and champagne for breakfast, when it was time for her to take to the stage.

Arms flailing wildly as she struggled to keep her balance, she stumbled in front of the studio audience, pausing only to smash her foot into a glass table. *The Jewish Chronicle* recalled the performance, claiming: 'Amy reportedly had trouble reading the auto-cue and kept shoving her head into the camera when it was focusing on other guests.' The audience began to scream: 'Sing it on your own, Charlotte!' as an increasingly confused Amy failed to remember the lyrics.

Charlotte later told *The Telegraph:* 'She was smashed… I had my hand behind her like a puppet the whole time, pushing her when it was her turn to sing. If you want to know what even the best singer can sound like drunk, then Google that performance. It was horrible.'

She continued, 'I think it's rude if you ask me. I always turned up and did my duties.' Some might have disagreed – a much earlier live show in her career had seen Charlotte repeatedly wandering off to check her mobile phone while onstage, seeking a sign of life from her estranged boyfriend. In addition, newspaper reports later sensationally suggested that Charlotte had consumed alcohol while pregnant, putting her unborn baby at risk of Fetal Alcohol Syndrome.

Whatever the truth behind these rumours, Amy was not amused. Feeling that Charlotte was taking an air of moral superiority, she branded her 'an arrogant cow'. She responded to the comments against her with the words: 'I don't promote myself to be a wonderful person. I know I can be quite foolish but it's not like I claim otherwise.'

She hit out at Charlotte again over concern about Amy's rapidly diminishing figure. 'It bothered me when someone said, "You used to be a role model for curvy women",' she raged to *Contact Music*. 'I was like, no, actually. Go and have a go at Charlotte Church when she loses a stone. People say you're too skinny, it's like saying you're too fat. It's weight discrimination.'

Aside from the war of words between the pair, the shambolic performance on *The Charlotte Church Show* continued to blight Amy's career. *Scotland on Sunday* reported that her vocals were 'completely incomprehensible', although one fan on the website insisted: 'This could make her an icon.'

For Amy's part, a journalist who interviewed her for the newspaper insisted that she was unapologetic, laughing off claims that the duet was 'diabolical' and simply saying that she'd love to watch it when it aired on TV.

In a further interview with *The Times*, Amy gave in to her addiction yet again with loud cries of 'Where's my vodka?' When a man following her command returned empty-handed, she turned to her minders and mocked 'There's probably a monkey in his brain rubbing two sticks together!'

Amy also confessed that she had been succumbing to drunken episodes of violence. When leaving one of her comeback shows in September, she had seen red and lashed out at a fan. 'Apparently the other night, some girl comes up to me [after the show] and she goes "Hello", gives me a kiss on the cheek, and as she went away, she goes to my boyfriend "God, she's really fucked, isn't she?" and I just saw red and smacked her,' Amy recalled candidly. 'I don't remember this at all. Then I took my boyfriend home and started beating him up.'

Another night in the Hawley Arms pub, a man incited Amy's fury when he kept 'punctuating his stories by slapping his hand on our table'. Whilst any other reveller might have ignored it or politely asked him to stop, Amy wasn't doing anything by halves – instead, she found the man responsible and gave him a 'well-deserved' slap. 'I push it over the edge and ruin my boyfriend's night,' she confessed. 'I'm an ugly dickhead drunk, I really am.'

Sophie Heawood, a freelance journalist for *The Times* who had spent time with Amy at one of her shows later commented, 'She told me she had tried rehab and decided it wasn't for her, so I asked her why she thought people went to the Priory. "To get crack obviously!" she beamed. We were backstage at Sharon Osbourne's TV show, on which Amy would perform, but the whole day was distracted by her need for the vodka. "'Appy times!" she announced when the vodka finally arrived, and poured herself and Blake a large one.'

Her insatiable appetite for alcohol came to a head at the Q Awards on October 30th. U2's lead singer Bono was accepting the award from the coveted Band of Bands category. An arena sat in hushed silence – some members of the audience were watching in awe, whilst others were simply conforming to etiquette by being polite and respectful. Amy, on the other hand, was thoroughly bored. 'Shut up! I don't give a fuck!' she screamed. That very same day, her much awaited second album hit the shops. Would it be career suicide, or the ideal advertisement for her comeback?

If it was an advertisement, it was certainly a truthful one, leaving potential buyers under no illusion about her frankness. The acid tongue was still very much in attendance, even three years on.

However, backing vocalist Ade Omotayo recalled how Amy was left shame-faced when irate music bosses at her label took her to one side for a stern talking to. '[She and Bono] were on the same label,' he laughed to the author. 'They said to her: "You do know he's responsible for you being able to do all the stuff you're doing, because his album sold like a zillion copies?" If it wasn't for him, the label wouldn't have the money to send her out on the road. She said "Oh my God, I'm sorry!" – she just apologised.' It might temporarily have smoothed things over but, to Amy, sorry was 'just a word' – and label bosses shouldn't have counted on her actually meaning it.

Her antics certainly didn't seem to damage her album prospects though. Reviews began to pour into the media, almost unanimously praising the musical change of direction on the new album, and often expressing surprise at the 'maturity' and 'otherworldliness' of her voice – one that many felt would sound more at home if it rose from the vocal chords of a heartbroken black American twenty years her senior.

The Telegraph claimed: '*Back to Black* sees a triumphant Winehouse slamming the door on those laidback lounge influences and strutting into a gloriously ballsy, bell-ringing, bottle-swigging doo-wop territory… think Ronnie Spector, Etta James, Edith Piaf and Marlene Shaw. Women whose favourite men are bartenders.'

The Guardian heralded it as a '21st century soul classic', a reference that made Amy beam with pride. The paper also claimed: 'Any album that features the line "What kind of fuckery is this? You made me miss the Slick Rick gig" demands close investigation.' Meanwhile reviewers understood her desire to escape from the pigeon-hole of commercial mainstream friendly jazz-pop – and believed she'd achieved her goal.

However *OMH Music* had a cynical theory that her heartbreak fuelled journey to hell and back had all been a carefully crafted PR stunt. 'Cue tabloid stories of record company worry at Winehouse's alleged excessive alcohol habits and paparazzi photos showing a dramatic weight loss. Then along comes a single which begins "They tried to make me go to rehab, I said no, no, no"…' it claimed cynically.

The website believed Amy's car-crash lifestyle was an act, a deliberate anithesis to distinguish herself from the good girl persona of 'boring' and 'wholesome' artists such as Katie Melua – whom Amy openly despised. The review continued: 'If indeed the conveniently timed newspapers are a PR stunt, it's a shame as *Back to Black* needs no such media manipulation… it's an amazingly confident second album which shows Winehouse moving on in leaps and bounds from *Frank*.' With a nod to its retro sound, the website praised 'Rehab' as a great example. 'Horns parp and blaze, strings classily swing and smoulder while Winehouse's extraordinary voice purrs and growls about old Ray Charles records being better than the Priory,' it continued. 'It's Motown rewritten for the 21st century.'

Yet the best news Amy could have received was the claim: 'It's staggering to think that Winehouse was compared to the likes of Katie Melua when she first arrived – it's certainly hard to imagine Melua extolling the virtues of cannabis, let alone in quite the same way as Winehouse does in the classy 'Addicted' ("It's got me addicted, does more than any dick did") or indeed conjuring up an album with half the passion, fire and good old-fashioned soul as 'Back to Black'.' Calculated or not, she had certainly got her point across.

'All I ever wanted was for the album to be honest,' she claimed later. Amy hadn't just humiliated one of the most acclaimed rock singers in the world when she heckled U2, but she had also humiliated herself – but she would feel no shame. Her brutal honesty extended to her own personal problems and, however harsh she was towards Katie Melua or Chris Martin, she seemed to be ten times harder on herself. She admitted to an insatiable desire for sambucas and that she'd had a flirtation with 'every eating disorder there is'.

Amy would now embark on a ten date tour across the country to promote the new album. She was celebrating her bid for artistic freedom – and her first major tour without 19 Management in tow – with a defiant new style that was just as 60s as her music. That's right, the singer was sporting a towering beehive hairdo.

Whilst men might have needed to feel large in the trouser department for sexual confidence and prowess, Amy needed a larger than life hairdo to strut her stuff onstage. She compensated for her lack of stature by six inches of hair above her head.

News travelled fast and, as she moved from city to city, the *UK Hairdressers' Forum* had the trendsetter in mind, writing, 'Love it or hate it, you certainly can't ignore it! Our inbox is divided over whether the new style is a super new trend or a bedraggled bird's nest.'

Amy was had no such reservations. The style was her way of honouring her favourite 60s artists, the Ronettes, who were famed for combining powerful vocals with equally big hair and dramatic black eyeliner. There was only one look in their visual vocabulary – and bigger was better.

However the look had originated around 3,000 years earlier in Queen Nefertiti of Egypt, whose kohl-lacquered eyes and bouffant-like black head-dress mirrored the trend. In 1958, a Chicago hairdresser known as Margaret Vinci Heldt unwittingly revived the style when asked to mould the perfect hairdo for a vertically challenged client.

Dusty Springfield, Brigitte Bardot, Audrey Hepburn and the Ronettes quickly followed suite. By 1964, sales of hairspray had overtaken lipstick as the nation's most popular cosmetic purchase.

Yet fast forward to the 1990s and the only sign of it was on the chronically unfashionable cartoon character Marge Simpson, who sported an eye-watering 2ft tall blue mop. Aside from Christina Aguilera's badly received attempt to relive the trend at a 2001 awards ceremony, the look had totally faded into obscurity.

Enter 23-year-old Amy Winehouse and the trend was bang up to date. *The Evening Standard* got in on the act, writing: 'Forget the Eiffel Tower and the Golden Gate Bridge – this is a real feat of engineering. Amy Winehouse's beehive attained epic proportions yesterday, when she emerged from her house with more than 12 inches of hair piled on her head... unkind observers might wonder if the singer is considering a career in the Grenadier Guards. If so, she could save the taxpayer the £6540 it costs to make a traditional bearskin hat.'

The scene was one of hilarity – and it recalled an episode of the Flintstones when a passing car destroys Wilma and Fred's matching new beehive hairdos and, meanwhile, Amy herself was also seen bending down to avoid low doorways.

Her hair had become a hot topic, with even national newspapers showing their interest. Alice-Azaria Jarvis, a journalist for *The Independent*, was keen to try out the beehive herself – purely for research purposes of course – and was sponsored by the paper to visit a branch of Amy's preferred hairdressers, Racoon International, for a makeover.

She started to have second thoughts when copious amounts of glue were applied to her scalp and employee Cinta Martello mentioned, just in passing, Amy's penchant for polysterene padding to increase the effect.

'In order to create my beehive, Martello is going to apply patches of adhesive to my roots, which will then be pressed together with an alarmingly large pair of forceps,' Alice-Azaria commented. 'Any doubts I might have about the wisdom of applying glue to my hair are only slightly dispelled by the fact that Winehouse is one of Racoon's clients.'

However Mortello had a slightly different look in mind, claiming: '[Amy] sometimes looks as if she's been dragged through a hedge backwards, bless her. But when Karl Lagerfeld did it, he really made it classy. The beehive should be much more about old Hollywood glamour. It should be fun, but sexy and elegant too.'

Alice-Azaria continued, 'She starts with a thorough hair teasing (although the process is so vigorous, I wonder if bullying might be more accurate) and then gathers together the tangles to form a sort of heavy clump around my crown… Out of the corner of my eye, I can just make out the photographer's sceptical expression… but at the last minute, she gathers up some loose strands… smoothing them elegantly over my emerging hive.'

Amy's trademark style, just a few months into its conception, had been recreated by a national newspaper. However Alice-Azaria soon found that Amy's hairstyle was unenduringly showbiz. 'By the time I get home, it's irretrievable,' she lamented. 'Where once I had a beehive, I now have a soggy mass of knotted hair... Glamorous the beehive may be, but for life in the real world? Maybe not.'

However, Amy would soon be gloating, as – in later years – Paris Hilton, Lady Gaga and the French catwalk model Noemie Lenoir all sported the style. The top New York hairdressing school Bumble and Bumble even introduced beehives into the curriculum, creating a dedicated module to teach aspiring students how to perfect the look. An unusual style icon at best, Amy was transforming the hairstyles of the Western world. The style was also seen on female farmers in Yemen for outdoor work, although they had probably started the trend first – and for more practical reasons such as shielding the sun.

And so Amy set off on tour with an exaggerated six inch hair-do – two inches taller than the average beehive and around the length of the average penis. Flaunting her phallic symbol as a female penis extension, she found that with it, she exuded confidence she might otherwise have lacked. 'I've never met anyone with bigger hair than me,' she boasted. 'If I do, I'll be so gutted. That's my secret weapon – I'm nothing without my hair.'

Flatteringly, it was the hottest topic of conversation when she descended on the Koko club in Camden on November 14th, along with her tiny figure – three dress sizes smaller than the one she'd exhibited on the *Frank* tour. It was described as both 'horrifyingly emaciated' and 'fashionably skinny'. Amy, meanwhile, dismissed her weight altogether, telling a fan outside after the show: 'Its simple – I want the music to speak for itself.' Fortunately for her, onlookers had not neglected the vocals from their reviews either. All in all, with her eccentric style, irrepressible rock 'n' roll persona, chic but borderline dangerously skinny frame and of course, her distinctive vocals, she seemed to be a very interesting prospect for the UK media.

Consequently, the buzz around her much anticipated Camden concert was on a whole new level. Her name now came with the implicit promise of misdemeanours – and, on the night, the press weren't disappointed. Her huge voice, combined with a dress so tiny that it barely covered her underwear, led *The Evening Standard* to call her a 'premature foal revived by rum'. She cracked jokes, coquettishly pulled up the hem of her barely there dress and shook her hips while pouting like Betty Boop – all the while seeming to be surgically attached to a pint glass. However, disappointed that she'd only earned tabloid column inches since her weight loss – despite boasting a voice far more voluptuous than her body – *The Evening Standard* set out to redress the balance.

'If this was America, she would be our Courtney Love,' the newspaper claimed, 'only more talented and interpreting Sixties soul with lyrics to make Kurt's widow contemplate swallowing a thesaurus. A genuine singing genius.'

The paper went on to praise that 'where debut album *Frank* noodled around in the sub-jazz stratosphere, her current album shows Amy's talent for proper song-writing'. This might have reassured a visibly nervous Amy that her forte was firmly in writing smoky jazz numbers and soulful Motown inspired beats rather than the 'torturous pop' her previous management had coerced her to try before. Amy wasted no time in admitting at the show that she couldn't wait to 'get the old songs out of the way first'.

A BBC review described the show as an 'unequivocal triumph', challenging, 'How could tonight be anything less? The larger question is why La Winehouse is perceived to be toiling in the shadow of paler counterparts such as Joss Stone, Corrine Bailey Rae and Lily Allen.'

Amy enjoyed the show just as much, announcing to a packed out audience that – despite the tiny venue – she wanted to do a residency at Koko every week. Within walking distance of her Camden flat, she wouldn't have had far to travel.

But her pressing touring schedule soon saw her dragged away. Three days later, she was performing in Birmingham at the Academy 2, on November 17th. 'I wanna put my blowjob lips on! Excuse me a minute!' Amy cried controversially within moments of arriving onstage, after begging the audience for a lipstick in her favourite shade of gaudy red. 'And so the striking young lady in a skimpy dress… proceeds to apply some lipstick that she's just acquired from someone in the front row for about two minutes,' *Glasswerks* wrote of the night. 'Welcome to the crazy world of Amy Winehouse.'

However, anyone hoping for debauched antics would be disappointed. The review continued: 'After finishing her make-up routine, she stumbles around the stage, croaking inaudibly, causing many to worry that she's perhaps a little worse for wear. It turns out she's [just] got a stinking cold. The poor lass can barely talk, but there's no way she's going to let that stop her tonight. Behind the media image of the mouthy, boozed up hellraiser is a total professional who puts her heart and soul into every performance, and she appears visibly frustrated and even upset at times that her voice prevents her from reaching her own high standards tonight... she needn't worry. An off-form Amy Winehouse gig is still a unique, captivating experience.' Back in those days, her lifestyle hadn't yet overshadowed her music – neither as a topic of conversation nor as a stage show.

Amy would also have been delighted to learn that the reviewer placed much-hated rival Katie Melua as hopelessly below her league. Speaking just a day after she repeated on TV show *Never Mind the Buzzcocks* that she would prefer to have 'cat aids' than work with Katie, the review claimed: 'Amy jokes that it doesn't matter if she ruins her voice anyway, as Katie Melua can just take over the rest of the tour. Such an idea seems preposterous, but remember how she was originally placed in the easy listening category of Melua and the other Radio Two favourites? An injustice that thankfully seems to have been corrected with the new album.'

Meanwhile, if Amy had been worried that her shambolic performance on *The Charlotte Church Show* had detracted from the music, she would be pleasantly surprised by journalist and blogger Robert Jackman's review of the concert at the Norwich Waterfront the following day. Held on November 18th, it was an opportunity to showcase the album to both students from the local university and jazz aficionados in a town she had never taken to the stage in before.

It might have been just three weeks since the show and her showbiz rival might have seized the high ground morally and the upper hand vocally – even if only because she'd managed to finish the song without slurring – but Amy was the one listeners would remember. Far from seeing it as a humiliating experience, she had laughed it off – and many found her laidback attitude refreshing and appealing. Plus, while Charlotte's sound had often been dubbed as one of an angel, Amy's seemed to tap into several decades of heartbreak experiences. Even though she seemed more self-destructive than a soldier wielding a machine gun then turning and shooting herself, back then the music was still on everyone's lips.

Robert Jackman blogged 'It's not hard to see why jazz fans hail Winehouse as a messianic figure. This is much more than everyday wine bar jazz from a girl who'd feel more at home in an off license; Amy offers talent and chutzpah in abundance… Alcoholic – she may well be, but with a voice this great she could never be anonymous.'

Unfortunately, the last sentiment was proved correct in more ways than one when Amy allegedly went on a drunken rampage at the local student bar that night. She confronted a male student and, in the altercation that followed, had to be led away from the area. A spokesperson for the bar claimed: 'After the concert finished, Ms. Winehouse was socialising. She took exception to a comment made by a young male… there was a bit of a fracas… the young man was led away and Ms. Winehouse was asked to leave the area.'

Wherever Amy went, it seemed that trouble would follow. However, the glowing praise of the reviews made no mention of the fisticuffs. For now, in the battle between the music and Amy's comedic extra-curricular side-show, the music was definitely winning.

Amy continued the tour, concluding with a headline show for the Little Noise Sessions at the Union Chapel in London's Islington – a 800-capacity Victorian church. Other headliners that season had included Liam Gallagher, who was also renowned for a ballsy attitude and a penchant for heavy drinking as well as, according to his fanbase, 'artistic brilliance'. The concert was a fundraiser for Mencap, a charity that helps young people with learning difficulties.

After that, Amy managed to spend Christmas with her family before taking part in a New Year's Eve special edition of *Later with Jools Holland*. It was a perfect way for her to see in the New Year, doing what she enjoyed the most – singing her heart out. She first sang solo on a cover version of 'Monkey Man' by Toots and the Maytals. She then joined Paul Weller for a joint performance of Marvin Gaye's 'I Heard It Through The Grapevine' and Etta James's 'Don't Go To Strangers'.

Dressed in a feathery black dress and with a colourful band adorning her ever unruly hair, Amy played the role of a 50s movie star, swaying her hips provocatively to the rhythm of the music, while Jools Holland played a piano accompaniment. A studio employee revealed to the author: 'Jools has played onstage with some extremely competent performers, but never anyone like Amy. He tried to keep his cool, but it was pretty clear that he was flattered just to be gracing the same stage as her – he even said as much when the cameras stopped rolling.'

Paul Weller agreed with the praise, stating that she was one of his all time favourite singers. 'She is a great talent,' he told Radio 1 after their gig together, 'and despite what all the papers say, she is a great role model for people.' Indeed, just months later, Amy would be voted Ultimate Heroine in a nationwide youth poll. However, her detractors remarked that the nomination would have been more appropriate if organisers had removed the 'E' from 'heroin'.

Paul continued to sing her praises, however, defending: 'I don't think the drugs and the drink and all that make a scrap of difference, really. I think you should judge people on their talent and on that level she's up there, a major talent.'

This background of glowing praise was the ideal climate for Amy to release her second single, 'You Know I'm No Good'. Amy's first ever collaboration would appear on this single – a remix of the title track by Wu Tang Clan's hip-hop giant Ghostface Killah. Other tracks on the single included a studio version of 'Monkey Man' and a live version of 'To Know Him Is To Love Him'. The release date was scheduled for January 8th, 2007.

However, two days before the CD was due to hit the shops, tragedy struck. Amy was due to play to her gay and lesbian following in an intimate gathering at the G. A.Y club. It would be her chance to compensate for the homophobia rumours that had blighted her ever since she released 'Stronger Than Me'. Housed in the basement of the Astoria rock club in London's Charing Cross, the night regularly received celebrity guests. Some were too candy-coated, camp and kitsch for Amy's tastes, such as Atomic Kitten, Boyzone, Britney Spears, Girls Aloud and the Minogue sisters. Meanwhile, Amy's opinion of Tatu, the manufactured lesbian pop duo who hit the charts in 2003 and G.A.Y shortly after, was an unprintable expletive. 'I think it spoiled the lesbian illusion when one of them got pregnant,' she had chuckled sarcastically. 'The men can kiss goodbye to their girly fantasies.' That said, even some of the largely gay crowd at the Astoria had shunned the group due to its 'fakeness'.

On the night of the show, flyers were handed out with the message 'They tried to make me go to rehab, I said No, No, No! They tried to make me go to G.A.Y, I said Yes, Yes, Yes!' Convinced of Amy's commitment, fans arrived in their droves. There was a buzz of anticipation in the tiny hall, which was filled to capacity. Arriving way behind schedule at 1:45 a.m., Amy was met with relieved rounds of applause – but the crowd's temporary elation was to be short-lived. After just a few verses of 'Back to Black', she began to clutch her stomach, retching violently. She tried desperately to hold the group together but failed and was allegedly seen vomiting before she'd even reached the backstage area. The visual evidence that she was genuinely ill did little to assuage the fury of clubbers, many of whom believed she was merely drunk. Apologetic staff took to the stage to promise that she would return shortly, but despite a furious audience's bays and cat-calls, she never did. The scene was reminiscent of rock princess Courtney Love's notoriously diabolical tours of America in the 90s, when angry concert-goers would lie in wait outside her tour bus after shows to demand their money back. On occasion, they were even successful.

However, there was no such reward for the disheartened gay followers that night. A club goer reported: 'Amy looked drunk and after singing a few lines of the opening track, put her hand over her mouth as if to be sick. Then she legged it. When the organiser came out to say she wouldn't be coming back, the crowd got really angry and started to boo. A lot of people had paid money to see her perform and all we got was one half-hearted album track. It wasn't good enough.'

Rumours circulated that Amy's illness was the result of a drunken date with Kelly Osbourne earlier in the day. According to the list, however, Amy's only drug of choice during that time had been fruit smoothies to ease her sore throats. She had flown back from a trip to Miami the morning before the show and blamed a bout of food poisoning contracted on the aeroplane. She remained adamant that she hadn't had a drink in days. Unfortunately, the rumour that she and Kelly Osbourne had been partying hard remained a persistent one.

The two had been firm friends since the Brit Awards three years previously, bonding over a shared loved of tattoos and wild child excess. Both boasted unconventional beauty and displayed an awkwardness far removed from the self assuredness of the celebrity circuit. 'She came up to me drunkenly, grabbed my boob and said she wasn't being forward but just really liked me,' said Kelly of the moment. 'We started talking and just became friends. I think we got on because we both have a big lack of vanity.'

That lack of vanity was seen at its worst during the G.A.Y performance where disgruntled concert goers saw her vomit in public. G.A.Y, meanwhile, found itself in the embarrassing position of having to negotiate refunds with furious customers. Amy's reputation with the gay community had been a difficult one ever since 'Stronger than Me' had been deemed homophobic in the press. However, despite this divide of opinion, a large crowd had warmed to Amy and been there to cheer her on that night. Regrettably, this latest episode would only rub salt in their wounds. Meanwhile Amy's arch rival Kanye West might have won over some of her fans with the admission that he had a gay cousin. He promised that, in spite of previous lyrics that had been perceived as gay bashing, he had a new found respect for the community. Months later, he would form dangerous competition for Amy when he was nominated for eight prestigious Grammy awards to her comparatively paltry six.

It had been a disappointing and embarrassing start to the year for Amy, and she was a little relieved when the time came for her to flee British shores. However, the pressure wasn't going to cease, as she was about to face a bigger challenge than ever before while abroad – that of breaking America. For a British girl who hadn't released so much as a single song stateside, it was a major undertaking – but this proud British girl was ready to do her best.

CHAPTER 9

Amy stepped tentatively off the aeroplane into the path of a bitterly cold wind – she'd touched down in New York at the height of winter and, for a girl who preferred to spend the season in Miami, it would take all of her endurance to brave the sub-zero temperatures.

Yet she had more pressing matters on her mind – her first performance on US soil at the 160-capacity hangout Joe's Pub. To the outsider, it was a tiny scruffy dive of a bar without a single speck of glamour to its name. Yet despite the peeling paint on the walls and the diminutive down-market vibe, it had been the venue for Norah Jones, Alicia Keys, Mos Def and Eartha Kitt to launch their careers in the USA. There could have been few better places for a virgin artist stateside to start out.

Indeed, the venue proved lucky for her. She was legendary before she'd so much as publicly stepped a foot on US soil, with tickets selling on auction website Craigslist for more than $200 each – a higher price than many established acts could command on the black market. Tickets sold like gold dust, while musical icons such as Mos Def and Jay Z, and even Jimi Hendrix's sister made the guestlist. She would be playing to an eclectic crowd and her mixed audience was fitting. Amy had a head-start with the older generation, who – through her music – could relive the nostalgia of nights out in 60s supper clubs. Yet Amy was edgy and exciting enough to earn a nod of approval from a younger crowd too.

As *The Observer* commented in anticipation of her stateside adventure, 'Given the uproar in America a couple of years ago when Justin Timberlake exposed Janet Jackson's left nipple at the Super Bowl, trying to imagine what our American friends would make of Amy Winehouse and the word fuckery, was worth the price of the ticket alone.'

Her mixture of sophistication and 21st century raucous rock chick would arouse the interests of young and old alike. There would also be a nod of recognition from the black community as she referenced African soul artists both past and present. Amy's management were hoping she would dominate on many levels – and, if early ticket sales were anything to go by, she certainly would.

Amy arrived on time in a black strapless dress and sporting hair that a reviewer would describe as 'piled a foot above her head'. As the audience drank in her appearance, she spoke. 'Awwight?' she cackled, by way of introduction. 'I'm Ad-Rock from the Beastie Boys!' She then launched without further ado into the lazy reggae vibe of 'Just Friends'.

Clamouring for amaretto almost the moment she arrived onstage, she then popped a Maraschino cherry into her mouth while she finished the song. Her excessive alcohol consumption was part of what America seemed to love about her and that was alright with Amy – she'd simply incorporate her demons into her onstage act.

Bill Bragin, director at Joe's Pub, explained the key to Amy's instant appeal. 'She's coming with a larger than life persona,' he commented. 'She's got all the elements of a star. She's got the talent, but she's [also] got something that gets her into [gossip columnist] Perez Hilton when she doesn't even have an album in the US. She's the real deal.'

Mark Ronson, a mutual guest at the show night, also had ideas about why she was catching on. 'Amy is just so refreshingly honest and raw and pure,' he enthused. '[Britney Spears et al] aren't bad people but it's just cookie cutter.' He believed that the USA was filled with harmless yet meaningless love songs, designed neither to offend nor to stand out and that the country was crying out, whether they knew it or not, for an artist like Amy. Terrified that the obligatory parental advisory stickers might damage their sales if they stood out, Mark believed many contemporary artists were playing it safe at the expense of being real. 'No-one's making music that's really going to be around to listen to in ten years,' he continued. 'But you come to Amy and it just feels incredibly real.'

It was against that backdrop that she took to the stage for just over an hour for the punters of Joe's Pub. What would the media make of her performance? Music blog *A Deeper Shade of Soul* recalled of the event, which took place on January 16th, that instead of being known for her 'tumbling BMI' and hard partying, she had 'redeemed herself with a triumphant debut performance in New York'.

The backing band had been criticised with the words 'They were holding back because they have one eye on their playing and one eye on making sure Amy's holding it together.' Again, however, it didn't detract from the music. Meanwhile the *Daily Mail* spoke of 'jazz-infused vocals perfectly backed by her tight funk band. Reports that Ms. Winehouse is in dire need of rehab… judged by this brilliant performance, are very premature.'

However it was the critical American audiences that Amy needed to cater to and impress that night. Soon, the stress of trying to win over a critical public so far from her comfort zone would prove overwhelming for Amy. The following morning she arrived at a photo shoot for *The Washington Post* confused, disorientated and more than a little drunk. Her arm showed signs of recent self-harm and she eventually dissolved into tears before fleeing the room and claiming that she 'didn't feel pretty enough'.

The Washington Post took up the story: 'Amy Winehouse arrives an hour later with her tour manager, looking frail, apologising again and again. None of her trademark bravado is on display. She's shy and she's shaking. She stutters and searches for words, eyes welling with tears. Her left arm is abraded and raw – she won't share why. "I got drunk and I don't remember."'

With a little champagne to warm her fragile nerves, Amy regained the bravado they loved, refusing to wear a dozen or so outfits she didn't believe were her style. The light-hearted ambience saw Amy laughing and joking with her entourage and new American friends, before the mood suddenly – and dramatically – changed again. 'Five minutes later, as a photographer snaps her picture, she starts smacking herself in the face – hard – and then abruptly bolts, in tears. Later she will say that she just didn't feel pretty enough and was worried about disappointing everyone.'

The drama that unfolded would see *The Washington Post* describe her as a 'train wreck with talent'. Speaking of the interview, one of six crammed into a seven hour slot, the magazine recalled: 'She makes awkward chitchat in that Cockney twang. Tugs distractedly at her trademark ratty 'do. Yanks nervously on the strapless shift that's sliding dangerously south. Finally, she requests an amaretto sour – to hoots of approval. It's part of her shtick, what her fans have come to expect.' Dropping a potential line for a future song, Amy told an interviewer: 'They keep trying to keep me from drinking, but they forget it's my gig.' Was this Rehab Mark Two? These were exactly the same words the singer used the previous night to introduce the show's highlight – 'Rehab'.

Amy was certainly living up to her 'train wreck with talent' reputation, but was it enough to launch her? Breaking the USA as an outsider was always going to be tough. Amy's label had been trying desperately to promote this diminutive Jewish white girl to black America, the nation that some might say had created soul. It was going to take some doing. Yet some African American members of the audience, including those old enough to remember the soul classics from the first time round, had already given Amy their stamp of approval. This meant she wasn't seen as a mere copycat version of the golden oldies. All that was needed now was boundless enthusiasm and rabid determination – although, puzzlingly, Amy seemed devoid of both. Where was her ambition to be successful stateside?

'I always thought I'd be a roller skating waitress singing songs to my husband while I'm cooking grits somewhere,' she laughed. 'What I'm doing I'm so grateful to be doing – it's so exciting, so fun. But I've never been the kind of girl who knocks on someone's door and says "Make me famous."' What was more, she'd been vocal about her desire for the simple life too, claiming 'I've always been a little homemaker. I know I'm talented, but I wasn't put here to sing. I was put here to be a wife and a mum and to look after my family. I love what I do, but it's not where it begins and ends.' Although Amy's beehive was growing rapidly, her ego had perhaps not caught up to the same speed. Asked how she felt that Jay Z had appreciated her album, she even used the word 'surreal'.

It might have given Amy a confidence boost to learn that, in her absence from the UK, she had been nominated for two Brit awards and, on January 14th, *Back to Black* had reached No. 1 in the UK album chart. It was time to leave New York behind temporarily and double her efforts in England. On her return, Amy threw herself into a hectic promotional schedule, which would see her win gongs at both the Elle Style Awards and the Brit Awards on the same day.

The Elle Style Awards, hosted on Valentine's Day at the Roundhouse Theatre in Camden, was an annual ceremony designed to recognise style, design and entertainment achievements. Yet Amy, who won the nomination for Best British Musical Act, was not a conventional candidate for *Elle* to describe as chic. Attending alongside the 'impossibly gorgeous' actress Thandie Newton and the renowned catwalk model Naomi Campbell, Amy and friend Kelly Osbourne arrived together, to defiantly fight their corner as square pegs in round holes, unconventional icons.

In her photograph, Amy wore a long black satin dress that skimmed a few inches above her ankles. Her best signature fuck me pumps were also on show, with an open toe design to reveal blood red nail polish. Meanwhile she clutched what appeared to be a white Chanel replica purse. So far so good, until the errant Amy confessed that her grandmother was her ultimate style icon. And, despite her otherwise immaculate appearance, her arms were also criss-crossed with scars, rumoured to be the result of self-inflicted razor cuts. Amy, on the other hand, brushed off the marks by insisting they were the result of a drunken fall on the streets of New York. While the cuts raised suspicion, her painfully thin, almost skeletal figure barely raised an eyebrow amongst the dieted and disciplined models and fashionistas that joined her for the awards bash. Her weight would be the only area where she did match her contemporaries.

Posing as she collected her award, Amy was on a mission to be different – her hand was on her hip, whilst her surly sideways glance, slashed arms and piercing just above her lip were conspicuous reminders that – to a throng of dedicated fashionistas – she just didn't fit in.

At the Brit Awards however, Amy was universally welcomed. Competing against the Arctic Monkeys, Muse, Snow Patrol and Lily Allen for the Best British Album Award, Amy lost out by a whisker. However she beat away the competition to claim the gong for Best British Female Solo Artist. The voting public seemed to confirm that, by and large, they found

Corrine Bailey Rae and Lily Allen insipid entertainment compared to the intense darkness of *Back to Black*. Other losers in this category included Nerina Pallot and Amy's close friend Jamelia.

Amy had her war paint on and would mark her victory by changing clothes several times – most notably wearing a bright yellow dress, combined with a heart shaped purse, implausibly high stiletto heels and Louis Vuitton earrings. In the eyes of showbiz reporters, she put more under-dressed contestants contestants such as Jamelia – who wore minimal make-up, a plain black dress and hair tied into a bun – to shame. It was in this canary yellow coloured outfit that she collected her award, giving gushing thanks to her parents. She also managed to upset Lily Allen's actor father Keith, who spluttered to the press: 'No, I didn't have a good time tonight. My daughter didn't win a fucking thing.'

Meanwhile, for Amy, the celebrations had only just started – and for her own father, they were in full swing. 'My proudest moment of the night was coming off the red carpet and seeing my dad already pissed,' Amy recalled, 'and he doesn't even drink!'

By now Amy had made a name for herself as a drinking, smoking, swearing, spitting urban circus sideshow act, complete with a novelty Cockney twang who also – as an afterthought – happened to sing fantastic songs. The tables were about to turn on this perception of her, as she behaved impeccably at the Brits. In fact, the only controversy surrounding her was a comment by comedian Russell Brand that Amy was a woman 'whose surname sounds increasingly like the state of her liver'.

John Walsh of *The Independent* published a tongue in cheek review of the night, suggesting that the biggest shocker of all was that she was on her best behaviour. 'Her behaviour was nothing less than shocking,' he joked. 'Everyone agreed, she let the side down pretty badly. You think you know people, you think you can trust them to turn in a reliable performance – and they go and ruin it. Amy Winehouse just flatly refused to get drunk, swear, vomit, smoke a joint or storm out. Not once did she tell the writhing popinjay Russell Brand to eff off with his smart remarks about her incipient alcoholism. She sang Rehab with a sweet uncertainty, hitching up her red frock to mid thigh level, but delicately, carefully, as though primly fastidious about revealing her knickers… She declared "I'm just glad my mum and dad are here" and exited, probably for a nice family night out. It was hopeless. They tried to make me go to rehab? More like "They tried to persuade me to have a small sherry and enjoy myself but I said no, no, no."'

The comments were clearly intended as irony, but would a shame-faced Amy have perceived them that way? According to one acquaintance who was a regular on the party circuit, she was chronically insecure without her trademark tipple in one hand – and actually felt embarrassed to abstain.

"She'd blush if she wasn't drinking for any reason and if someone insisted, she was pretty quick to give in,' he told the author. 'It was like she relied on drinking to make her more popular – I guess because it was what she was known for.'

Amy was competitive by nature – she was reportedly never happier than when outdoing fellow exercisers in the gym – so could it be that she was trying to outdo friends and rivals in the binge drinking stakes too? Or did it give her confidence, acting as a social lubricant? Perhaps it even blunted her senses enough to provide a coping mechanism for the pressures of fame. Whatever the reason, Amy was determined to be seen with a drink in her hand at all times – and tellingly, she'd even admitted her shame publicly on national TV, claiming: 'If I'm not drinking], I have to say I'm on a course of medication, because I feel ashamed.'

Could the media's seemingly harmless jokes be perpetuating her problem? After all, according to psychotherapist Charley Shults, 'Negative attention is better than no attention at all.'

The review in *The Independent* had even more ruthless words when it added: 'At no point did she pass out from drink, forget the words or punch her guitarist. It's just not good enough... at this rate, we'll soon have to stop waiting for her to self-destruct and start listening to her singing.'

Yet that change was exactly what Amy had in mind when she returned to the tiny basement club of G.A.Y on February 20th, with promises not to vomit or self-destruct this time. 'I'm surprised they let me in,' she cackled later, showing she hadn't left all of her mischief behind. 'I thought there would be crowds of angry homosexuals at the door, waiting to batter me. I know I look like I can handle myself, but....!'

It might have seemed somewhat surreal that a girl with a No. 1 album and a handful of recent awards was playing a venue she'd have been able to sell out three years previously – a tiny club with barely enough room for the average chart-topping singer's ego. Yet she was present – and ready to make amends. *The Evening Standard* even reported that she was just as calm as she had been at the Brit Awards. The paper insisted: 'There was no danger of any drama this time... Perhaps it was her father cheering her on from the balcony, but she was on her very best behaviour. She may not have returned Russell Brand's hair after the Brits; she may still be painfully thin... but there were no too-short skirts, no smoking, no swearing, no projectile vomiting and unless looking reasonably happy counts, no signs of insobriety. This might be the moment she has chosen to refocus on her day job rather than the bacchanalian debauchery which threatens to relegate her music to a sideshow.'

Indeed, Amy was dressed down in blue drainpipe jeans and a nondescript white polo shirt. Gone for now was the glamour and gone was the misbehaviour. What she lacked in unpredictability, however, she compensated for by being consistent with her music.

The Observer agreed, renarking of the show: 'Tonight, the Winehouse fists remain in check... Despite the broken bottles and the bruises, history will remember her as a lover, not a fighter.'

Even the *NME* stepped outside its indie rock comfort zone to attend the gig. To the magazine's surprise, she was an instant in-house success. Winning over the *NME* crowd represented one of Amy's most important conquests yet. It was an assault on the unsuspecting mainstream. Normally the *NME* stuck to a prescribed list of indie music, but Amy swept aside any musical snobbery and tricked them into singing along to 'Valerie'.

'Yep, for one night only, Amy Winehouse has made us sing along to The Zutons,' the review blushed. 'And we continue singing along despite an innate hatred for insipid pub rock with over-enthusiastic saxophonists... Because Amy, despite looking like a mashed hybrid of Cleopatra and Faris Rotter and inventing words like 'fuckery', is irresistible. And of course, she has that voice, a voice as pretty as a lily in the snow, even when she's singing about adulterous blowjobs in bathrooms.' The magazine concluded finally 'We'll let her off making us look like twats.'

Returning to the Astoria had also brought her back into favour with the gay and lesbian community. *Sapphic Central* was eager to catch a lusty glimpse of the star, reporting on its website of the reviewer's position several rows from the front: 'My girlfriend was becoming increasingly frustrated... at 5"6 at least I had a view of her head.'

Amy's opinion of the show? She was hoping that the music stood taller than both the drunken altercations and the beehive put together. She would have a chance to prove this as the tour continued, passing through Northumbria, Liverpool, Manchester, Birmingham, Glasgow, Nottingham and Sheffield. It was then due to culminate with headline shows at the Shepherds Bush Empire in London – but this was not to be.

The previous day, on March 7th, Amy had been in high spirits and it had seemed that all was well. She had performed a secret concert at the Porchester Hall that would be filmed by the BBC for their Sessions series. A small number of fans in the know had beaten the barrier of their television screens to be there in person, where they were greeted by a chatty and happy Amy.

Roars of 'Amy, we love you!' flowed from the audience and she appreciated their sentiments, answering back, 'You're really doing your job's worth – I'll have to pay you more. Fifty quid next time!' She laughed at the crowd's jokes, occasionally objecting: 'You're just picking on me 'cuz I'm drunk!' in her slow Cockney drawl. Racing through a fast-paced set of the hits, she interspersed them with impromptu cover versions including a rendition of Lauryn Hill's 'Doo Wop (That Thing)' to liven up the end of 'He Can Only Hold Her'.

Occasionally a dark shadow crossed Amy's glitter studded path and one such moment was the admission that performing several depressing' songs 'all in a row' had brought back some painful memories. Yet despite the glitches, Amy seemed to be – for the most part – healthy and contented. It came as a surprise when, at the first of her two headline shows in Shepherd's Bush the following day, she was a no-show. Both concerts, scheduled for March 8th and 9th, were cancelled at short notice due to 'unforeseen circumstances'. Perhaps she was ill, but there was one complication.

The same morning, Amy had been snapped by paparazzi in the Camden branch of Tesco, chatting away merrily on her mobile phone while perusing the supermarket's alcohol section. In the evening, at around the same time she would have taken to the stage, she was allegedly seen in the local pub with the TV presenter Alex Zane and the comedian Noel Fielding. Journalists were less than sympathetic. Newspapers assumed the worst and *The Evening Standard* printed details of her no-show that commented between the lines exactly what they suspected. 'Here is a picture of Amy Winehouse buying booze in a North London supermarket at 11 in the morning,' the paper wrote. 'There is no picture of her performing at the Shepherd's Bush Empire [later the same day] – chiefly on account of the fact that she did not show up. The two events are, of course, completely unrelated.' The newspaper went on: 'The singer cancelled the show saying she was ill – obviously one of those nasty bugs where you're fit and well and chatting away in Tesco one minute, completely laid out the next.'

However Amy had a more sinister explanation for her absence. 'My tooth got knocked out,' she told MTV. 'I bit down on an ice-cube and felt it come loose. I was sitting with my boyfriend and told him he had to pull it out because it was going to come out at some point and it would be horrible and bloody. He wouldn't pull it out so I had to do it myself.'

Amy told the website that she was rushed to the dentist for emergency surgery on the 'massive gap in the front of my mouth'. Meanwhile the media questioned whether the loss of her front tooth was related to the increasing reports of her drug and alcohol abuse. Addiction consultant Dr Ken Checinski told the *Daily Mail:* 'When taking cocaine and heroin, people can experience a deterioration in their appearance due to general dietary deficiency and the inability to absorb Vitamin C and calcium. Snorting cocaine… can also make gums recede.' He also added that, due to a plummeting immune system, teeth could easily rot away and fall out. The controversy surrounding Amy Winehouse had just become even more complicated.

By the following week, she had recovered, finding herself on a transatlantic flight, headed for New York. She jetted in on March 13th, the day that her album was released in the USA. That night, she would headline a Live from London triple bill designed to showcase the best up and coming artists in British music. All three acts would perform at the small but sophisticated Bowery Ballroom. Singer, song-writer and producer Jamie Woon was the first contender to take to the stage. Like Amy, he was a cross-over artist mixing heartbreak blues with modern garage.

His brand of blues was followed by the Pipettes, an indie rock trio with a penchant for polka dot dresses. The three front women quickly set about making the style their trademark look, with almost every photo-shoot seeing them parade the fashion. In fact Amy joined them, donning her own polka dot outfit for the evening. Generally the group was well liked, but it was also criticised for its painted on persona – one which gossip columns labelled a 'gimmick'.

Finally the headline act, the star of the show, would be Amy herself. For her, the escape to New York was not so much a chance to pursue the American dream but more a way to regain her musical footing. Back in Britain, the paparazzi were in hot pursuit, following her every move – from Camden's Hawley Arms pub to the local Nando outlet when she would pick up fried chicken takeaways. American would provide Amy with the anonymity she lacked at home and might offer her the opportunity, after all the chaos, to be viewed as a serious artist again.

However, if she'd hoped word wouldn't have spread about her misdemeanours of the previous year, she was in for a disappointment, as even in New York, her reputation seemed to precede her.

American website *Popwatch* said of the show: 'Perhaps the biggest surprise was that she showed up at all. [But] we got her on a comparatively good day: the sold out room welcomed her with palpable adoration. In the end, her singular voice broke through. There it was, undeniably, the sonic fierceness that, when matched with her melancholic, autobiographical lyrics, brought tapping foot and aching heart together.'

Fans were equally enamoured, with one concert goer, known only as Ray, claiming: 'Amy Winehouse will fare better than Lily Allen in America, simply because Amy's music is just so much more American. She sounds like she's straight out of Motown. I swear there's a big, black lady in a choir uniform living inside her vocal box!'

Amy, who had worn a black and white polka dot dress herself in a nod to the Pipettes, had a larger than life accompaniment to back her up too. Her ten piece band dwarfed the tiny stage of the Bowery, with three guitarists, a trumpet player, two saxophonists and two backing singers complete with a sequence of dance moves, who flanked her at the front of the stage.

Prefix Magazine also attended the show and suggested that – far from her alcohol issues alienating punters – her alcohol issues could be drawing them in. Perhaps people could live vicariously through her adventures. 'Fans ejaculated premature adoration,' the review claimed, 'but she only responded to one question – "What are you drinking?"'

Amy's reply? 'Ladies don't drink.' After a brief pause, she corrected, 'They gulp.' *Prefix* added: 'The crowd responded loudest when she knelt to take her first sip, as if that represented the first taste of liquor for an attentive nation of 21 year olds.'

The final word on the show came from blogger Patrick Meaney, who wrote of his experience a week later. 'She joked with the crowd about her love of alcohol, bringing back some vintage drinking jokes like "I have a drinking problem, I can't seem to get it in my mouth",' he recalled. 'I'm not sure how much of that is an act, playing up to her image, but it gets pops from the crowd, so it worked... If you get the chance to see her, don't pass it up.' She hadn't quite shaken off the alcohol comparisons, but it didn't appear to be to her detriment – yet.

Amy's next major show was in Austin, Texas on March 15th. Performing at the SXSW festival, it would be her first show outside a major contemporary city. A notoriously Bible belt region, known for its largely conservative dress codes and devout religious beliefs, how would the public react when a dishevelled drunkard (who was proud of it) descended on their peaceful city for a velvety voiced singing showdown?

She had no plans to adapt for the Texans, remaining as frank as ever. 'I never thought I'd be opening for Razorlight,' she announced sarcastically before launching into 'Just Friends'. The next time she spoke, it was to let loose a string of profanities and painfully honest disclosures. 'I wrote my whole album about being heartbroken and I realised that every night, I'm singing for the audience about sad, fucked up things. This song's about a break-up,' she added before 'Wake Up Alone', before conceding 'Well, they all are.'

She even made a cryptic comment about her boyfriend Alex, introducing 'You Know I'm No Good' by dedicating it to someone she'd cheated on. 'I told him, "I do love you, but I get bored! I told you I'm no good,"' Amy recalled. How a region of monogamous Texans reacted to this knowledge was unknown. To add to the sense of drama, Lily Allen, who'd wrongly been accused of a feud with her at the Brit Awards joked, 'Me and Amy have made up now – we're lesbian lovers!'

Jesus is Savior, a Texas based website, had reviled fellow performer Katy Perry for her flirtation with lesbianism, making it clear how some of the members of the state felt about such issues. 'She's promoting and glorifying the vile sin of homosexuality!' it argued. 'Shame on *[America]* for promoting such an immoral and Godless heathen as Katy. This is apostasy! Katy Perry is of the Devil. It is a shame that a young woman who grew up in church, had religious parents, sang in church, and even released her own Gospel CD would grow up to be a spokeswoman for homosexuality… Katy Perry is headed for the Lake of Fire.'

Katy had done little more than sing about kissing a girl, while Amy was at least one step higher in the bad behaviour and debauchery stakes. Yet if she had been worried about how Texans would react to her language, she needn't have been, as the reviews were glowing. 'Fuckery – it takes a certain type of girl to write a song that uses such a word and to say it with such snorting disdain,' one blogger ranted. 'In a fantastic performance, Amy Winehouse showed why she is just that kind of girl and a whole lot more.' The review lauded *Back to Black* as the 'best soul record since 1998's The Miseducation of Lauryn Hill'. Meanwhile renowned rap group The Roots described it as 'the album Lauryn Hill wanted to make'.

This was praise indeed for Amy, who would then move onto the Roxy Theatre in Los Angeles, not far from the Chateau Marmont hotel, where she had once been a regular. Her show was equally well received there and attended by rock songstress Courtney Love, whom her band mate Neal Sugarman of the Daptone Kings had been delighted to ignore. 'We snubbed Courtney Love,' he chuckled to the author. 'Every day hanging out with Amy was crazy. It was a great time - it was her first US tour and behind a record every one loved. And she loved taking us out for great dinners. There were lots of celebrities - I met Bruce Willis and Danny

Devito back stage. One of Amy's favourite restaurants was Fish Bate on 23rd Street I think she really liked it because at the time we could go with lots of people and this was before her big success in the States so she would go unrecognized. There were some great Sushi dinners in LA that I remember being great too.'

As Amy flitted from city to city, leaving almost no location uncovered in her bid to introduce America to her Motown melodies, some good news emerged. Back to Black had entered the Top 10 in the notoriously unbreakable US Billboard Chart. It soared straight to No. 7, making Amy the highest debuting British female artist to date. She would hold that accolade for a week, until Joss Stone made the No. 2 spot with her third studio album, *Introducing Joss Stone.*

This was the confirmation Amy had needed that the USA was warming to her. However, the euphoria was marred by tragedy when Amy had a painful breakup with her partner of nine months, Alex Donnely Jones.

A one-time Radio One executive, Alex had once been hailed in the media as one of the most important and influential people on the music scene. In 2005, he was headhunted by EMI, becoming the senior vice president of the publishing department. Less than a year later, he was working on Amy's publishing contract for *Back to Black,* when the two had their first date. He would be a stabilising influence that would take Amy's mind off her ill-fated former relationship with Blake. Unusually however, they first met not through work but in a pub where Amy was, as ever, playing pool. She was also nursing a large bruise on her forehead, courtesy of a drunken fall the night before.

She recalled: 'He walked in the Mixer and I was literally like "Fucking hell!" So gorgeous. And I had a massive bump on my head the size of a fucking golf ball, because the night before I woke up in hospital. I'd been unconscious and I looked around and all my best friends were there and I looked at the doctor and was like [helplessly] "What happened to me?" and they were like [resigned] "You had a fall." I'm like [sweetly] "Why? Was I drunk?"'

Amy thanked the doctor profusely for saving her life, causing some irritation among those gathered at her bedside. 'My best friend Catriona was like, "Oh what, now you're nice? Now you're not trying to hit anyone? You're all thanks to the doctor, what about me, when you were fucking swinging at me?" I was convinced I'd been spiked. So I got out of hospital and went back to the pub and said to the barman "I got spiked last night, bastards! Did you see anyone funny around my drinks?" and he said "Yeah, you! You drank about 30 Sambucas!" Such an idiot!'

Amy was still trying to disguise her blushes when Alex walked in the following day. Despite the alcohol in her brain, she soon devised a cunning plot to both get another drink and break the ice with the charming young man who'd caught her eye. 'I went up to him and went, "Would you do me a favour and take this two pounds and buy me a tequila? They won't serve me shots today because I was drunk yesterday." With this fucking bump on my head. And he goes, "Put your money in your pocket, darling, I'll get you a drink."'

Several tequilas later, Amy found herself spending the night at the mystery man's flat. It was just the beginning of a nine month romance. However, it was a flawed one as Alex already had a girlfriend at the time. 'I'm not very moral,' Amy had cackled by way of explanation – and neither was her new lover.

Initially a mere stop-gap to take her mind off her traumatic break-up with Blake, Amy had not at first taken the relationship seriously. However, she had grown close to him over time and he was important enough to her to be her date for the evening at the 2007 Brit Awards. The two shared a passion for fitness and would attend the gym together – Alex often trailing a few steps behind, carrying his lover's handbag – and he had also accompanied Amy on her February UK tour.

However, things had come to a head when reports suggested that the songstress may have been two-timing Alex with ex-lover Blake – on one occasion meeting up with both on the same day for passionate trysts. An anonymous friend of Amy's spoke of her behaviour backstage at *The Sharon Osbourne Show* the previous year, saying, 'She had Blake with her. All the time she was talking about her 'boyfriend' Alex – but was sitting on Blake's lap and snogging him. She was saying "Read me out those text messages I sent you – the filthy ones".'

Whilst she might have found temporary comfort in the arms of Alex, it was clear that Blake had never left her mind. She had tattooed an 'A' for

Alex across the ring finger of her left hand in a bid to reassure her increasingly possessive boyfriend that her heart was his. However her promises were fooling no-one, perhaps devised to fool herself more than anyone else. It wasn't just the tell-tale clues of the song 'You Know I'm No Good', which advertised her struggles with infidelity. Amy still had the words 'Blake's' emblazoned across her left breast. When a journalist in New York asked why she had not had the tattoo removed, Amy had replied, 'I need reminding of what a fucking idiot I am all the time.'

That reminder didn't make Alex feel much better. Although she liked both her men, Amy couldn't resist alternating between Blake and Alex – the one she loved with an obsessive passion and the one she'd used as an emotional crutch to distract her from the loss of formally being Blake's girlfriend. No doubt her father's romances with both Janis and Jane at the same time had normalised casual infidelity for Amy. In her eyes, it was perfectly acceptable to cheat. It was possible to sleep with a second man without it detracting from her love for the first one.

Psychoanalytic theories suggest that a child's parents, as early significant attachment figures, provide a model of how the world is and how oneself and others ought to behave. In Mitch, Amy had a role model whose values didn't outwardly embrace loyalty or exclusive commitment. Perhaps as a consequence, she now felt – as she'd explained in interviews – that cheating 'wasn't a big deal' and was 'like smoking a joint'.

Yet there was more to this than mere sexual greed or a distorted view of what traditional relationships were. As a self-confessed unhappy, insecure woman, bed-hopping would protect Amy from one of her biggest fears – being alone.

In 'You Know I'm No Good', Amy sings of her struggles with monogamy. She cheats to distract herself from emotional pain, but then punishes herself if her chosen course of action hurts other people. As she repeats in earlier songs like 'I Heard Love Is Blind', she cheats on her man because he isn't there at the time and, in low moments, she doesn't want to succumb to loneliness. Yet when her actions upset a boyfriend who expects loyalty, this confirms her hypothesis about herself – her suspicions that she's 'no good'.

Yet where had these negative thought processes originated? Was it the well-documented issues with her father that tugged at her heart-strings so sharply? As one psychoanalyst comments, 'A child's brain has limited ability to process that something isn't her fault. She can't say "My dad left but that's his problem, not mine. It says more about him than me. It doesn't mean he doesn't love me or that he's gone forever." Children are egocentric – in their view, the world is focused around them. And they will interpret it as "It's my fault. I'm not good enough."'

Not feeling good enough could draw Amy into a constant search for validation that she was lovable after all – and this could perpetuate her tendency to be unfaithful. According to some psychoanalytic theories, each new notch on her bedpost would provide both instant comfort to bandage her pain and a feeling of conquest, that people demonstrably found her attractive after all.

Beneath what appeared on the surface to be bravado or merely a high sex drive was a need more likely driven by vulnerability and low self-esteem. Amy cheated because he was 'no good', but doing so temporarily gave her the feeling she was 'okay' and lovable after all. Then, as soon as her boyfriend discovers her infidelity, being 'no good' yet again becomes a self-fulfilling prophecy.

Behind the vicious circle of loneliness and self-loathing, however, was love of a depth and quality she hadn't felt before – and that was her relationship with Blake. In a world of fame and superficiality, her affection for him was something realm, unique and tangible. It was time to start making tough decisions.

Amy recalled of her lingering love affair with Blake: 'We were always close but it got to the point when it was hurting other people for us to keep seeing each other.' Neither one of them was content to continue living a lie and snatching brief illicit fumbles before returning to their partners. Something had to give - and it did.

The final reason for the break-up with Alex was uncertain. Perhaps Amy's drunken misdemeanours had played a part, becoming too much for him. 'It really embarrasses me to hear that I've punched him in the face six times,' Amy told the media of her bouts of violence. Even the hardest-partying libertine might have found Amy a little too hot to handle – and if the words of 'You Know I'm No Good' were anything to go by, monogamy just wasn't in the contract.

Amy had been due to play a small venue is Los Angeles, known as Spaceland, on March 10th, but in the wake of a brutal breakup, she was labelled 'too heart-broken to perform'. Internet reports claimed that 'due to her busy concert schedule in Britain and America, she hadn't had the chance to grieve the loss of the relationship'. Cancelling her second Los Angeles show with just hours to spare, Amy clearly needed some recuperation time.

A friend was quoting as saying: 'Amy loved Alex so much and was so upset when they split. Normally she would take time out to wallow like most normal young girls, but she's just been on the road performing and doing interviews non-stop. She's exhausted and miserable. She doesn't feel she can give the audience her best while she feels this sad.'

The drama continued all the way up to the end of the month, intensifying on Amy's return to London. On March 29th, she reportedly spent time with both of her long-suffering exes, despite having a current relationship with neither one.

The Sun captured the uncertainty, reporting that Amy had started the afternoon holding hands with Alex on a walk in Camden, spent the evening flirting with revellers at a Teenage Cancer Trust gig and finally ended the night with passionate kisses in the arms of Blake. The two had been drinking at the fashionable Maddox Club in Mayfair. The newspaper summed up: 'Even who she's going to date – and who she's going to be just friends with – seems to be a tough call for the soul singer.'

Even worse, Amy had made a major gaff at the Teenage Cancer Trust show, candidly announcing 'I don't normally go to celebrity parties but this one's free booze and I haven't got no money!' She added, less than tactfully, 'The record company won't pay me until I come up with the next album.' She was neither in the party spirit not in a charitable mood, following her tumultuous love affair.

The split was not an easy one and Alex was equally traumatised. A few weeks after Amy's return to England, he made an emotional very public blog post on his Myspace account that, for those in any doubt, pronounced the relationship over for good. 'After turning up at three in the morning at the

Hawley Arms, I saw [Amy] with her ex and I saw red mist. I was shaking like a leaf… while she sat there inebriated on the lap of her ex. I'm skint, heartbroken and homeless… but shit, what's a man to do?'

He found solace in drugs, adding: 'A friend gave me a little something I hadn't had in a while – MDMA. I always forget how enjoyable everything is after you taste that rank shit, especially with a couple of Valium, three lines [of coke] and a little dark rum to wash it down.' He continued: 'It's like she cut out my heart, bit a chunk out of it, threw it on the floor and stomped all over it. She's scared to be happy. I hope she finds happiness one day. She needs looking after but I'm glad that's not my responsibility anymore.'

In a bid for revenge, Alex then sold a kiss and tell story to the *News of the World* – a double page feature entitled 'Bondage Crazed Amy Just Can't Beehive in Bed'. Selling the tale under the guise of Alex Claire to protect his identity, he told of how he was once knocked in the head by her beehive during frenzied sex sessions. Lifting the lid none too discreetly on their private liaisons, he also revealed that she liked both to dominate and be dominated, but that her fondness for the former had almost risked his life one night. In a Jacuzzi, whilst on top of her lover, he claimed Amy had diced with death, pushing his face down and holding him under the water. 'She had a very striking face with big brown eyes that suck you in,' he told the paper. 'I was gazing at it when suddenly she pushed me down. I was under for several seconds. I couldn't breathe and started freaking out. Then she pulled my head up. I was gasping for breath but Amy carried on as if it was perfectly normal behaviour. I thought, "Wow, you've got balls!"'

However Amy also enjoyed the submissive role according to Alex, asking him to tie her up, spank her and pull her hair. The ultimate fantasy for Amy, by his account, was bondage. Alex also recalled an occasion when the adventurous lovers were ejected from a London cinema for their romps. 'We were kicked out because we were getting it on in the back row,' he claimed. 'Amy was astride me and we were warned a couple of times [but] being told off got her going even more.'

However, listeners were left unimpressed by tales of their antics. One fan wrote on an Internet forum: 'That just sounds like a normal night of sex to me. Why can't he keep it quiet?'

146

The revelations would humiliate an already devastated Amy, whose relationships never seemed to end well. Her subsequent return to America would be an opportunity for her to take her mind off her woes but, far from being the bubbly all American girl the media was used to, Amy was dreading the prospect of more interviews about her album. In fact, her self marketing proved so haphazard that anything other than the vocals was best left to her promotional team. Whether she was upset about her turbulent love life, she felt shy in the spotlight or she just didn't care, she had no intentions of playing up to the media hype. She wasn't ruthless, she wasn't ambitious, and she couldn't have been less archetypally American if she tried.

In interviews, Amy was devoid of earnest, rigorously prepared PR jargon. Some would-be stars might have carefully prepared responses, calculated to titillate their target audience. Yet when Amy was asked the demographic of people buying her music, she confessed bluntly, 'I have no idea'. Not one for over-analysis, Amy was a girl who was simply passionate about performance. The formalities that came with it were – to her – merely a necessary evil, an irritating inconvenience.

One interviewer asked about her change in musical direction between *Frank* and *Back to Black,* inviting her to expand on the key moments in her life that had inspired it. Amy's response? 'I'm not interested in writing songs so that people can find out who I really am. I don't give a fuck.' Cue a shocked silence.

In another interview, she playfully thrust her carefully stacked beehive into the microphone, giggling, 'I'd rather you did the whole interview about my hair.'

It might have been near impossible to get a sensible response about her music, but – just as Simon Fuller had overlooked her less flattering idiosyncrasies when he signed her – so had America. In fact, it was still being debated that this approach was what drew some of the crowds to her.

On April 24th, she braved the intense heat of the desert-based Coachella Festival in California for the first date of a mammoth tour that would take in San Francisco, Colorado, Minneapolis, Chicago, Philadelphia, New York and Boston, before ending at the Mod Club in Canada's Toronto for a double date on May 12th and 13th.

While she was singing her heart out in America, the record company released her third single – the album's title track, 'Back to Black'. The single, which hit the shops on April 30th, included a studio version of 'Valerie' by the Zutons, which was by now a regular fixture at Amy's live shows and a self-proclaimed 'song of the year'. It also contained a cover of 'Hey Little Rich Girl' by the Specials. Despite the new songs, the single peaked in the UK chart at just No. 25. While that might have been a disappointment, Amy had other things on her mind to soothe the blow – she had fallen firmly back in love, and was as far from her former black moods as she could have imagined. Would this be a new start for Amy?

CHAPTER 10

Previously casual about affairs of the heart, Amy had fallen head over heels in love with Blake – and her feelings had shell-shocked her in terms of both ill-fatedness and intensity.

She had been drunk on a daily basis since they first got together and, when he finally broke off the affair, she had pined for him every day. The relationship had been profound enough for Amy to change her on many levels. From the ballsy teenage feminist who wouldn't alter herself for anyone and would put no man before her own needs, she had gladly transformed into a self-professed 'fool for love'. Inspired by groups like the ShangriLas who gave themselves wholeheartedly in trysts, she had penned most of *Back to Black* in Blake's memory.

'I like the Shangri-Las, because it's the opposite of feminism,' Amy had recalled. 'They were girls who would lie in the road for their boyfriends. They did have songs like 'He Cried', stuff that's quite heartless, but at the same time there's 'Dressed in Black' and 'I Can Never Go Home Anymore', where she's signing "My life has no purpose if I don't have my boy."'

Fortunately for Amy, her life *had* found a purpose again – she and Blake were back together. Making up for lost time, the two moved in with each other straight away and Blake quickly popped the question – would she marry him? Amy had previously stated: 'I've never been a marriage kind of girl – I'm too selfish,' but she had also found when she met Blake that he'd 'kick-started her domestic instinct'. Taking just a day to consider the proposal, her answer was a resounding yes. 'I think it was the right thing to do,' she explained.

Amy was elated and took the opportunity to flash her £3000 Tiffany engagement ring, which was inset with diamonds, at her very next show. Descending on the Dublin Castle pub on April 19th as part of the Camden Crawl music festival, she was in better spirits than her fan base had seen her for a very long time.

MTV reported: 'Amy Winehouse has brought the first day of Camden Crawl to an electrifying close. Getting a bit of thirst on, Winehouse offered sexual favours to anyone that dared brave the struggle to the bar and back to bring her a shot and one man rose to the challenge. Some 15 minutes later, he cashed in a shot of a tequila for a snog… then demanded a second after remembering it was a double… it was a top set from the vocal star and she didn't even fall over or puke, unlike most of the audience.'

This small local pub atmosphere surrounded by her close friends meant that Amy was in her element. And, unconcerned that his wife to be was jokily masquerading as a prostitute, Blake was proudly waiting in the wings.

He would take the same role on her US tour a few days later and, after the final show had drawn to a close, the two jetted off to Miami. Their goal? To make the wedding the two had dreamed of a reality. Shunning a traditional Jewish affair, they had settled for the unglamorous alternative of a £60 no frills ceremony at a registry office. Guilded wedding invitations and celebrity magazine deals just weren't Amy's style. On May 18th, at the Miami Dade County Marriage Bureau, the pair were officially pronounced man and wife.

Even in Miami, Amy was a minor celebrity, but the couple had planned ahead, instead simply turning up at the nearest registry office. Wedding clerk Sammy Calixte told the author: 'They were very eager to get married - when I asked them when the ceremony was to take place, they both answered "At once! RIGHT NOW!" They were giggling and carrying on and seemed very happy. They were both covered in tattoos and Amy explained the meaning of them all to the clerks. Especially the one on her arm that was done for her grandmother. It was a very exciting day for all the clerks that were present.'

After a ceremony that was emotional by all accounts, Blake called his parents and told mother Georgette, 'Mum, congratulate me, I'm married. Would you like to speak to my wife?' She told the *Daily Mail* later, 'I spoke to Amy and they both sounded so happy – but I can't pretend that it was what I had hoped for my son.' Nevertheless, Amy and Blake were living their dream.

Amy's mother was even less complimentary, claiming that Blake had to have talked her daughter into the ceremony. 'I think they were both drunk, he said "Let's do it", and she said "OK then!"' Janis surmised.

Just months earlier, even Amy herself had doubted she could ever tie the knot, claiming: 'I don't know any man that would be able to handle me – I'm a bit too mad.' If it was a shock to her to discover her wifely instincts, it was even more of a shock for Alex. Not long before, she had told the press that marriage and children were off the cards for the foreseeable future because the two were little more than 'babies' themselves – yet here she was, beaming proudly, with her new husband.

On the night of the nuptials, the two were photographed strolling down Miami Beach hand in hand, but it was to be the last public appearance for the newly weds. Checking into the Shore Club, a boutique hotel boasting understated luxury and the best party scene on South Beach, their only aim was a 48 hour lock-in.

Allegedly spending almost £1000 on champagne, the pair treated themselves to a relaxing in-room couples massage and – the morning after the wedding – an understated breakfast of burgers and French fries. For the North London girl who felt more at home in Nando's than an upmarket restaurant, there was no other way she would have preferred to spend her big day.

Yet Amy had to face the music on returning home. 'Dad is going to kick my head in,' she had grimaced. 'He's still got to pay for the proper wedding.' Yet Mitch didn't even know about it yet. The event had been shrouded in secrecy with Amy's parents, who'd thought she was simply taking a last-minute holiday, finding out in the newspapers. Media reports suggested that Janis had been 'crying hysterically' to have missed her only daughter's wedding. Amy took a more stoical view, telling the *Daily Mail* : 'I would have loved my family to have been there but it was something just for us.' To mend the wounds, she promised to have a Christmas party to celebrate the nuptials with all of her friends and family.

Yet it wasn't just the absence of a wedding invitation that sparked their tears – and Amy's parents had other concerns about their daughter's new husband. Mitch had attended her concert in New York earlier that month, where he had met Blake for the first time. The scene that awaited Mitch had shocked him – instead of socialising, his daughter's new husband had allegedly spent 23 hours in his hotel bedroom, not even surfacing for the concert. It added to his worries to read allegations that Blake had been spotted walking through the corridors of the Shore Club singing 'They tried to make me get a pre-nup, I said no, no, no!' to the tune of 'Rehab'. Was Blake genuinely in love with Amy or had he just been seduced by the promise of notoriety, fame and fortune? Either way, Blake had now almost irreversibly entered his daughter's world.

Before the dust had settled, Amy was due to appear at the Ivor Novello awards for song-writers, where she had been nominated in the Best Contemporary Song category with 'Rehab'. Amy turned up late to the lavish ceremony at the Grosvenor House Hotel in London, arriving just in time to claim her gong. She had beaten off Hot Chip and Bodyrox to win the title but joked in her acceptance speech that she had arrived so late that she hadn't even had time to get drunk yet.

On May 28th and 29th, she played her rescheduled shows at London's Shepherd's Bush Empire. Crooner Elton John and his partner David Furnish were among the audience. Amy had personally apologised to them when the shows had been cancelled the first time around, promising 'There'll be a next time', and this incendiary performance was her chance to make it up to them. On both nights she had a parting shot for the audience – 'I don't know if you heard, but I just got married to the best man in the entire world!'

Following this show, award nominations started flooding in. Despite her unwholesome habits and penchant for excess, she was nominated for the best Breakout Female Artist with 'Rehab'. The awards were voted for purely by 13-19 year olds. She also appealed to a young audience when she won Best British Pop Single of the Year at the Woodie Awards. This ceremony was home to the MTVu Channel, which provided a musical fix for college students at over 750 university campuses across America.

However one of the most exciting stateside appearances for Amy was her invitation to perform at MTV's first ever live Movie Awards, on June 3rd 2007. 'Booking unpredictable singer Amy Winehouse… seemed like a recipe for trouble, but her sultry hit single 'Rehab' was climbing the charts and audiences were clamouring for any glimpse of the talented British songstress,' MTV's website explained. Not wanting to let their fan base down, the channel organised for her to play the track at the ceremony, staged at the Gibson Amphitheatre in California.

The trouble began at rehearsals, when according to MTV executive Garrett English, Amy wandered off stage during 'just about every song'. The day before the event itself, rumours surfaced that she was planning to board a plane to Las Vegas for a party hosted by top fashion photographer David La Chapelle. What's more, it was too late to confront her – as she had already left. Terrified producers were on tenterhooks, but the following day – just half an hour before the show went on air – Amy got in touch to confirm that her return plane had landed. Arriving with just moments to spare, she did a performance of 'Rehab' that onlookers described as 'phenomenal'. Unlike with most artists, it had been employees' jobs to 'babysit' the unpredictable singer and keep her out of trouble. An insider revealed: 'We had to just hope for the best, but if she'd been a no-show on the night, I'd have feared for my job.'

In fact, drummer Nathan Allen revealed that Amy had been seduced by the glamorous lifestyle of jet-setting model and actress Pamela Anderson when she left for Las Vegas the night before. 'Pamela invited her to go in her private jet,' he recalled. 'When Amy started getting big, people like that wanted to hang out with her.'

Recovering quickly from a cocaine-fuelled party where she and Blake had allegedly crept off to the toilets at regular intervals for nose candy and even stolen some from Kate Moss's bag, she had ended up performing well. 'They wanted to do something really special for the MTV Awards,' Nathan confirmed. 'There was a really big stage so both the Dap Kings from New York and her English band were playing at the same time, when there's normally only one on stage for budget reasons. We ended up with six horn players, three from each band.' Amy didn't do anything by halves and she ended on the note of huge sighs of relief from MTV producers, whose risks seemed to have paid off.

However, behind the scenes, Amy's marriage was proving to be more of a gamble. Just a week earlier, she had gushed 'Every day is like a honeymoon – Blake is the best man in the world'. Yet on the day of the awards, there was trouble in paradise when Amy was seen pushing her husband into a hedge and screaming obscenities at him. A witness at the couple's hotel remarked: 'Amy was shouting: "You always fucking do this! Don't fucking touch me! Fuck you!" She was in tears but Blake tried to walk away. It wound her up so much she pushed him into a hedge. She calmed down a bit and walked over to Blake. Then she sat between his legs and they embraced. They were both crying and Blake said: "Why do you always fucking do this? I'm always propping you up". They were on the kerb for over an hour, sobbing.'

This new drama might have brought relief to fans of Amy's confessional musical style as she had promised her marriage was so idyllic that her next album would be about Care Bears. 'Some of her best songs were meaningful and melancholic and people in pain can relate to that,' a London fan enthused. 'I don't think if she wrote about being deliriously happy, that it would be quite the same.' There was no chance of that yet – the rollercoaster of ups and downs would continue to plague her throughout the year.

Yet what was the truth behind Amy and Blake's tearful public meltdowns? They'd been the picture of happiness at their nuptials in Miami, both grinning broadly for the camera, but now the marriage was more grizzly bears than Care Bears – and their luck was rapidly running out. According to an anonymous friend, the pair's biggest problem was Blake's insecurity about his wife's career.

'Music was the other man in Amy's relationship – something she loved as much as she loved him – and it drove Blake insane with jealousy,' she revealed to the author. 'He was terrified of losing her to someone in showbiz and he generally saw her musical career as a bit of a threat. If she ended it all there and then, she'd still be considered an icon with Number 1 CDs, but he had nothing. He was afraid that one day Amy would see him as a good for nothing guy and chuck him out of her life. If she was off her head on drugs, there was less chance of that happening, so some might say he was trying to sabotage her singing career.'

She continued: 'To begin with, he was also Amy's supplier. He could decide if he was going to give her drugs and he liked that because it gave him a type of control in their relationship that he'd always been lacking. He was constantly pushing Amy to the limit and testing her love because he felt powerless in their relationship. She was the one with the money and the adulation and she could call things off at any time, so he wanted to be reassured she'd stay.'

The pair also had a penchant for 'emotional S&M', inflicting cruelty on each other with words. While they were desperately in love, they seemed so fearful of losing what they had that they were sabotaging their own marriage. 'It was very manipulative,' the friend explained. 'The more Blake was cruel and unkind to Amy, the more she felt she needed him and vice versa.'

According to her, the pair also found the ever-changing power structure in their relationship arousing. 'They got off on playing the games,' she explained. 'It was emotional S&M.'

She added: 'When Amy thought she was about to lose Blake, it made her want him all the more. She'd start off hating him for something he'd done and then the fear of being abandoned would kick in and she'd beg for him to come back.'

Regaining his lost power became a reward in itself to Blake in the pair's toxic love affair. To prove to himself he was still relevant in their relationship, according to Amy's friend, he'd 'pretend' to break up with her, threatening to end it if she didn't spend more time with him or prioritise him over her family and career.

'Blake didn't mean to do it, he was just ridiculously insecure,' she added. 'He knew being abandoned was Amy's Achilles heel – she'd been through it with her dad – but he didn't stop taunting her. He'd make her feel like she was nothing without him, when actually he was projecting onto her how he felt about himself.'

Clearly the two were manipulating each other to pacify their own fears – Blake would leave her if she didn't do what he wanted, while she'd threaten likewise if he didn't give into her. It was a matter of mutual co-dependency – as a reaction against feeling helpless, both would constantly try to assert control. The power struggles appeared to be driven not by a need for dominion, but by desperate insecurity.

With that in mind, it seemed as though there was now a drug in Amy's life that was even deadlier than heroin. The substances she used might have been poisoning her body and addling her mind, but that seemed nothing compared to the destruction her relationship seemed to be wreaking in her life.

'Amy soon found a way to manipulate him right back – she threatened suicide if he left,' her friend explained. 'If the stress got too much, they'd self-harm to punish themselves or get attention and a shock reaction from the other one. All this was so unhealthy, but Amy was addicted and couldn't let her go, whatever he did to her. She was a fool for love. If she ever did have a rethink and back away a bit, she'd see him talking to another girl and go mental. She was under a lot of pressure to let him go, from the people who said she'd never put another album out while he was around to the people who bullied her to leave him, who she thought wouldn't love her anymore if she stayed. But that backfired in the end – people pulling her in all these different directions made it easier for her just to withdraw into drugs and escape from it all.'

Her friend added: 'From what I read in the papers, people think Amy brought tragedy on herself. After all, how could someone have bestselling CDs out, a voice that's raved about in every newspaper, a bank account stuffed full of money and STILL be unhappy, still be drawn to these self-destructive relationships? Well, they say money can't buy you happiness – and do you really think anyone who could write something like 'Love Is A Losing Game' had ever been happy?'

Less than a week after their public altercation in the street, Amy was up on stage again for the Isle of Wight festival on June 9th – and it was a double bill. On arrival, she got into the spirit of the event by trying out some of the funfair rides, but suddenly had a change of heart, letting out a blood-curdling scream and demanding to be let off. What was more, it wasn't a fear of heights that had motivated her, but a new found vanity. 'Get me off! What about my hair?' she asked, concerned that when the ride plunged upside down, it would make her carefully arranged beehive go awry. That evening, she took to the stage alone, offering up crowd-pleasers such as 'Valerie' and 'Cherry'.

A day later, she appeared again with headliners the Rolling Stones, who were celebrating their first festival performance since 1976. The group had coyly hinted to the *NME* that they'd have liked a chance to sing with Amy, sparking rumours of a collaboration, but it wasn't until she appeared on stage that there was finally an end to the speculation. Watched by a 60,000 strong audience, including actresses Sienna Miller and Anna Friel and Amy's close friend Pete Doherty from Babyshambles, she did a duet with front man Mick Jagger for a cover version of 'Ain't Too Proud To Beg' by the Temptations.

The Stones were high maintenance, earning a reported £1 million for their one hour appearance, and arriving by private ferry with an entourage of 200 aides. But Amy fought back for diva status, demanding 24 bottles of free champagne for her rider, and being flanked by several bodyguards wherever she went. Yet that wasn't the only way for her to compete in the diva stakes. *Uncut* magazine divulged: 'Backstage gossip suggested the Stones had been calling her a madam for refusing to rehearse with them... but it certainly adds a spontaneous air to tonight's performance that gives the show a certain frisson.'

Rumours were rife on the showbiz circuit about an overdose of champagne that night. However Mick Jagger was convinced Amy's celebrations were a normal rite of passage for a musician, or — in the words of the Stones' 1974 album — only rock and roll. He told the BBC: 'Everyone goes through this sort of thing when they become very famous so hopefully they will come out the other side with equanimity and a new lease of life.'

That might not have been so for guitarist Ronnie Wood, when a mischevious Blake coerced the recovering alcoholic into having a drink. He told *The Sun:* 'I asked Ronnie if he wanted a drink. He said, "No, I can't — my counsellors will have a go at me." There were about 15 people and they were part of his recovery team. I said, "Don't be a mug — just have a drink. You're a grown man, ain't ya?" He started downing all the half bits on people's tables like a tramp. That was one of the best nights ever.' He added sarcastically 'Ronnie later said Amy should stop hanging out with losers — I think he probably meant me.'

Yet Amy's rock and roll dream continued as she was nominated for a string of awards at the annual ceremony for *Mojo* magazine on June

18th. She arrived fashionably late after becoming caught in traffic and collected two awards – Woman of the Year and Best Song of the Year for 'Rehab' – before Terry Hall of the Specials announced: 'It's a shame Amy wasn't here earlier – she's the only woman here tonight I wanted to shag!' In spite of her blushes, she was the flavour of the evening. The magazine's editor, Phil Alexander, also spoke of Amy, warning: 'Now the sky is the limit for her. There is nothing that can stop her – apart from herself.'

Behind the scenes, the truth of that statement was beginning to unfold. The public didn't yet realise, but Amy and her husband were becoming increasingly addicted to heroin and crack cocaine. Add to that Amy's penchant for strong alcohol at all times of the day and her live shows were car-crashes waiting to happen. She had been skipping performances, once turning back seconds after boarding an aeroplane at the estimated cost of £80,000.

When Amy did turn up, reports quickly noticed something was very wrong. At her Glastonbury festival performance on June 22nd, the Guardian noticed her clenched jaw and rolling eyes – classic symptoms of drug abuse. The review continued 'Though Winehouse's live voice is flawless, she bears more than a passing resemblance to a rabbit caught in the headlights… she never loses her slightly traumatised expression.'

His review echoed one of her performances at the Isle of Wight festival earlier that month. *The Spectator* reported 'It was like seeing Bambi bounce into a clearing to find himself faced with a firing squad… she fidgeted and scampered on the spot, calming down only when she sang and it looked as if it took every ounce of muscle and morphine she could muster not to run for the hills.'

After the show, Amy reinforced fears for her well-being when she confessed, 'I almost didn't come to this concert… I almost didn't go to the Isle of Wight. I just want [Blake] to be happy and if for some reason he's unhappy, then it just floors me.'

Blake might have had good reason to be unhappy, as his wife was fast becoming a weapon of massive consumption. 'I always get my way,' she confessed, admitting that she regularly beat him when drunk. 'If Blake says one thing I don't like, then I'll chin him.'

Why was Amy taking her unbridled passion for Blake to such unhealthy extremes? Many people find it challenging to balance the demands of significant relationships with the pressures of work, but few would allow their partner to destroy every aspect of their lives simply to stay together. And Amy was making the ultimate sacrifice – her multi-million pound career.

The examples were endless – turning back seconds before boarding an aeroplane to be with her husband, rushing back to her hotel room moments before a concert due to Blake's insistence and abandoning video shoots with little regard for the astronomical financial losses she'd incur, because she was at home with her beau and couldn't bear to leave his side. Most poignantly of all was the hysterical crying and screaming as she went through the gates at a Eurostar terminal, trying to jump back across to the other side as the reality hit her that boarding the train meant being parted from Blake.

Yet she wasn't bidding him farewell as he went to war in a foreign country – the two would be reunited less than 24 hours later. Her behaviour had the signature of a distressed toddler suffering from separation anxiety and fearing the loss of their parents at a tender age when their presence could mean the difference between death and survival. Perhaps that, a deep-rooted syndrome from childhood, was the key to Amy's alarming behaviour as an adult. Had something taken place in her young years to leave her helplessly predisposed to love addiction?

As one psychotherapist from the website www.loveaddiction.co.uk theorises, 'The routes of love addiction are grounded in childhood experiences. If the child is nurtured fully by their primary caregivers from birth, then the child will likely develop a healthy sense of self-identity, self-esteem and appropriate boundaries. If such nurture is not received, then the child may develop a shaky sense of self and non-existent or distorted boundaries. A deep need for security from another rather than from within is laid down and the seeds of love addiction are sown.'

He adds, 'Love addicts escape at an early age into the realm of fantasy, a rescuer, a perfect love, in order to escape from an intolerable reality that their primary caregivers have failed to transmit to them through appropriate nurture; the messages that they are important, they matter and they are loved.'

Amy's parents clearly loved her – and yet those messages were evidently not getting through. She had told national newspapers in her darkest moments that she felt unlovable, talentless, 'hideous to look at' and 'nothing at all without my Blake'. She'd added that she needed to be with him to combat her otherwise unshakable feelings of self-disgust.

Those would be unusually negative opinions for anyone to hold about themselves, let alone someone with a number one album under her belt. What was the root of Amy's excessive pain and vulnerability? Mitch had addressed in interviews his belief that he might have been responsible due to his divorce from Amy's mother, something which he described as necessity as he 'simply wasn't happy'.

In the Western world, marriage breakdowns are commonplace and are not usually synonymous with symptoms as extreme as Amy's. Yet arguably, this was no ordinary divorce. Mitch had openly flaunted his infidelity in front of both his children from a tender age and, by a child's logic, had demonstrably chosen the other woman over her and her mother.

As the romance with Jane had been played out in public, it had gone beyond 'Mummy and Daddy don't get along' and had become a matter of choice between Janis and Jane. In many marriages, new partners tend to be concealed from the children until after the divorce proceedings, but for Amy it hadn't happened this way. Had this scenario given her the subconscious message that she wasn't good enough?

Internationally acclaimed psychotherapist, author and leading authority on love addiction Pia Mellody, explains: 'People fall into love addiction because of the unhealed pain from childhood abandonment and the feeling that they cannot be safe in the world without having somebody else to hold them up.'

In Amy's eyes, Blake had become the fairy-tale saviour to rescue her from the trauma within - the dissatisfaction she felt in her own skin, and the fear of being alone. Perhaps when he threatened to leave Amy's tour and head back to the UK after a fight, or even when they'd separated amicably for short periods, being parted from the man she relied upon for security and a sense of self-worth might have tapped into childhood loss. The nine-year-old within her could have come surging back into play, recalling the time her father had left the family home for someone he'd openly admitted to 'loving a little bit more' than her mother. Perhaps she was willing to prevent that re-enactment of loss at all costs – even if it meant sabotaging herself.

As www.loveaddiction.co.uk claims, 'At an unconscious level, the love addict is [addicted] for a very good reason. The lover to whom they are attracted in some way reminds them of their opposite sex primary caregiver from whom they failed to receive proper love and nurture. If they can receive love and nurture from this partner, symbolically it will put right the relationship with the primary caregiver. It is of course a strategy that is, by its very nature, doomed to failure.'

One psychologist added, 'When someone, deep in their subconscious, just doesn't feel loved, relationships that to some people are just one facet of their happy, balanced lives can become all-consuming and all-important for them, just to be okay and to emotionally survive.'

Psychoanalytic psychotherapist Charley Shults also believed that the intense addiction Amy had to Blake, seeing her refusing to spend time apart from him and descending into self-hatred whenever he wasn't around, was linked back to the trauma of childhood abandonment. In his eyes, it tapped into primal life and death issues in the subconscious.

'Imagine you're abandoned in the wilderness of Alaska, staked to the ground and left there,' he explained. 'You'll do anything you can to survive. That's how a child feels when they don't have a secure connection to their parent. It's the same terror, as if they were in the Arctic wilderness. Adults don't look at it that way. We say, "The child will calm down soon and go to sleep." We don't get that in a child's mind, there are wolves, bears, monsters under the bed. For Amy the relationship with Blake was about having an attachment figure that relieved her from that terror. It gave her brain the message, "You're going to survive" and everything else paled into comparison.'

Charley believed the problems may have begun early, with Amy's primary attachment figure. 'If you're nine months old and your mom leaves you, you will die,' he continued. 'If you have a consistent loving relationship with her, then you feel secure and have the feeling "I'm lovable." If mom isn't consistently available to you, that need is not met and if it's not met, that need stays prominent – the belief that I have to stay connected to my attachment figure in order to survive.'

Crippled with physical pain from then undiagnosed MS and smarting with emotional pain from her husband's betrayal might not have left Janis in the best position to give Amy her all. To top it off, in addition to two young children, she had a demanding job as a chemist.

'If she gets abandoned by her husband, what chance does she get to be loving and emotionally stable towards her child?' Charley theorised. 'She'll be preoccupied. We don't have to blame mom – maybe she didn't get the parenting she needed either – and parents are human beings, they do the best they can. But if Amy's relationship with mom was sufficiently disturbed and unsatisfying, her interactions with dad would have been all the more important. She may have looked to dad to give her messages about being okay – and he left.' He added, 'Self-hatred, feeling "I'm a bad person, I'm worthless" – that comes from these earliest attachment experiences.'

According to the theory, because Amy's childhood traumas hadn't been resolved, they loomed large in adult relationships too. She hadn't been able to fulfil her need for security in her earlier life, so she still had 'attachment hunger'. If Blake had divorced her, that might have reinforced her subconscious fear from times past that she was unlovable – a theory supported by her claims that she was 'nothing at all without my Blake'. In stark contrast, if he was by her side she mentally shifted from a wretched woman on the verge of suicide to one who felt invincible, her thirst quenched by the elixir of her love.

Suicide threats came flying back and forth, symbolic of their addiction to each other, Amy was inseparable from Blake not just because she loved him, but because – buried deep in her subconscious – was the fear that she needed his love to stay alive.

'In the 1970s, studies showed that babies in orphanages who'd been abandoned by their parents would die at incredibly high rates even though there was no reason for them to die as they were medically healthy,' Charley explained. 'When children have been abandoned, they lose the will to live.'

'Adults who perceive they've been abandoned feel, "Life is not worth living without you" and "If you abandon me, I might as well be dead",' Charley continued. 'If a well-adjusted person's partner leaves them, then they grieve a while and then get on with their life – but to someone who has this really insecure attachment, their whole world is over.'

It seemed that Amy was indeed addicted to love, even taking Blake along to a photo shoot with *Spin* magazine in the USA. Photographer Terry Richardson watched in horror as Amy pierced her stomach with a shard of glass and calmly began to carve 'I love Blake' into her skin. If it was agonisingly painful, she didn't show it, stopping only to exchange sweet nothings and whisper in the ear of her husband.

A friend of Amy's revealed of her self-harm: 'She's told me they egg each other on. Privately she's said she cuts herself because of work pressure. She's struggled with depression and says a blade piercing her skin makes her feel alive.' The friend continued that Amy had mourned her original break up with Blake by 'cutting wildly' at her tattoo of his name as a sign that she was hurting her. Allegedly she had celebrated her reunion with him the same way, with a frenzied bout of cuts to her arm. Rumours circulated that Blake not only encouraged this means of relieving pressure, but was also harming himself, sometimes cutting in the genital area to avoid detection. He was later quoted as saying he had introduced his wife to self-harm.

Amy had hinted that she'd enjoyed the pain – receiving a tattoo in memory of her grandmother Cynthia, she had shunned anaesthetic, claiming: 'It's a way of suffering for the things that mean a lot to you – I like the pain.' And like the poets of the early 1900s – especially Lord Byron, whose work Amy read avidly – she believed that physical pain was nothing compared to emotional loss.

Indeed, according to psychotherapeutic theory, children can handle a broken leg far better than a broken heart. Thus it is said that, of the two types of pain, they favour the physical variety – nothing to distract from the more overwhelming emotional ache.

However, the two might have been more similar than Amy had thought. Recent studies have indicated that psychological and emotional pain are both processed in the same part of the brain – in fact, some researchers argue that they are one and the same.

Self-harm is known to produce a surge of natural pain-relieving chemicals called endorphins, which will course through the sufferer's bloodstream, provide a feel-good factor to counter the negative effects of the pain. If emotional suffering is on-going in the victim's day-to-day life, then – after self-harm – the body's natural pain relief will recreate the endorphin rush again and again, making self-harm a chemical addiction as real as any drug habit – and just as seductive.

According to this theory, the prospect of getting relief can over-ride the unpleasant side-effects of wounds and scars. 'Amy was in so much emotional pain, she didn't really care,' surmised psychotherapist Charley Shults. 'She just wanted relief at any cost.'

He added, 'If you don't have a viable plan for what you're doing to relieve yourself of the pain, you're going to keep seeking the relief to the point of death – you feel you're going to die anyway if you don't get some relief.'

Yet it harming herself was about self-medicating, how had Amy first discovered that it would have that effect? What had first made her reach for the razor blade or the scissors?

Various theories speculate that harming oneself is about a masochistic desire for self-punishment. Blaming themselves both for their condition and for other problems around them, they attack themselves to express their guilt. Acting out her pain allowed Amy feel physically something which matched and related to the negativity that she already felt inside. The pain-relief effect would then allow her to break through her emotional numbness.

Another theory is that Amy may have been with other people and if the target of her anger wasn't available to her at that time or wasn't an appropriate figure to express it towards (especially if the rage was subconscious) then she'd turn it inwards. Even more likely, Amy was simply angry with herself.

As mentioned earlier, opinions in the psychological world are divided between those who blame childhood abuse for those feelings and those who believe it has other origins. Either way, whether deliberately afflicting abuse on herself or enduring the pain of a tattoo etched into her skin without anaesthetic, Amy had entered a dark place where the only thing that could heal her pain was more pain. It was a catch 22 situation – and it was hardly surprising that she felt she had little to live for.

Her self-harm took an even more sinister turn when she reached for the bottle. 'I didn't like the way that I looked,' Amy admitted. 'I'd drink a bottle of champagne and start slapping myself in the face. I try to please everyone all the time and then it all builds up. I get frustrated.'

The *Daily Mail* dismissed her behaviour as the 'sinister cult of ego' but it seemed at times as though painfully insecure Amy had no ego at all. Desperately unhappy, the flattery of her fame could never hope to have healed her low self-esteem. In fact, if anything, pressures of work life seemed to be making her problems worse. Now, with a husband who expressed misery in the same way, there was a risk that the two would perpetuate each other's dangerous thrills. It was clear that Amy needed help – and in more ways than one.

The tour continued but Amy's performances had become increasingly erratic. Her priorities lay with Blake and she would sometimes run off-stage to kiss her husband mid-concert. Some reviews reported that Amy was aggressive and incoherent, whilst others described her voice and attitude as 'flawless'. At times, she would display all of these traits in one day.

At the Cornwall Eden Project on July, a Radio 1 blog hinted at a Dr Jekyll and Mr Hyde persona, naming no fewer than seven personality types to manifest themselves during her one hour set. These included Nice Amy – ('came out for the first half hour. Sang beautifully, in tune, exchanged happy glances with her backing band, danced, attempted to talk to the audience a bit, failed, but charmingly!'), Angry Amy ('Disappeared off stage after half an hour, then came back on in a foul temper. Glared at her band for daring to fill the empty stage time with some jazz noodling… then after a couple of brilliant songs made famous by 70s punk ska legends The Specials, tetchily asked the audience if we wanted to know who the people in her band were, and when we failed to hoot with delight, swiped "Whatever – I'm going to tell you anyway!"') and Dirty Protest Amy ('spat on the stage in a venomous fashion, kept hitching those denim shorts up, pulling her vest down and generally acting as if she is uncomfortable in her own skin.')

Amy also made an admission that she knew little of the Eden Project, claiming: 'I didn't even know those, what are they? Bio domes? I didn't know they've been here for what, four years? I'm so ignorant – I know nothing, I really do…'She clearly hadn't researched the venue of her concert – and she wasn't afraid to say so. However, when the confusion extended to her own gig, Amy crumbled. As a room of horrified fans looked on, she started to repeatedly scream 'Fuck it!' into her microphone, before using it to bash herself over the head, when she forgot her own lyrics. It was the outward manifestation of Amy's battle with heroin – sometimes the real Amy would come shining through, someone who was devastated to let a crowd down. Yet, all too often, she would descend back into drug abuse and leave the same crowd unspeakably disappointed.

Talking of her many personalities, the blog then claimed: 'That's got to be the definitive Amy Winehouse experience, right? It's hard to think of many other people who can treat their audience with such disdain at times and still get away with it… Despite all this, whatever is going on with Madame Winehouse is a massive part of how she gets to write the kind of self-lacerating, truthful songs that she does… The terrible irony is that people love Amy for being emotionally raw in her work, but actually being around someone who is that emotionally raw while at work is pretty uncomfortable. But then who said going to gigs has to be a comfortable experience anyway? It's music, not massage.'

Other people were less complimentary, with one gig goer telling the *Daily Mail* 'The gig became absolutely awful. Members of her entourage were coming on to the stage, obviously worried she couldn't go on, and she would just shout "Fuck off" at them. Everyone in the crowd just felt sorry for her.' Another fan recalled sympathetically: 'She seemed to wipe away tears on two occasions and by the end she looked a very distressed lady.'

A spokesperson for Amy defended 'She is a bit ring rusty after not having played for a while and was upset after making a few mistakes in the set.'

After Amy's 'shambolic' set at the Eden Project, her mother Janis was finally able to deliver a wedding gift to her in person – almost two months after the nuptials. 'Sometimes I don't phone her because if I don't phone her, I don't get hurt,' Janis told the *Daily Mail*. '[That way] she can't just brush me off and say she's too busy or too tired.'

Consumed by her destructive relationship, these ailments were becoming increasingly common excuses in Amy's repertoire. Contact with her father, who had been managing her accounts, had declined from four times a week to just once. Amy had been in constant contact with her mother, but when her career took off in America, she had become more and more distant and Janis had not seen her daughter in months. When she visited Amy's 'filthy' home, the true extent of the problems she'd been trying to hide emerged. She gave the couple a kettle as their wedding gift – not a show-biz gift but an essential for their spartan, barely stocked house.

One bone of contention between Amy and her mother had been Blake. Janis was concerned about him in many ways. There were indications that Amy was financing her husband's lifestyle due to his tongue in cheek remarks on Myspace. His profile described him as a 'rent boy' who earned in excess of £250,000 per year. In addition to this, Amy had been flying her husband across the world to be with her, at her own expense.

It wasn't just her parents - even former lover and long-term friend Tyler James came to blows with Amy over her choice of husband. The two had known each other since their early teenage years and had dated briefly, but this was the first boyfriend that Tyler had seriously disapproved of. At Amy's July 20th concert at Somerset House, she was introduced by Kelly Osbourne before arriving on stage to the roar of 3500 expectant fans.

The show was a successful one, with *The Sun* reporting that 'after the most controversial weeks of her turbulent career, she gave the sort of soulful performance her fans had been begging for... She acted like a woman on the edge in Cornwall earlier this week, but at Somerset House she... looked happy on stage again. Amy is a huge talent and without too much wine, she deserves a champagne reception.' The headline was 'Great Return for Amy Wineless', demonstrating the prowess that the paper felt she had when she wasn't clouded by alcohol. She admitted herself on the stage: 'I rarely know what side of bed I'm waking up on, but I've been looking forward to this gig forever.'

However, there was one very unexpected – and, in this case, unwelcome – guest in the front row of the audience. *Digital Spy* reported: 'She spotted Tyler taunting her in the front row. [He] repeatedly tried to wind her up. Then she just snapped and stuck two singers up at him on stage. Amy clearly wasn't finding it funny. She told him to "cut it out" at one point during the show. It was obvious there is a mutual dislike still there between Amy and her ex.'

Yet the two had been close friends long after their break up, pictured together at numerous events on nights out. It was Amy's husband who had reportedly caused a rift between the two. She had boasted to the crowd 'I've been here at least an hour and I haven't even collapsed!' but Tyler didn't find her antics amusing. 'Tyler kept it up even after Amy let rip at him,' the report continued. 'It was only when a friend of his told him to stop that he gave up. Amy was furious – she was doing her best to put on a good show. After the gig, she demanded to know why Tyler had even been allowed in.'

Another of Amy's friends was more up front about the issues facing her and her husband. She reported 'To be honest, Blake doesn't help. I've known Amy since she started going out with him and I've never seen her so fucked up as she is now. The house has become a drugs den. It's filthy, covered in ash and the stench of rotting food. Blake wants to be like Pete Doherty, with Amy as his Kate. But Amy is just tumbling and tumbling and all her mates are terrified.'

It had reached a point where Amy could no longer deny the accusations. Her last performance before tragedy struck was the Lollapolooza festival in Chicago on August 5th. Dressed in a black and white gingham dress, Amy played a set which the *NME* reported 'failed to excite, as Winehouse seemed eager to get through it quickly'. *The Chicago Tribune* also noticed Amy's problem, claiming: 'The very gifted Ms Winehouse seems to be ripping a page from the book of Janis Joplin i.e. a dynamic, soulful voice mired in a web of drugs, booze and bad relationship choices. In this day of talentless hip-hop soulsters, she is peerless. It is always sad to see someone waste their gifts.'

These cautionary words of advice would ring in Amy's ears as it would be her last day of public normality. Just three days later, the newspapers would be emblazoned with shock headlines of a collapse, sandwiched between photographs of the emaciated and skeletal looking star on her way home from hospital. This was the day that Amy would die in her husband's arms for a few terrifying seconds.

After the show in Chicago, she and Blake boarded a plane to London, arriving back at around 1 p.m. As soon as they touched down, the pair were already in search of a fix, asking a taxi driver to take them to the nearest pub. They duly arrived at the Robert Inn in Hounslow, just a few miles from Heathrow Airport. There, Amy was loudly boasting to anyone who would listen that she had not slept for a day and was already on a high. Yet that was just the beginning.

She then invited some friends to her flat in Camden for a party she hoped would be an all-nighter. At first she did what she loved best – sang, played guitar and entertained. But the evening quickly descended into chaos, with Amy taking a cocktail of cocaine, ecstasy, heroin, vodka, whisky and the horse tranquiliser ketamine.

A friend of Blake's told the media: 'At one point she strummed her pink guitar and sang and I thought "Yes, the girl is back!" But then she started rocking like a six-year-old and was wailing and sobbing.' The friend continued: 'She looked like a zombie, white as a sheet and trembling – and I'll never forget her eyes, They were dead, like a shark.'

By 10pm, things had come to a head. Amy and Blake had been lying on the bed together chatting and smoking heroin when she suddenly started convulsing, forcing Blake to telephone friends, screaming: 'Fuck! Fuck! She's having a fit!' Then, his wife slipped out of consciousness altogether.

Blake told *The Sun* of the moment: 'She started having a fit on the bed. She slid down to the floor before I could stop her. She started quivering again and it suddenly grew into what seemed like a full-blown epileptic fit.' He continued: 'I was panicking and I didn't know what to do to help her. I was out of it on drugs as well and was sobbing and crying out "Amy!" I knelt over her as she kept on fitting. But then suddenly she just passed out and stopped breathing.'

Despite his anxiety, Blake managed to calm down enough to put her into the recovery position, an action which may have saved her life. He recalled: 'It was the most frightening thing I had ever seen. I felt sure I was watching her die right there in front of me… but somehow I managed to open her mouth and breathe air down her throat. At first nothing happened, so I did it again. I was feeling for her pulse because I thought her heart might have stopped. Then she spluttered – and I saw her chest rise. I was still sobbing and panicking but I just felt this huge relief that she was alive.'

Heartbreakingly for Blake, who was still reeling from the near miss, Amy failed to recognise him and instead called out for more drugs. Ignoring her pleas, friends called a taxi and she was rushed to the University College London Hospital, held up by Blake and best pal Juliette. Amy made it as far as the reception desk, before she let out a blood-curdling scream, her legs buckled and she fell to the floor.

An onlooker, seeking treatment after an accident, told the author: 'We figured it was pretty serious because despite there being a huge crowd of people, she was rushed straight to the front of the queue.' Amy was placed on a drip, had her stomach pumped and received an emergency adrenaline injection, before undergoing a brain scan to see whether her fit had caused permanent brain damage. The scan came back clear, but Amy had experienced a drug related seizure – she could no longer deny that she had a serious problem.

Meanwhile, Blake was racked with guilt, later telling *The New York Times*: 'My wife, who I love with all my heart and soul, just started shaking violently in front of me. It was heartbreaking seeing someone you love more than yourself, someone you would die for, someone you would kill for, on the floor shaking. I knew fucking then that I had ruined something beautiful. It was all my fault.'

Amy consoled him by insisting that he had saved her life. She told the German magazine *Stern*: 'I really thought I was on the way out. My husband Blake saved my life and brought me to the hospital.' Speaking of her drug related antics, she continued, 'The next day the memory returned and then I was engulfed with shame.'

The Sun dismissed Blake's guilt as amateur dramatics, reporting with heavy sarcasm, 'Amy has admitted she thought she was "on the way out". She certainly came close, but she has a rather strange take on why she is still with us. Ignoring the work of the doctors and nurses who saved her life, Wino once again claimed husband Blake Fielder Civil was her saviour. This is the same man who left her in hospital to go for another fix.'

Facing the music, Amy's parents were distraught, arranging for her to recuperate in a £3000 a night suite at the Four Seasons Hotel in Hook, Hants – far away from the drug scene of London. The day before her collapse, Amy had been nominated for three MTV Video Music Awards, including Best Newcomer and Female Artist of the Year. The musical world had been at her feet. Legendary musicians held her in high regard and her album had reached the No. 1 spot in both the UK and the USA. Yet nothing could stop Amy from pressing the self destruct button – in fact, she was suicidal.

Simply, it seemed that the trauma that had driven her to write music in the first place was ever-present. She suffered from depression, bulimia, anorexia, self-harming, alcoholism and drug abuse – and reports seemed to suggest that her issues had been looming since long before she ever hit the tabloids, or became famous.

In the past Amy had told the press: 'I never wanted any of this', 'I'm not ambitious' and 'I write songs because I'm fucked in the head and need to get something good out of something bad… I'm going to die if I don't write down the way I feel – I'm going to do myself in.'

That was the scene that met Amy's brother and parents when they drove down to the luxury hotel where she had been recuperating. 'I thought I was prepared for what was to come, but when we walked into her room, she looked terrible. She was lucky to be alive,' Janis told the *Daily Mail*. 'Alex [Amy's brother] said to her, "You're going to kill yourself. You're not going to live to 25 – you know that, don't you? Are you happy your life is like this?" She didn't have an answer. She didn't say anything, not a word. She was curled up on the bed and we told her she would have to go to rehab. She was saying "No, no, no, I don't want to go."'

Tragically, the song which had once been introduced as a humorous parody, the one which had won her awards nationwide, was now becoming more and more true to life. The light-hearted joke was now a stark reality, and Amy was at the centre of it.

Janis looked on in horror as her daughter lay lifelessly on the sofa, her face streaked with tears, refusing to get help. It was the first time that Janis had seen Amy alone since the previous Christmas. She had claimed that, since her marriage, she had always been with Blake – and that his presence had been a barrier to connecting with her daughter. 'I hugged her and kept saying, "What are you doing to yourself?"' she continued. 'I wasn't angry. I'm past anger. It's as if her whole life's turned into a stage performance.'

The next morning, the couple had a heart to heart with Amy's family – and Juliette had some bad news for them. She had been a constant companion over the two days of mayhem and had walked into the couple's hotel suite at breakfast to find pieces of charred foil scattered across the floor – a sign that the two may have been smoking heroin.

Even the day after her heart has stopped for a few terrifying seconds, Amy hadn't been able to restrain herself from taking another hit – it had gone much too far. Over chocolate cake, the family had a secret pow-wow where Amy tearfully confessed that she and Blake were addicted to both heroin and crack cocaine. Mitch was devastated that his daughter could have turned to drugs again just a day after her life-threatening seizure – and insisted that she talk. After months of holding back, the confessions came pouring out. The pair had made a pact, promising each other that if either's drug use became out of hand, they would tell the other. Yet Blake had eerily predicted his own fate, jokingly commenting to Amy in the previous month's edition of *Spin* magazine: 'You wouldn't tell me. Not right away, anyway. You'd wait till I had a needle hanging off my eyeball and then you'd be like, "Blake, I think it's gone too far."' By all accounts, however, the events of the last few days had gone way too far.

Later that morning, Amy and Blake's parents, Amy's manager Raye and four of her closest friends were all gathered for a meeting at the hotel – and emotions were running high. Blake's mother, Georgette, who had been trying to try to contact her son constantly by phone on the day of the incident, told *The Evening Standard*: 'We had a call from Mitch to say Amy had been in hospital and the pair of them had a problem that we needed to address. We were frantic with worry and we raced to the hotel for a very hastily arranged emergency summit… by the look of anger on Mitch's face, we could see he was unhappy about something. He launched straight into a torrent of abuse at [Blake's stepfather] Giles, shouting that everything was Blake's fault, then he tried to grab him round the throat. I was looking on, horrified, while Amy was yelling at her dad to get off Giles… we had done nothing to deserve it.'

In the midst of the chaos, Raye had calmly prepared a dossier of media cuttings that chronicled Amy's downfall. He told her to look at the pictures, spread out across the table, depicting her stumbling out of nightclubs looking tearful and gaunt, and tell him she didn't have a problem. She couldn't.

When the dust settled, Mitch apologised 'unreservedly' to Blake's parents and told the media that he believed Amy's new husband was not responsible for her drug habit after all. He claimed: 'He didn't coerce her in any way. I wish he had because she would most likely have said "I don't want to do it."' He knew his daughter's stubborn nature, her strong will and her desire to contradict too well to place the blame on her husband. Yet it was no longer a question of fault for Mitch. Amy now needed urgent help and who was to blame had become irrelevant.

Yet many people were keen to know the truth behind her behaviour. Why was Amy self-destructing at such a rapid pace? One theory was that she had only wanted to be a singer, not a public personality – and she was desperately unprepared for fame. She outwardly appeared not to care what others thought, but she later berated herself for being 'cripplingly stupid and hideous to look at'. She'd also admitted that – as she was a musician and not a model – she'd feel insecure, and be driven to drink.

Surrounded by beautiful rivals, to disguise her awkwardness and to get through a day packed with interviews, she would end up drinking copiously. That way, she anaesthetised herself from the pressures of fame, the twinges of stage fright and the fear of not being good enough. Perhaps it became tempting to reach for the bottle to become less vulnerable. It was something to hide behind, to mask her insecurities so she didn't have to face the realities of life and all the horrors that level of consciousness entailed.

Her relentless media coverage might also have made the problem worse. Originally, magazines had branded a healthily voluptuous Amy 'fat' and, later, when she reacted by slimming down to a tiny size six, she seemed to be jeered at for being dangerously thin. She confessed in interviews that she was keen to please everyone, but would often fail and the frustration would build up until she reached breaking point. But had her problems been triggered by fame or were they already there in the background to begin with? For example, the curvy Adele – also a big hit in music – was proud of her size 16 figure and refused to change to please anyone. She seemed to have a healthy opinion of her own self-worth. Yet Amy had already been depressed, succumbing to self-harm since the age of nine.

When she met Blake, the coping mechanisms reached a new level and Amy gravitated from smoking weed to smoking – and injecting – far harder drugs such as crack cocaine and heroin.

Perhaps a key factor in her growing reliance on alcohol and drugs was that – according to psychoanalysis – substances served as a defence against anxiety. A commonly used acronym in therapy is HALT, denoting that users battle with feeling Hungry, Angry, Lonely and Tired.

This certainly seemed to describe Amy. She was constantly hungry due to her anorexia and was furiously angry, as evidenced by her physical attacks on her husband and ex-partners when drunk, her tendency to trash dressing rooms and her repeated attempts to punch walls after arguments. She'd often complained of loneliness, while exhaustion was simply part and parcel of a demanding tour.

In the presence of these weaknesses, cravings can move in that are too powerful to resist – and that's what a controllable habit becomes an uncontrollable addiction. Dangerously, substance abuse numbed Amy's ever-present anxiety and allowed her to enter a comfort zone that she couldn't reach when held back by sobriety. Yet it wasn't enough to acknowledge that Amy was suffering – to stand a chance of conquering the addiction, she needed to know the root of why she felt so desperate.

While chemical addiction usually has a biological basis, it has been indicated time and time again that medical detoxification alone, which weans the user off a drug in a safe and supportive environment until the withdrawal symptoms have disappeared, is insufficient. Even when the entrapment of the biological cravings has passed, a detoxified addict will often return to their former ways. Therefore the psychology and psychiatry industries usually advocate treating not just the medical symptoms, but the original cause of dependency.

According to Harvard psychiatrist Edward Khantzian, addicts are often totally unable to regulate their moods and soothe themselves when distressed. Further to that, he adds that the critical window for learning how to do so is the first three years of life, 'when a toddler normally internalises such a function from caring parents'.

Amy was within this age group when she was first introduced to Jane, her father's second lover, whom he dated in hear early childhood whilst simultaneously maintaining a family life with Janis. The knowledge that she was sharing her father and risked losing him might have proved damaging, but either way, the status quo of life as Amy knew it had changed irreversibly.

What was more, her original loss of Blake to another woman might have reminded her of the time her father left the family home, sparking off a deep-seated, long-held sense of abandonment. Her obsessive relationship with her husband seemed to hold her back, while living out her pain and distress in public in front of the scrutiny of a camera lens could have been another culprit that triggered her meltdown. Whatever the cause of it, sobriety had gradually become too terrifying, too overwhelming, to contemplate – and it was time to call the experts in.

Clinical psychologists were called into the hotel and advised that it would be counter-productive for the pair to attend rehab together – they needed to battle their demons separately. Amy, on the other hand, insisted she would not attend a clinic unless she could go with her husband. It was far from ideal, but it was a start. Mitch and his son Alex immediately started to make arrangements.

Meanwhile, *The Sunday Times* released a report that couldn't disguise the extent of the singer's problems. 'Amy Winehouse should have been basking in glory, triumphant in the knowledge that, with three MTV nominations to her name and an album rocketing up the US charts, she had achieved the kind of success that most British artists can only dream about,' it wrote. 'Instead the jazz singer-songwriter was engulfed in a flurry of speculation about her increasingly unpredictable behaviour... after abandoning yet more gigs and ending up in hospital. The latest episode... fuelled concerns that one of Britain's hottest young singing talents is on a dangerous downward spiral.'

Meanwhile, Amy's competitors were moving in. Sharon Jones, whose band, the Dap Kings, had played on Amy's album and accompanied her on tour, had released a new album – *100 Days 100 Nights* – that threatened momentarily to usurp *Back to Black*. A slice of gospel, soul and funk with a Motown element throughout, the album was described by the media as 'the illegitimate love child of Tina Turner and James Brown'.

On the dawn of its release, Amy found herself at the centre of a backlash when Sharon complained that Amy, nothing more than a 'little white girl', had not only been heavily influenced by her but had also stolen her sound. 'Amy Winehouse ain't got nothing on me!' screamed the headlines.

'[Amy and Mark Ronson] came to us to get the sound that they wanted behind their music,' elaborated Sharon to *Jezebel* magazine. 'We were just sitting there minding our own business doing little 45s and albums and, all of a sudden, they were like "I want your sound." First, I felt kind of angry about it [but] if it took Amy to get the Dap Kings heard, it's a good thing.'

Originally a school choir girl who went on to become a corrections officer at a women's prison, Sharon had at first failed to secure the musical career she'd always wanted. She blamed discrimination in the industry, claiming numerous record companies had told her she didn't fit the bill because she was 'too black, too dark-skinned, too short, too fat, too old'. Reeling from the rejections of an increasingly image conscious industry, Sharon had been annoyed that Amy commanded so much press attention, supported by the sound of her band, while she – 'the original jazz artist' – struggled financially.

When an interviewer asked whether she would prefer to duet with Amy or Tina Turner, she made her feelings clear. 'Tina Turner – what do you think? Stupid question. Didn't I just tell you that Amy said I inspired her to sing?' she asked. 'Tina inspired me. I want to do a duet with Tina.'

However, she then assured the press: 'There's nothing negative between me and Amy. I just wish she'd get herself together and get back to the music.'

However, Sharon's discrimination claims had caused a race debate, with Amy at the centre of it. One fan wrote on an online forum: 'It's well documented that companies look to market black soul music with a white face wherever possible, because Caucasian people seem to feel more comfortable consuming it in this package. Amy Winehouse is just one more example of that product packaging. Elvis, the Shangri-Las, Dusty Springfield, the Allman Brothers... people who have studied the music industry in the last 100 years know what's up. Amy Winehouse is a knock off who happened to have a whole lot of money behind her and truth be told, she's got nothing on the authentic black soul singers of the past or present.'

Another fan wrote: 'It's sad that it took an over-rated faker like Amy Winehouse to use Sharon Jones's backing band in order to make people recognise her, but still, it's great that she's finally getting the attention she deserves.'

Even Amazon got in on the debate, writing in the album's product description: 'Despite... the volcanic popularity of new soul crooners like Amy Winehouse, the champions of the new generation's purist strain are Sharon Jones and the Dap Kings.' Mark Schlesinger, director of the Columbus Blues Alliance, also brought Amy's authenticity and originality into question, exclaiming: 'If Sharon Jones acted like Amy Crackhouse, would she make as much money and as much news? Maybe the British bozo used the mighty Dap Kings as her band (never heard it, don't care to) but Miss Jones rules!'

However another music fan countered: 'Amy might well have been influenced by the greats of the past, but she reinvented their sound and actually ended up doing it better.' Former Musical Director Ian Barter went a step further, discussing rumours of copying as 'A load of rubbish – and certainly not my opinion. Everyone takes an amount of style and approach from things they listen to, then subconsciously or deliberately put it into their work. But no, she is not copying. She's good – and that's rare.' He added: 'She's on a par with Dinah Washington.'

The hotly contested argument raised some questions. Was the sideshow of Amy's addiction struggles, previously in the background, now threatening to overshadow her music and her credibility as an artist? Were the comments of Sharon and her fans justified or had she become the scapegoat of a race debate?

In no position to fight back, Amy reluctantly postponed her September tour in the USA. She also cancelled a flurry of August appearances, including two in Germany's Dusseldorf and Hamburg which would have seen her opening for the Rolling Stones. A slot at Chelmsford's V Festival and shows in Denmark and Norway were among others to be ditched. In fact, on the day of the hotel meeting, Amy had been due to play the Oya festival in Norway. The band was already sound-checking when the news came through that she wouldn't be making her appearance. A statement was released by her management stating: 'Amy is putting all her touring commitments on hold until further notice in order to address her health issues. Her family has requested that the media respect Amy's privacy at this time.'

However, that was unlikely to happen. Everyone – from the gossip columns to the broad-sheet newspapers – had their own opinions on what had happened to Amy, and weren't afraid to share them. Even astrologers had their say on her tormented lifestyle, questioning: 'How did this woman with a tightly wound perfectionist Sun-Mercury conjunction in Virgo get so out of control?'

Someone had to step in, and Amy's musician friend Remi Nicole defended her with strong words. 'First of all, leave her alone. Second of all, if she's got a problem, why are you following her and making it worse? It's romanticising it, making people think it's funny or cool and that's not a good thing.'

Meanwhile *Daily Mirror* journalist Eva Simpson, who broke the story about Amy's hospitalisation, defended the media's right to publish details of her downward spiral. 'They would do what they did even if we didn't write about them,' she insisted. 'We write about Pete taking heroin and Amy being a junkie because that's what happens and I don't think we glamorise it. We are not fuelling what they do. We first became interested in Amy because she is the best female voice – if not best voice – we have. It is because her life took this soap opera turn that she is always on the front pages.'

It was that soap opera that had dominated the media's coverage – tabloid headlines about her collapse threatened to overshadow the release of fourth single 'Tears Dry On Their Own'. Debuting on August 13th in the UK, it was accompanied by B-side 'You're Wondering Now', a tale of misbehaviour, and various remixes of the lead tune. It peaked at a respectable No. 16 in the UK charts.

Meanwhile in a desperate bid to heal away from the prying eyes of the media, Amy and Blake finally accepted that they were not in control of their drug habit and agreed to attend the Causeway clinic in Maldon, Essex. Amy had joked the previous year that addicts went to the Priory not to get better, but 'to get crack'. If that was what she thought, she'd be in for a sore disappointment as the clinic had a strict policy that forbade contact with the outside world.

The Causeway was a drug addiction and mental health clinic on Osea, a private island connected by an ancient causeway to the Essex coastline. Access by car was dependent on the tide, but the island also had a helipad and visitors could arrive by helicopter within 20 minutes from central London. The clinic offered rehabilitation at a cost of £10,000 per week – not to just celebrity guests, but also to corporate workers – particularly those in highly pressurised and high-flying jobs in investment banking and law.

Amy benefitted from luxury four poster beds, LCD screen TVs, a gym, a yoga room and – best of all – a recording studio that had once been the hang-out spot of reggae giant Bob Marley. Yet all of this held limited interest for the restless Amy. Within 48 hours, the couple had made a dash for freedom and – as soon as they arrived back in London – were sighted in their local pub. The pair had a meeting with Blake's parents in the Old Eagle in Camden, before returning home – but later that evening, Amy returned to a second pub, the Hawley Arms, for yet another drink. Blake told the press that they had come back solely to collect a guitar, but the facts of their 24 hour break told a different story.

The news sparked outrage. 'I can't stop talking about Amy,' a Californian fan blogged. 'She represents so many women in the world who are strong and talented and yet succumb to addiction, poor self image and destructive relationships. It breaks my heart to see her this way. I watched a video from only a year ago and it shows a vibrant, well spoken diva in the making. I watched one from July this year and it was frightening to see what had happened to her.' It wasn't long before the blogger also took on Blake, the man she believed was responsible for the downfall. 'How could a man marry someone and let them go down this road?' she asked. 'He shouldn't be taking her to a pub just days after her overdose. Is that love? Your man just ain't good enough for you.'

A former musical assistant of Amy's also placed the blame on Blake, reminiscing about her musicianship before targeting her husband as the catalyst for her addiction. He anonymously told *The Observer:* 'She has enormous talent and deep roots in jazz and blues, she didn't suffer from the lead singer syndrome and unlike most she knew her sharps and flats… she knew exactly who she was and how she wanted to sound – which some singers only know when they've got £40,000 worth of equipment, but which Amy knew by standing on top of a piano in a pub… Amy is not the idiot [people] think she is from the papers. She drank too much, but at 23 that doesn't make you an alcoholic… I've been around a few junkies but I never saw any sign of that until Blake came back. He was introduced as the ex-boyfriend and as soon as he arrived, the coke started arriving. He had these rings around his eyes – as I said, I've known enough junkies.'

He continued: 'He stuck to her like glue and they soon became inseparable. I think Amy's wonderful and that's the tragedy – think Billie Holiday, Edith Piaf and her favourite, Dinah Washington.' All three had suffered from substance abuse problems and Holiday in particular endured domestic violence in an addictive relationship that was played out in the media at that time before an early death. 'The worst thing is that she knows what she is doing. You can't tell her anything about what she is doing that she doesn't know.'

Tyler James concurred of her addictive personality, 'Amy will say "I shouldn't say this, and then five minutes later she'll be doing it."' And indeed, Blake would later admit that, against all odds, the pair had managed to smuggle Valium and a heroin substitute into the Causeway. Of their time in rehab, he told the *News of the World:* 'We never really took it seriously.'

Yet for his part, Blake defended himself when questioned outside the pub that night. 'Everyone thinks that everything that's happened to Amy is my fault and I'm portrayed as the bad guy,' he said. 'But I love her so, so much. She's so precious to me, she's my wife and I want to take care of her – that's why I'm taking her back to rehab.'

He continued: 'We only came back to get a guitar but of course in the paper that's interpreted as we're both so weak we left. It's the inevitable way the papers are trying to put you down when you're trying to do something positive. The main thing is that me and Amy are getting better… she's fine, she's loved and looked after.'

Amy denied the allegations of a drug problem altogether when she was asked on her return if the reports of substance abuse were true. She replied with the curt response: 'I wouldn't say so, no.' She also added, 'Cocaine isn't my thing and I was never really on it.'

However the couple duly returned to the clinic, staying for a few more days before finally abandoning it. One source indicated that their departure had been well timed. 'It was supposed to be a peaceful backdrop to help people deal with their problems, but Blake kept rowing and spoiling the ambience,' the source said.

Back home, Amy claimed to have gained half a stone during her short stay in rehab and – for her father, who had described her as a concentration camp victim – it was a huge relief. Blake's parents reported: 'Amy has had five days away from drugs and her self esteem and confidence is slowly coming back. I hope that she and Blake can now take control of their lives.'

Were the world's most tortured couple finally on the road to recovery?

CHAPTER 11

A distraught young woman crawls into a hotel elevator crying hysterically, a mixture of mascara stains and tears pouring from her bloodshot eyes. Oblivious to the shocked guests around her, the frail figure – clad in blood-soaked satin ballet pumps – bolts through the elevator doors and out into the night. That young woman, of course, is Amy Winehouse.

The ill-fated night had begun when, on August 24th, fresh out of rehab, Amy and Blake decided to spend a night at the fashionable Sanderson hotel in London's Soho. Swish and centrally located, the hotel's recent clients had included Justin Timberlake and Madonna. However, more importantly than any connotations of celebrity, it was a chance for them to escape from the drug culture of Camden.

The pair enjoyed a relaxed meal with Amy's father that evening but, after he left, things began to take a turn for the worse. At around 11pm, Amy greeted a young woman in the lobby, embracing her before taking receipt of a small package. Moments later, the couple's hotel suite erupted with the sounds of screams and the thuds of furniture hitting the floor. An eerie silence followed before Amy made an emergency call to the concierge for assistance with wounds to her arm. This fuelled rumours that Amy was self-harming or, even worse, that she was a victim of domestic violence. Meanwhile the reception desk was flooded with calls from aggravated neighbours who'd heard the fight break out.

By 2:30am, after a brief respite, the drama began again. Concerned for her safety and desperate to appease their angry guests, hotel staff called police to the scene. However, before they had a chance to arrive, Amy was seen fleeing to the elevators with her heavily bleeding husband in hot pursuit.

One horrified onlooker told the press: 'Amy was in floods of tears. [Blake] was screaming at her. She was cowering in the corner and I thought he was going to hit her. When the lift door opened, she took off across the lobby at a real pace. He was chasing after her… about five paces behind.' Other eyewitness reports claimed that a 'terrified' Amy was begging with her eyes for help' as she tried to escape.

Fleeing out of the front entrance to freedom, Amy flagged down a passing car with the plea:

'Quickly, I have to get in, I have to get away, please help me.' The driver obliged and sped off into the night, dropping Amy at Charing Cross railway station, where she appeared to have calmed down, stopping to buy some cigarettes. Meanwhile Blake was left behind, calling out his wife's name forlornly as he searched doorways without success.

By 4am, after a frantic phone call, the passionate pair was reunited. They then left the hotel arm-in-arm, Amy clutching her purse in one hand and her wedding photograph in the other – all the two lovebirds had needed for their one night stay. However, both bore the scars of what had happened to them that night. Blake looked as if he had borne the brunt of the altercation, with his neck and face covered in scratches. In fact, newspapers claimed that he looked like the victim of a sustained knife attack.

An onlooker revealed: 'It was a horrifying sight. Blake had all these deep scratches on his face and neck, like he had been scratched by a wildcat. They were still open and weeping… he'd obviously tried to stem the flow of blood with what looked like a T-shirt tied around his neck. But the attach marks went down to an angry looking red patch and an open wound on his chest. It must have been a frenzied onslaught. And God knows what injuries he was covering under his clothes.'

Blood was also dripping from Amy's sodden ballet pumps, leading to rumours that she had injected heroin between her toes. Ballet shoes were ordinarily a symbol of discipline, elegance, sophistication and femininity – yet that night, their wearer looked anything but. Seemingly oblivious to their condition, they casually walked around central London, stopping to check out the cult Entertainment Megastore, before heading off back to Camden.

Was this a normal argument that could happen between any volatile hot-headed couple, or was it an out of control act of violence? Either way, with press photographers in hot pursuit, the difference was that their fight was played out in public.

Amy's plight soon attracted the attention of high profile celebrity blogger Perez Hilton, a personal friend of Amy's whose pseudonym was a word play on socialite and heiress Paris Hilton. Perez, real name Mario Lavandeira, was a controversial writer based in Hollywood. Over his career he had made a name for himself as one of the most hated media personalities of all time, with pop singer Fergie writing a song, 'Pedestal', in retaliation to his negative comments about her. Yet in July 2007, Perez alleged that his website had almost nine million hits in one 24 hour period – it seemed the world was addicted to celebrity.

Openly gay, the blogger courted controversy when he made a video post savaging a Californian Miss World contestant who had said in an interview with him that same sex marriage went against her religious beliefs. According to Perez, the would-be beauty queen was 'a dumb bitch' with the most bigoted response in pageant history.

As well as getting political, Perez was also unafraid to cause offence. He flirted with danger after linking to a photograph that allegedly showed the underage vocalist Miley Cyrus without underpants. Under American law, Perez could have faced child pornography charges for distributing and publicising the image.

He caused yet more offence when one blog posting saw him claim that news of Michael Jackson's death was a 'publicity stunt', before sarcastically egging on ticket holders to get their money back. The post was sheepishly removed soon afterwards, to be replaced with his condolences.

Finally, a week before the Winehouse story broke, he had falsely reported the death of the Cuban president Fidel Castro. He announced that his website was the first in the world to report the news, although it then emerged that this was because Castro was in fact still alive and well. Perez would go on to describe the story as the biggest mistake of his career.

By August 25th, he had recovered enough from the humiliation to post a blog about Amy that didn't hold back. 'Fuck this fake Hollywood bullshit,' he wrote, referring to the glamour that at times surrounded drug use. 'Amy Winehouse is going to die if she continues down this destructive path! Click here for graphic pictures of a bloody fight that erupted... in the wee hours of Thursday morning... Ditch that loser husband!'

Amy instantly retaliated, sending a series of text messages to Perez to try to prove Blake's innocence. With the determination she spoke of in 'Some Holy War', she was prepared to defend his honour to the death.

'Blake is the best man in the world,' she declared. 'We would never, ever harm each other. Take back what you said on the blog. I was cutting myself after he found me in our room about to do drugs with a call girl and rightly said I wasn't good enough for him. I lost it and he saved my life.'

Determined to get her version of events into print, Amy followed it up with a second text, claiming: 'For the last time, he did not and has never hurt me. Say I told you what happened on your blog. He has such a hard time and he's so supportive. Please make amends.' She ended the message with a persuasive kiss.

Her third and final message pleaded: 'Can you put up the truthful version straight away?... I know you love me but he deserves the truth, he is an amazing man who saved my life again and got cut badly for his troubles. All he gets is horrible stories printed about him and he just keeps quiet, but this is too much. I'll be alright. I need to fight my man's corner for him though. Thanks, girl. Amy.'

Perez obliged in printing her responses but it was too little, too late. The news of Amy's night out had circulated around the world, in all its gory detail. Everyone had something to say on the matter. Amy's heartbroken father was so sickened by the pictures of his vulnerable daughter that he 'wanted to die'. According to rumours, he'd even begun to write a eulogy for Amy's funeral.

Meanwhile a music industry insider revealed that not only was her lifestyle damaging her health, but her record sales too. 'If they want to fuck themselves up on heroin, they could do it at a house in the middle of the country,' claimed the anonymous insider. 'But they don't. They do it before running around the streets of Soho. The idea that all publicity is good publicity is not true. There comes a point when you cross the line and staggering around the streets with blood on your face is not good publicity. How can it be in Island's interests to have Amy dead when the company is hoping for five more platinum albums?'

Mike Leonard of Parlophone, Pete Doherty's record label, agreed: 'There's a big difference between someone with a serious problem destructive to themselves and a colourful lifestyle and that's where the boundaries are blurring. With Amy, we have seen a desperation reaching the point of no return. I don't necessarily think it's self-promotion by the artists. But if it is, it will have diminishing returns. I see all this beginning to have the opposite effect, working against the artist and therefore against the label and, in the end, against everyone involved. Most fans don't want to see their artists like this.'

However journalist Mark Ellen believed Amy's outrageous antics were relatable, elicited sympathy and perhaps even served to increase record sales. 'There's an appetite for authenticity at the moment,' he commented, hinting that Amy – troubles and all – was the real deal. 'People are drawn towards singers who appear to inhabit the songs they perform and a sense of suffering has never damaged the integrity of an artist.'

However, for those who cared about the singer personally, record sales were the last thing on their minds. While Amy was almost indisputably the antithesis of the average squeaky clean, manufactured pop star, was it at the cost of her health and sanity? Her family and friends certainly seemed to think so.

Her father in law, Giles Civil, believed that Amy and Blake were the modern day Sid and Nancy. The couple were tragic icons, avatars of excess and were both adored and reviled, until one day their fast-paced lifestyles came to a head. Rock star Sid Vicious and his girlfriend Nancy Spungen were famed for living a decadent, hedonistic lifestyle but in 1978, in a seedy New York hotel room, Sid murdered his girlfriend in a heroin-fuelled attack. The couple had been arguing when Sid woke up the next morning to find his lover dead on the bathroom floor with stab wounds. Before he could go to trial accused of her murder, the star died of a heroin overdose just four months later.

Comparing Amy and Blake to rock 'n' roll's most dangerous couple seemed sensationalist, but perhaps it wasn't so far off the mark. According to Ade Omotayo, the couple were 'dangerous' for each other and Amy was becoming increasingly violent. Not only did she punch anything she could get her hands on after a dispute – including Blake himself – but she had reached a point where she was 'always up for a fight'.

'She only ever backed down from a fight once,' Ade told the author. 'We were at the BBC for a Children In Need show and Javine [singer and partner of rapper Harvey] heard Amy had been saying things about her. She's nearly 6ft tall and Amy is tiny – and she came up saying, "What's this you were saying about me?" in a really aggressive manner. Amy backed down instantly and said: "Oh no, no, I didn't!"'

While the threat of a punch in the nose from an intimidating Amazonian woman nearly a foot taller than her might have been enough to make her back down but she couldn't claim the same where Blake was involved.

'She could be nice one moment and tell you to fuck off the next. Someone she was showing love to, she could tell them to go away within the next second,' Ade explained incredulously. One trigger than changed her from angel to devil could be something as small as an insult directed at her beloved husband. 'You'd have to tread carefully and watch what you said, because she'd over-react,' Ade continued. 'One time we were playing pool and the singer from Towers of London – who thought he was the new Johnny Rotten – said something to her jokingly about Blake. He didn't mean anything by it but she snapped and punched him immediately. He reeled back and was like, "What's wrong? What's wrong?!"'

Yet her fury with those who criticised her husband was nothing compared to how she reacted when the criticism came from Blake himself. Violent arguments followed by passionate reunions became commonplace in her marriage and, by now, everyone was worried for the pair's safety. Fearing a repeat performance of the Sid and Nancy tragedy, based on Amy's history of violence and self-harm and the bloodbath of their night at the Sanderson, both families were urging the couple to separate – at least temporarily.

The Civils made an impassioned public plea on BBC Radio 5 Live, with mother Georgette claiming: 'Blake and Amy are like two separate accidents waiting to happen. Their meeting simply exacerbated everything that was wrong with their lives to the verge of tragedy. Our greatest fear is that if one of them dies, the other will commit suicide, such is their love for one another. If Amy died, Blake's life wouldn't be worth living because he'd be vilified. He told me that if Amy died on a Monday, he would be dead on Monday night… I'm so desperate to get Blake away from drugs that I'm even considering having him kidnapped and taken to a safe house where we could get professional help for him.' She added: 'All we can think about as we lie awake at night is: will we be burying our son in the next few weeks?'

Both families were by now desperate for the pair to take a break from each other. Yet the relationship between the two seemed to have reached a whole new height of co-dependency when Amy ranted to *The Mirror* that she had no intention of leaving Blake behind. 'Look at me, I'm a mess,' she said. 'I'm nothing special. In fact, I'm nothing at all. I don't feel good. I don't have talent. I'm nothing without my husband. I love him so much sometimes it hurts. Without him I would be nothing which is why it is so important we are together. I can't beat the drugs without him. He's my rock. Blake says he isn't going back to rehab – but I can if I want. But I'm not going without him. I know I need help but Blake is the only one who can help me. I don't want to lose him. I won't lose him. I want to make him happy like he does to me. I feel disgusting and Blake's the only person who stops me feeling like this.'

Realising it would be futile to try to split up the reluctant pair while emotions remained high, Mitch instead arranged for them to have a break in the Caribbean island paradise of St Lucia. This not only kept their dirty laundry out of the British newspapers but it gave them a chance to recover away from the many temptations of the London drug scene.

Amy and Blake booked into the luxury Jade Mountain resort, described as 'one of the Caribbean's most mesmerising experiences'. All of the rooms featured 15ft high ceilings and panoramic views of the mountains flanking the sea, and their suite boasted its own private pool. With its policy of no telephones or televisions and no contact with the outside world, it was not just a place for harassed professionals to unwind but a form of drug rehab in itself. The hotel's website described the accommodation as a 'stage like setting from which to embrace the glory of the eternal Caribbean sea'. Mitch hoped this backdrop would prove a peaceful sanctuary for his daughter to beat her demons.

Unfortunately, the reality was a little different. The couple seemed to have patched up their volatile relationship, stealing tender kisses on the beach as Amy lazed in a bright green bikini, but the paparazzi had tracked them down and relentlessly pursued pictures during their stay. It was not the private retreat that the two might have hoped for. *The London Paper* also broke a story that the couple had used heroin during their stay. Critics dismissed the allegations, asking how Amy could have got access to heroin abroad without her contacts and how it could have passed through airport security. As it turned out, however, Amy had a penchant for swallowing drugs to get through long periods abroad without needing to go through cold turkey.

The same newspaper claimed that Amy had vomited blood all over the bathroom of her suite and had then vomited again while drinking in the resort's restaurant, which had to be closed temporarily until it had been cleaned. She had allegedly refused an intervention from the hotel's on site doctor. A source told *The Mirror* of Amy and Blake's stay, 'They're not like our typical guests. They stand out because they're both covered in cuts and have tattoos all over their bodies. They both behave very strangely.'

All in all, the trip was far from the private haven the couple had hoped for, with so many people willing to discuss their relationship. Amy returned from the airport with fresh puncture wounds on her arm which the media believed to be a sign of heroin use. If the newspaper reports were to be believed, she was descending down a slippery slope – and her loved ones were beginning to doubt whether they would ever see her alive again.

Amy's manager was quick to step in and deny reports that she had vomited or was unwell on her trip. However Amy's in-laws were fearful that there had been no improvement and spoke again to the press. Georgette Civil claimed: 'We didn't ask for the tragedy of our son's drug addiction to be played out so publicly, but that is the beast we are dealing with because of Amy's fame.' Meanwhile Giles Civil urged fans to boycott Amy's album in a bid to shock her into cleaning up her act. He also claimed that she should no longer be nominated at music awards, saying, 'We should not be condoning her addiction by awarding her.'

His words matched those of Francis Rossi, an ex-member of the rock group Status Quo. 'I have been subjected to so much of Amy and her antics that I just think "fuck off"', he raged. 'What message does giving her [awards] send to young people? She's not a good role model. They should have said to her "You're not getting [the award]. You would have done but you're not cutting it anymore.' Francis, however, received many an accolade in his time despite admitting to an out of control cocaine habit and claiming that he had once lost part of his septum after it fell down the plughole of a bath tub. Was he a hypocrite? Moreover, was Amy even sober enough to care whether she won an award, let alone to acknowledge that she'd been rewarded? Her problems reached far beyond whether or not to present a trophy.

Meanwhile, a cynical source close to Amy was unconvinced about the motives of her detractors. 'The Civils are behaving like groupies,' the anonymous friend revealed. 'They have seemed a little too keen to share the spotlight with her. It's right that they have begged Amy and Blake to get help, but do they honestly think people will stop buying her records? And even if they did, Amy's too far gone to care right now. Nobody's saying Blake's parents aren't worried sick, but you get the impression they are rather in awe of Amy's fame and are enjoying their own moment in the spotlight.'

The source had been correct – people did continue to buy Amy's CDs, and even more so than ever. That month, on the same week as Amy's 24th birthday, Back to Black sold its millionth copy in the UK. In the wake of a personal tragedy, Amy's popularity was only increasing.

And even if Giles Civil's seemingly well-intended fatherly advice was for Amy's award nominations to be withdrawn, it didn't stop her from receiving one the very day she returned from St Lucia. On September 4th, she attended the Mercury Music Prize's annual award ceremony at the Grosvenor House Hotel in London. The overall winner of the Best Album nomination would net a cheque for £20,000 for their efforts. Alongside competitors such as the Klaxons, Arctic Monkeys and Bat for Lashes, Amy was one of the hopefuls. She took to the stage in the same yellow dress she had worn at the Brits for a stripped down acoustic version of 'Love is a Losing Game'. 'There wasn't a dry eye in the house,' an eyewitness recalled.

The Sunday Herald had equally glowing praise for her, commenting that the viable pain she held within made for a mesmerising performance. 'It was an incredible performance, brimful of vulnerability and strength, one of those rare moments when pop music on television achieves an emotional honesty that transcends the essential fakeness of the medium,' journalist Peter Ross wrote. 'It was encouraging that Winehouse was capable of such heights, though there was the awful thought, too, that her troubles had sharpened her talents.'

Producer Stefan Skarbek agreed with this version of events, telling the author, 'Amy needs tragedy in her life to creatively inspire her. She is a classic self-saboteur – the edge is where the magic is.' Sadly, this was to be just the beginning of the self-sabotage for Amy, as the events of that month would reveal.

The Sunday Herald compared her Mercury Music performance to watching Kurt Cobain's rendition of 'Where Did You Sleep Last Night?' Live on MTV Unplugged. 'In both cases, an incredible voice articulated incredible pain and yet the very fact that a human being could express itself so powerfully seemed to pit hope against despair,' the feature said. 'It's probably pointless to speculate on why Winehouse behaves in a self destructive way. One answer is obvious – she has a depressive personality and uses drugs and alcohol to cope. But I'd say another reason is that she is still enchanted by the romantic rock and roll myth that personal turbulence... is what it means to be a true star.'

Despite her rousing performance, Amy did not win the award that night. Instead the Klaxons were triumphant with their debut album, *Myths of the Near Future*. The judges applauded: 'Rock meets pop meets dance – the Klaxons take us on an ecstatic musical adventure.'

Front man Jamie Reynolds expressed sadness that Amy had lost out, but said he was unsurprised at the outcome, as if anyone deserved the prize, it was him. 'It's a retro record and the Mercury is about pushing music forward,' he claimed. 'We've made the most forward thinking record in I don't know how long.'

However one media source had a different opinion, crowning Amy 'the undisputed star of the night', with other reports claiming that the Mercury Music Awards had a reputation for choosing unlikely candidates as winners. Blake claimed that Amy 'was robbed' while it was alleged on the grapevine that the pair had stormed out on learning who the winner was to be. Photographers finally snapped a tearful and tired looking Amy leaving the event in a silver BMW.

It might have been disheartening to lose out, but just two weeks later, on September 19th, Amy was nominated at two award ceremonies in one day. She was due to appear at both the MOBO awards at the 02 Arena in Greenwich and the Vodafone Live Music Awards at Earl's Court's Brompton Hall. She chose the former and, shaking off rumours that she had vomited all over the dressing room, sang renditions of both 'Me and Mr Jones' and 'Tears Dry On Their Own'.

Amy's nomination seemed over-ambitious as the MOBOs represented music of black origin and, battling it out against Beverley Knight, Jamelia and Corrine Bailey Rae, she and Joss Stone would be the only white artists in the building. In spite of that, she still won a gong. She was introduced as having 'the best voice you're ever likely to hear', before picking up the award for Best UK Female alongside Dizzee Rascal, who won the male equivalent.

Meanwhile back at the Brompton Hall in Earl's Court, Amy had recruited the landlord of her local pub the Hawley Arms to collect her award for Best Female Live Act. Known only as Dougy, he stepped onstage to tell onlookers that the gong would take pride of place behind the pub's bar.

Yet despite her prestigious awards, the consequences of Amy's unpredictable behaviour were now beginning to set in. Her edginess was the very reason magazines and movies craved her, but – when she took it to the extreme – it repelled them. *US Vogue* editor Anna Wintour was allegedly desperate for the 'iconic' singer to grace the magazine's front cover. She had been chosen for the September edition – traditionally the highest selling issue of the year – and the deal was characterised by mutual excitement.

A source told *The Mirror*: 'An order from Anna Wintour is like a royal command and the order was "Get me Amy". Anna loved Amy's album so much that she just had to have her. But at the end of the day, it's not just about the music, it's about her rawness, her kooky style and her outspokenness. She's very much a one off.'

Amy had been an avid reader of *Vogue* and other "high fashion Bibles" in her teenage years, so the invitation must have been flattering. Yet what was troubling about it was the connotation that Amy was being sought after and marketed not just on her music, but on her "rawness" –[something that was currently causing her a great deal of pain.

Arguably, magazines capitalised on Amy's behaviour because it won them headlines and, in theory, increased their readership. Yet did their appetite for shock reports make Amy feel obliged to live up to expectations and, like a 'sad clown' at the circus, self-destruct on command for the entertainment of a baying audience?

She'd already made it known how much she hated to disappoint the media, feeling she wasn't pretty, articulate or talented enough to impress – but one thing she could reliably put on was a hedonistic show. She never disappointed at that.

Amy saw herself as unlovable, yet drinking and drug-taking to excess, whilst enhancing her status as a rock 'n' roll hell-raiser – something which was probably encouraged by the likes of new buddy Pete Doherty – also created attention and concern around her. For someone who felt chronically starved of authentic love, perhaps the attention was positive reinforcement for her, making her all the less likely to change her behaviour.

The column set up by national newspaper The Sun to monitor her debauchery would have been humiliating for most, but the reality for Amy was that she was probably too far gone to notice or care.

So was the media perpetuating an insecure woman's difficulties by rewarding her with attention each time she descended into drug addiction? By continuing to validate her with magazine covers and awards, even after she slurred her way incoherently through yet another disastrous concert, were people sending ouit the message that her debauchery wasn't a problem?

The implicit message was that her misdemeanours made her cool, reinforced by the deafening cheers when she made light of her addiction by performing songs like 'Rehab'. Left unmonitored, her down-fall could turn into a modern-day Bedlam, where visitors paid to watch patients in a lunatic asylum acting out their issues. Here it seemed Amy's pain was a commodity to be bought into, something to be watched by casual sadists for amusement.

From the fans who purchased concert tickets to the magazines and TV stations which offered up footage of her latest mishaps, was complicit. Each time she took to the stage, it wasn't for a musical concert but for the latest instalment of a theatrical tragedy. What was more, that tragedy didn't seem likely to stop any time soon.

Amy, who still courted high fashion and had dreams of opening her own beauty salon in her late grandmother's memory, was devastated when it turned out that her drug battles had put the *Vogue* magazine cover deal in jeopardy. She had already taken part in a photo shoot in Miami but when September came, the cover went to the more wholesome Sienna Miller instead.

Amy had also been singled out as a candidate to record the theme tune for a forthcoming James Bond movie. Composer David Arnold, who had produced the music for the previous four movies, had publicly announced that Amy had 'the best album of 2006' and, according to insiders, her participation was a given.

A source told *The Sunday Express*: 'Amy's voice and musical style was in perfect sync with what Bond is all about. There was even talk of her having a cameo by performing the theme tune is a smoky club Bond visits, but that's all out of the window now. After all the reports of hard drug use, self injury and domestic violence, it's fair to say bosses here aren't keen on the idea.'

Blake told *The Sun* afterwards: 'She told me she was writing [the title song] about me and her and our relationship. How cool is that? To think, in 30 or 40 years time, people would still be watching this film and still hearing the song about us. That was really amazing. But she messed it all up.' Again, it was a classic case of self-sabotage – just moments from clinching a legendary deal, Amy had lost out due to her lifestyle.

It was clear that she needed to slow down with work commitments while she fought her personal battles. In early October, Amy was interviewed for *Blender* magazine, but – overwhelmed by exhaustion – repeatedly fell asleep. Her manager informed the magazine that she was on prescription medication which made her drowsy, but refused to elaborate, saying: 'That's between Amy and her physician.' His words sparked rumours that Amy could have been taking methadone or morphine in a bid to slowly wean herself off drugs – both drug substitutes are known for their extreme sedative effects.

'The singer has never exactly been a picture of health,' the magazine wrote, 'but tonight she looks especially worse for wear; hunched, heavy-lidded and frail. Now her words are slurred, her eyelids drooping… her head wobbles into a nod. She falls asleep for a second, wakes with a start, mutters and drops off again. The smouldering cigarette in her left hand falls to the floor.' Repeatedly falling asleep mid-sentence, Amy apologised profusely but was unable to shake off the sleepiness. Despite remembering the exact date that she first met her husband and proudly informing the interviewer, soon enough, 'she's gone, words trailing off, eyelids fluttering... she shakes awake again. "It's too dark in here – it makes me drowsy," she says finally. "There's no windows. Maybe we could do it another time in a corridor with windows. Some place with more light. I'm really, really sorry – from the bottom of my heart."'

The magazine had jetted from America to join her in Paris, where she was due to take to the stage for *La Musicale*, a TV show broadcast across the country. What they witnessed was an example of the Russian Roulette style paradox of a typical Amy Winehouse gig. During the first of her pair of two-song sets, her performance was erratic. 'Winehouse is in fine voice, but she stands nearly stone still at the mic, wearing a vacant expression,' the interviewer claimed. 'Her eyes roll back in her head as she sings. When she finishes, *La Musicale's* perky host mounts the stage and attempts to conduct an interview. But Winehouse can barely muster a syllable in response... outside of Winehouse's dressing room, her manager pulls Naomi, the stylist, aside and hisses: "Go back in there and get rid of that wine".'

An hour later, Amy was due for the second segment of her performance, 'looking more awake than she has all night'. What followed was surprisingly explosive. The magazine continued 'Winehouse is transfixing: rocking on her heels, gesticulating, shimmying, singing. Her singing is magnificent. She lingers behind the beat and unspools jazzy syncopations, purrs low, burly blue notes... you cannot help but be struck by the case of her virtuosity. For Winehouse, living is evidently exceedingly difficult, but singing is as natural as breathing.'

The review concluded, 'When the song ends, the studio audience erupts into the biggest ovation of the evening, a burst of sheer relief.' The show had evidently given onlookers a taste of what Amy might achieve if she was able to conquer her drug addiction.

Amy also made some positive headlines when she accepted an invitation to endorse a charity for the hard of hearing and – according to *The Mirror* – even donated £50,000 to a Romanian orphanage. By now notorious for her beehive hairstyle, she was alarmed to hear that some hair weaves originated from real hair that was 'culled unscrupulously' from impoverished children with little option to refuse. She allegedly had a conversation with the human rights group Beauty Hurts before deciding to make the donation. A source revealed: 'Amy had no idea orphans were exploited. She knows where her weave comes from but she still wanted to help. Amy actually wants to keep the donation secret, but she's setting such a good example, it needs to be known.'

However, there were still some cruel jokes winging Amy's way. On October 8th, Amy was nominated for Best Album at the Q Awards, but was unable to attend due to illness. Just the previous year, she had been healthy and happy there, poking fun at U2's political prowess, while candidly screaming: 'I don't give a fuck!' across the auditorium. Now, however, the tables had turned and the jokes were on her. In her absence, Jonathan Ross jibed: 'I was on a three to one bet that Amy would die before Pavarotti. I'm really annoyed with Amy that I lost.'

Jonathan had hit headlines many times before for his risqué behaviour, once phoning a burlesque dancer's famous grandfather live on TV to leave profane messages on his answer phone. He and fellow comedian Russell Brand almost lost their jobs over the affair, which saw the two lewdly remark: 'I fucked your grand-daughter!' Unsurprisingly, however, in this instance Amy was unlikely to have seen the funny side.

That year, she was competing with a rock influenced collection of nominees, including the Kaiser Chiefs, the Arctic Monkeys, the Manic Street Preachers and Arcade Fire, but was again triumphant for Best Album. Producer Mark Ronson was on hand to collect the award for her, saying in his short speech, 'That's Amy – taking her pain and turmoil and making it into music we enjoy.' However, she never saw her award – it disappeared soon after Mark accepted it and, following a night of party fuelled fun, was left languishing in the toilets of a Soho bar.

The following evening, Amy cheered herself up with a late night shopping spree at Harvey Nichols after she made an appearance at the new fashion line of Hollywood twins Mary Kate and Ashley Olsen. Meanwhile Blake disappeared in a car with ginger-haired teenage catwalk model Lily Cole and another mystery companion. The trio reportedly enjoyed each other's company, with Mary Kate sharing Amy's struggle with eating disorders. The twin had completed a course in rehab for food related issues at the tender age of 18. At around that time, Amy's hairdresser Alex Foden blamed the pressure of fame for their weight issues, telling the celebrity gossip magazine *Closer*: 'When Amy shot to fame, she was a size 10 and people called her fat. Celebrities say they don't read their own press, but they do. She's managed to put on a little weight recently, but it's an ongoing battle.'

An unhealthy relationship with food rang alarm bells for Ade Omotayo too, who revealed she'd eat virtually nothing on the road. 'We'd go to restaurants and she wouldn't really eat what was in front of her,' he told the author. Meanwhile, although Amy would order an abundance of health food for her rider, she could barely be persuaded to sample it. 'The stuff backstage was quite healthy but it was just a question of whether she ever ate any of it,' he sighed.

After many miserable nights of picking at her meals, Amy would go on stage so weak that it seemed as though her tiny legs would buckle under her at any moment. At times, it even seemed as though her beehive weighed more than she did.

Yet Ade agreed with Alex Foden that all the media attention that was focused on her weight could have been counterproductive. Since entering the limelight, Amy had been supplied with a stylist – something she'd always scoffed at before – and she suddenly found herself battling an obligation to take to the stage looking sassy every night. 'If it was left to her, she'd have performed in Reeboks with a Fred Perry top and some jeans,' Ade explained. In fact, the only fashion accessory she prized was her beehive.

Amy was trying to get better, but the humiliating media coverage of her weight battle was relentless – and at times, unstoppable.

On the other side of the coin, the newspapers – which had once poked fun at her curves – were now claiming that Amy was unnaturally emaciated. Trips to takeaways were regularly photographed, whilst a purchase at McDonalds and Nando's made national headlines.

However Amy had the last laugh when she was invited to appear at an exclusive Paris fashion show – irrespective of her weight. She was headed there the following day, leaving her husband behind, when she suddenly seemed to experience separation anxiety. Seconds after she passed through security at Waterloo's Eurostar terminal, she had a change of heart. After a hysterical altercation with a guard who had to restrain her, Amy hurled herself over the security barrier and ran back to her husband. A passenger recalled: 'She was crying, gesticulating wildly and shouting, while the man with her was trying to calm her and get her through the gate. It was pretty clear she was not keen on getting on that train to Paris.'

Although she was finally persuaded to take the train, Amy couldn't bear to be parted from Blake and friends continued to worry about their possessive relationship, which seemed clingy, co-dependent and a long way off perfect. In fact, their love proved to be almost as addictive as the heroin that threatened to part them.

Blake would also be joining Amy on her European tour, which kicked off in Berlin on October 15th. The *NME* was present to capture the action, writing: 'Amy Winehouse's first gig since it all went a bit wrong was due to start an hour and a half ago, but there's still no sign of her. Understandably, given that Germany is a nation renowned for its almost compulsive obsession with time keeping and efficiency, the audience are getting increasingly restless. The occasional calls of "Come on!" have escalated into a full-on chorus of catcalls and, worryingly, *NME* just overheard a roadie admitting to an impatient punter that Amy's band arrived at the venue without her.'

When it seemed as though things could not get any worse and the boos of the crowd were becoming ever more raucous, the lights went down and Amy finally appeared on stage. The *NME*'s review continued, 'Suddenly Amy's sounding every bit the soul diva we all know she can be. Close your eyes as she launches into the prophetic 'Rehab' and it's almost, almost possible to forget that the last few months ever happened. By the time she returns to the stage for an encore of 'Valerie', all is seemingly forgiven. Amy Winehouse is clearly still some way from solving her problems but, for tonight at least, she's silenced the critics.'

In some people's eyes, Blake remained one of the major problems. Amy spoke onstage of her purpose to be a wife and mother, not a performer, something which many audience members who had paid to see her found insulting. Rightly or wrongly, Amy's priorities were now firmly with her husband.

The tour continued with Hamburg and Copenhagen before she arrived in Bergen, Norway for a performance on October 19th. The day before the show, she was hit by yet another drugs scandal when police officers seized seven grams of cannabis – and the star herself – from her hotel suite. Guests had complained of an overpowering smell originating from Amy's room at the plush Radisson SAS. A building full of mainly business guests, they didn't take kindly to the smell of marijuana drifting through their rooms – and a formal complaint had been fate. This was to be Amy's downfall – yet police who burst into the room to investigate were unprepared for the scene that awaited them. Amy was allegedly so high on the drug that she could barely stand up and was totally incoherent, slurring her speech. Officers were forced to wait almost four hours before they deemed Amy to be in a suitable state for interview.

Meanwhile, she, Blake and her hairdresser Alex Foden were held at the local police station until they had sobered up. Amy was reported to be cooperative, allegedly allowing a rookie officer to look into her eyes to be trained in how a person under the influence of drugs might look. The three were each fined £350, a signature of Norway's strict anti-drugs policy, and were released in the early hours of the morning. Amy turned to alcohol and a spa treatment to console herself, and by the next morning the mishap was all but forgotten.

However the drugs arrest remained on her criminal record and, unbeknown to her, would prove to have serious repercussions for her plans once the European tour was over. At the start of November, she had planned to travel to the USA for further TV appearances. Yet her popularity and future stateside hung in the balance as it emerged her behaviour had prevented her from being granted a green card.

The release form that the pair had signed in Norwegian had in fact been a written confession. Still not completely sober and desperate to escape the prospect of a night in a cell, they had signed the forms without question. Mitch told the newspapers outside his home: 'This is being dealt with now by the Norwegian authorities and the British Consulate because the ramifications are that she now can't get into the States and she was meant to go next week.' Vowing to battle the visa ban, Amy had little choice but to summon all of her strength and continue with the tour.

A show she performed in Amsterdam on October 22nd saw her face the audience completely sober and spectators wondered if Amy might be returning to her former glory. However at the Volkhaus on October 25th, the wheel of fortune dipped down yet again. Making her way through a humiliating performance that a local newspaper described as '50 minutes of tears, anguish and pain', Amy watched helplessly as many of the audience walked out halfway through the show. The newspaper *Tages Anzeiger* commented: 'It's rare that a concert is so terrible that one would rather not have experienced it.'

Yet this was the reality for Amy. She had performed just a few songs before Blake had taken her offstage, concerned for her health. Ten minutes later, she had attempted to take to the stage again, but was reportedly sobbing and distraught. During the encore, she hit a new low when allegations emerged that she had taken some cocaine from her beehive during the song and snorted it between words.

Although most people who had seen the video were convinced that she'd been snorting cocaine, hairdresser Alex Foden had a different explanation – that Amy was distraught and tearful at not being able to have her husband's baby. He told The Mirror: 'Before she went on stage, she told Blake she thought she was pregnant. She was so happy and excited. She sent a girl out to buy pregnancy tests, but when she did them, they came back negative. She was heartbroken and went on stage that night a shell of a woman.'

While it wasn't difficult to imagine that Amy's excessive drug intake and lack of nutritious food had been the reason her periods had stopped, she had taken the news badly. Alex added: 'She got slated for that gig. People said she was pulling drugs out of her beehive and sniffing them while she was on stage, but she wasn't. She was actually crying and wiping her nose.'

Either way, the performance was reportedly so shambolic that a spokesperson for Good News Entertainment, the concert's organisers, stated that they would not be inviting Amy to Switzerland again in the future. He added that this could only change if she took control of her drug, alcohol and emotional issues. Perhaps Amy had taken note of this, as her performance the following evening in Milan received rave reviews, with journalists describing it as 'flawless'.

In spite of this, significant damage had already been done − both to her health and to her reputation. Worried fellow celebrities − including Cheryl Cole of Girls Aloud − sent well-wishing messages to her via the newspapers. Justin Timberlake went one step further and performed 'Rehab' live on stage in honour of her struggles. Rumours also suggested that Justin, a huge fan, had written a song about her which appeared on his 2006 album, *Future Sex/Love Sounds*. The lyrics of 'Losing My Way', a tale of a talented and popular guy whose life is destroyed by crack cocaine addiction, talk of a man who makes just '40-something' dollars a day and whose life has gradually been destroyed by his insatiable cravings for the pipe. Consequently, his 'dreams fall down'. The character was an anonymous mid-American man, but Justin could just as easily have had Amy in mind.

Amy's dreams of conquering America were also futile. Despite finally securing a US visa with a little help from her lawyers, her appearance on *Saturday Night Live* was cancelled due to a script-writers' strike. It seemed as though things couldn't get much worse for Amy although her flagging reputation was improved when Mark Ronson released the single 'Valerie', featuring Amy's vocal on the Zutons classic. The song was released on October 15th and immediately hit the No. 2 spot in the UK chart.

Amy would come home to this news, having completed her European tour with shows in Cologne, Paris and Brussels − where she concluded the stint at the AB Club on October 30th. Her final performance before returning to London for a much deserved rest was at the MTV Europe Music Awards in Germany, where she had been nominated for the Artist's Choice Award. Her big moment was again blighted by bizarre behaviour when, hours before the show, she caused thousands of pounds of damage to her dressing room at the Munich Olympiahalle. In front of Snoop Dogg and an alarmed entourage of her band and management, Amy threw a tantrum. A source close to Snoop Dogg told *The Mirror*: 'An hour and a half before the show, Snoop said he wanted to see Amy. When we got there, she was in a right state. Everyone just stood there as she lobbed spaghetti up the walls. It went on for about five minutes, with her kicking the walls and throwing whatever she could get her hands on – even the tables and chairs. Then she started cutting up the rug. Snoop was just standing there open-mouthed. He was pretty freaked out by it and didn't want to hang out with her after that.'

Amy was later seen looking frightened and tearful as she wandered around the streets of Munich on her own. Her friends blamed Blake for her apparent melt-down. According to them, he was manipulative, controlling and self-destructive and his mood swings threatened to wreck her career. One friend anonymously told *Closer* magazine: 'They are constantly arguing backstage and whenever he gets bored, he demands they leave, no matter what she's doing. At one of her gigs, Blake even insisted they go back to the hotel half an hour before she was due on stage. Amy's team has told her they can't run a tour under these circumstances, but she runs straight to Blake who goes mental and threatens to fly back to the UK. Then she goes back to her team and tells them she can't do it without him around.'

However, Amy's loved ones were adamant that if her husband truly loved her, he wouldn't put her career in jeopardy.

Her eventual performance at the awards bash received mixed opinions. *The Mirror* claimed: 'Amy's rendition of 'Back to Black' was one of the worst I have ever witnessed – and she looked close to tears as she stumbled through the words.' However *The Sun* felt differently, claiming, 'The Brits compared to the EMAs last night with Amy Winehouse and Pete Doherty on top form. They produced the two stand-out performances… and it just goes to show how good they could be if they both steer clear of drugs.' Few people present could have disagreed with that.

The review went on to say Amy's appearance 'was the perfect example of both her genius and her frustrating desire to muck it all up. When Amy tottered on stage to accept the Artist's Choice Award, muttered "Fanks" and then wandered off, she left most of the crowd scratching their heads – the least she could have done was show a bit of appreciation for her fellow artists who had nominated her for the gong.'

Yet Amy had other ideas, sauntering off to kiss her husband the moment she left the stage. As it later emerged, she had not been keen to make an appearance at all. Astonishingly, she insisted that she was present not to further her career but to please her parents. 'I can't be bothered going to perform but my family love these kinds of award shows and watching me, so I'm doing it for them really. I'm knackered after my own gigs in Europe and was back in London chilling out when I got the call asking me to MTV. My family are so important to me that I agreed to do it for them.'

Some saw Amy as ungracious, while others blamed her chronic depression for clouding her desire to do what she had strived to do throughout all of her youth – perform. However, according to Blake, there was a more sinister reason that Amy had lost all enthusiasm for playing live – crack cocaine. In a revelation to *The Sun*, he claimed that Amy had been smoking the deadly drug between every single song, accounting for why she would often run off stage during performances. 'Amy would stumble off with her hands out waiting for the pipe,' he claimed. 'She smoked after every song and without her next hit, she wouldn't go on. It's no wonder she couldn't sing properly. The only thing she cared about was her crack pipe.'

She had disappointed her fans and she took it to a whole new level when she failed to show up for her promotional video for 'Love is a Losing Game'. She had been due to appear at Pinewood Studios in London on November 6th, but when the morning came, she was nowhere to be seen. Frustrated crew members waited for her all day, occasionally getting hold of her by phone when she assured them she would 'be there in a minute'. A source claimed: 'Her management were running around trying to get hold of her – they even sent a car round to her place in Camden. When they finally spoke to her at around 7pm, she said that she was still at home with her husband.' The crew couldn't play cat and mouse games with her much longer and, after an agonising 15 hour wait, finally abandoned the shoot at a cost of £70,000.

Furious crew members allegedly pledged there and then never to work with Amy again. It was a classic case of self-sabotage and people could only sadly speculate as to why it was happening. Amy had sunk to an all-time low when she missed her pivotal video shoot, but something was about to happen that, for her, would make all of that pale in comparison – something that would change Amy's life forever.

CHAPTER 12

Heroin was far from the only tragedy looming in Amy's troubled marriage. In a seemingly never-ending downward spiral, news emerged that her husband was facing criminal charges for a brutal, alcohol-induced attack on a barman the previous year. Defendant James King, who worked at the Macbeth pub in Hoxton, east London, was left with a fractured cheekbone and required metal plates in his face. For his part in the attack, Blake found himself accused of grievous bodily harm, a charge that could carry a lengthy prison sentence. Yet things were about to get a lot worse.

Two men known as Ant and Jay had approached *The Mirror*, offering to provide evidence of a blackmail plot and CCTV footage of the assault. The pair believed that the film showed in no uncertain terms that Blake was guilty. What was more, they also claimed he had attempted to bribe his victim to drop the charges and leave the country – adding a charge of attempting to pervert the course of justice to his alleged crimes.

The Mirror responded to the challenge by installing covert recording equipment at one of the men's flats where a meeting would take place to uncover the alleged bribery. After a drink in a local Soho pub, the victim was filmed withdrawing his evidence in return for £200,000 cash and an additional £10,000 spending money to disappear to Spain until the case had been formally dropped.

Facing the camera, the victim read out: 'I, James King, hereby without pressure or duress wish to withdraw any legal statement previously made or written concerning the arrest of Blake Fielder Civil and Michael Brown [his second attacker] over the GBH charges relating to my injuries. I have no intention of going to court or helping any further. I feel this is in the best interests of mine and my family's safety.'

Blake might have breathed a huge sigh of relief, but that was just the beginning. On November 8th, two plain-clothed policemen descended on the flat Amy shared with her husband, smashing the door down with a crowbar. Lap-tops, bank statements and mobile phone accounts were seized to be used in evidence. A distraught Amy watched helplessly as, before her eyes, her marital home was turned into a crime scene. The hysterical singer was heard hyperventilating and begging to go with her husband to the police station, but to no avail. As Blake was handcuffed and led away, Amy wept openly on the balcony, screaming: 'Baby, I love you! Baby, I'll be fine,' to Blake in the courtyard below.

The scene depicted a modern day Romeo and Juliet. By this time, *Back to Black* had reached the enviable status of 5x Platinum in the UK, with more than three million copies sold in just one year. However, it seemed that the ill-fated couple would never be free of the dramas and tribulations that had inspired its songs.

Insisting that her husband had done nothing wrong, Amy vowed to stand by him. Meanwhile his frantic mother Georgette claimed to *The Sun*: 'He would never try to fix his trial. It's just ridiculous.' Even Amy's father Mitch, who had previously remarked that he hoped Blake was jailed so that Amy could rebuild her life, had now relented. 'Despite what has been said, I have no wish for Blake to go to prison,' he claimed. 'I've no wish for that as Amy and Blake are very much in love.'

In spite of the support, things didn't look good for Blake. On November 11th, he went on trial accused of perverting the course of justice. A pale and dishevelled looking Amy along with her friend Pete Doherty, who sported an equally colourful rock and roll lifestyle, watched from the sidelines as Blake was refused bail.

Even worse, just three days later, Amy was due to start her biggest UK tour yet, playing to over 50,000 fans across the country. The night before her first show, Amy's frantic parents ordered an ambulance to her home after she failed to answer phone-calls, fearing that her life was in danger. The ambulance crew found Amy safe and well but – while she might have been putting on a brave face for the public – she was desperately unhappy and perhaps more so than ever before.

Her first show, at the NEC in Birmingham, proved to be a disaster. *The Times Online* wrote of the show 'The top selling star staggered about the stage, slurred her words and called the audience mugs for buying tickets to her concert… it was no way to celebrate the biggest headline show of Winehouse's career, a sell out in front of 8,500 fans.'

Unfortunately Amy was not calm enough to consider the consequences. She had taken to the stage an hour later than advertised and appeared intoxicated, forgetting the words to her most popular hit singles. At one point, she tumbled over. Rumours were circulating that the delay in her arrival had been due to Amy locking herself in a toilet cubicle backstage, sobbing hysterically and refusing to come out without the support of Blake. The audience, infuriated that they had paid to see her downfall, began to turn against her. In response to their jeers and boos, she yelled: 'Let me tell you something. First of all, if you're booing, you're a mug for buying a ticket. Second, to all the people booing, just wait until my husband gets out of incarceration – and I mean that.' Then the tears started falling and a furious Amy found herself resorting to four letter insults, calling the audience 'monkey cunts'.

Amy was branded an 'absolute disgrace' on her official forum by disappointed fans. One spectator recalled: 'I could not understand a word. She could barely stand up and it was embarrassing for the band who were desperately trying to keep the show going.' Another fan was even less complimentary, claiming: 'She managed four songs but was slurring her words and swaying all over the place. She fell into the guitar stand and dropped the mic. It was atrocious.' In a final caustic parting shot, she added: 'The song she dedicated to her husband was so bad it was like swinging a cat around your head.'

However, in an unexpected twist, Andrew Lloyd Webber also attended her show – and felt the opposite. Referring to her 'flashes of genius' on stage, he showed sympathy for her troubled and asserted that she had his undivided attention. 'She is a major, major talent,' he praised. 'She lives these lyrics.'

If that was the case, perhaps Amy's tendency to self-destruct, to play Russian Roulette with her career and her life, was understandable. She wasn't acting a role or playing a song assigned to her by a *Pop Idol* sponsored writer, but was living the authentic pain of her songs in her everyday life. Amy was a girl who seemed to have the weight of the world on her shoulders. Depression, heartbreak and drug and love addiction were just a few of her problems – perhaps chaos was inevitable.

A review in *The Telegraph* sympathised, 'If the "appalled fans" had bought their £20 tickets to see a slick, wholesome pop show, they'd have cause for complaint but... whatever else Winehouse might be accused of, the self-proclaimed "ugly drunk" can't be charged with mis-selling herself. She lives a life of high drama and she has used that troubled experience to create an excellent album's worth of highly dramatic songs about desperate love, alcohol addiction and drug smoking. Her "appalled fans" must have heard them or they wouldn't have paid for tickets.'

However, some fans refused to take it lying down or to accept that failure was inevitable. James Pasquali, a London based listener who'd travelled halfway across the country for the tour's opening night, argued: 'Amy's fans are attracted to the songs they hear on her albums and they come to see her for an emotion-infused live version of these – not to watch her painful, embarrassing demise. Drama is one thing but a complete inability to perform is quite another.'

The American website *Pitchfork* concurred. 'Winehouse's slow public wreck isn't just an unfortunate thing that's happening to someone who happens to be a star, it's part of her act and has been from the get-go – which means it makes her audience complicit in it,' the site claimed. 'Her deliberate affectation of Holiday's unmistakable vocal tics can't help but suggest the narrative we're supposed to buy into – "Great singer, tragically destroyed by her unhappy private life and bad habits, who turned her pain into universal art." What are we as her audience supposed to do? Stage an intervention? Winehouse is good enough that she was worth paying attention to for her music alone before her drama started ruining it, but in the light of her subsequent career, [the songs] came off as the first chapter in the romantic myth of the poet who feels too deeply and ends up killing her for her audience's entertainment...' Perhaps a little harshly, the review added: 'The self destructive tortured artist routine was bullshit when Kurt Cobain did it, it was bullshit when Elliott Smith did it and it's bullshit now.'

Even *The Cyprus Times* had a say in the matter, contradicting that Amy's colourful lifestyle, on stage meltdowns and myriad of personal problems were relatable, exciting and part of what made her attractive. The reviewer commented: 'I loved the message in 'Rehab', that she was still her own woman making her own decisions. She was still a rebel... but now, of course, it has all nose-dived into self-destructive burn-out. Living close to the edge, flaunting convention and surrounded by the cocaine driven media world has pushed her, like many other musicians, to the point of no return. She's gone in. Whether she will survive, we don't know. And even if she does, after the therapy and the zero tolerance expected in a clean up from drugs and drink, will she still emerge with the same creative drive? We've seen this pattern so many times before... how a clean life can mean losing that anger, that passion that can produce some extraordinary results. Rehab, like the lobotomised characters in *One Flew Over the Cuckoo's Nest*, can save your life but at a cost. If you're driven by an amazing creative energy, nothing must frighten her than the thought of losing it. Chrissie Hynde should know – two of the original Pretenders died from drug abuse, but in her fifties she's still on the road, still smoking, drinking and rocking.'

However Amy's nearest and dearest didn't want to take that chance. The lyrics 'You're playing with your life' from Michael Jackson's 'Beat It', which Charlotte Church had sung while staring pointedly at Amy during their duet the previous year, had never been more true of her situation. Even ex-manager Nick Shymansky, in spite of their well-documented differences, claimed he didn't care if Amy never wrote a song again, as long as she stayed alive. Her happiness and well-being was paramount, even if it was at the cost of her creativity.

Perhaps Amy needed a break to resolve her demons. Yet the tour continued. Nationwide, Amy's admirers were on tenterhooks, wondering whether the next show would be diabolical or merely brilliantly decadent. Would-be gig-goers took to the internet in their droves to query whether it would be worth attending the next show. They were perched over newspapers, analysing horrendous reviews, and wondering whether to sell their taker – that is, if there'd be any takers.

They didn't have to wait for long to hear some news. Amy was due to fly to Glasgow for a double night headlining slot at the Barrowlands, beginning on November 16th. However, on arrival at the airport, she was already behaving erratically. She appeared with scratches on her face, sporting fears that she was still self-harming and turned on minders who tried to protect her from an overzealous gathering of fans. As one accidentally touched her beehive, she screamed: 'Get your hands off me!' before telling an open mouthed audience: 'It's not you lot, it's him. I don't know what he's trying to do.' Uttering a string of obscenities at reporters and security alike, Amy was led away without signing a single autograph.

As news spread about Amy's public meltdown, fans posted a deluge of messages on her forum with titles such as 'Do I even go tonight?' Sadly the singer seemed too far gone in her grief to pay attention as her career and reputation took a sharp nose-dive – she felt she'd already hit rock bottom, before the insults started.

However, she surprised everyone in Glasgow when she was on top form again, introducing a cover of the Sam Cooke song 'Cupid' to an already well-endowed set list. Perhaps it was a night to start over again, something which Amy confirmed when she announced: 'This is the second night of the tour but it feels like the first night.' She showered adoration on a receptive audience but was candid about her personal plight too, introducing 'Wake Up Alone' with the words: 'This song is for people who are lucky enough to wake up every morning with the person they are in love with. This one's for my husband – I love you. I love you too, Glasgow.'

The Scotsman begrudgingly described the night in glowing terms, saying: 'It seemed like a car crash was about to unfold before us. But there was none, nor was there any of the drama that must have had gossip columnists rubbing their hands in anticipation. Instead, no matter what you think of Winehouse's voice and music, this was something approaching a triumph.'

However, drama was ever-present in the world of tabloid headlines, when it emerged on the same day of the show that Amy's tour manager, Thom Stone, had quit. He alleged that hospital tests had detected heroin in his bloodstream, a result of passive smoke inhalation over the months on Amy's tour bus. A source had told *The Sun*: 'Thom had just had it up to here. He was watching [Amy and Blake] get off their heads and wondering whether Amy was even going to get up on stage. It was a nightmare job.'

Yet the show had to go on. Amy's next gig was at the intimate Empress Ballroom in Blackpool. One of Amy's favourite seaside towns, she was reported as relaxed and stoical, urging her audience to each buy a red rose for her husband. She even gave out the address of London's grim Pentonville Prison, where he was held. After the show, a source suggested that Amy was considering putting on a show at the prison itself, commenting: 'Amy has been in pieces ever since Blake was arrested. She can't stand the thought of him being alone in prison and wants to play a song there. She thinks it would be a fitting tribute to him, it would cheer her up and it would also help her cope with being separated from him.'

There was some consolation for Amy in her time of heartbreak, as *Frank* was finally released in the USA, sailing straight into the Billboard charts at No. 61. She had feared that her visa issues and drug battles might have destroyed her chances of being a serious contender in America, yet the news of the chart position had given her hope.

She moved on to London, playing a two-night slot at the 4,000 capacity Brixton Academy on March 22nd and 23rd. speaking of the show, *The Observer* said: 'Even when crying for Blake, she still performs better than Britney. She may dress her head like a tear-stained Sixties prostitute, but her body is that of an onshore sailor. It takes strength to cope with all that drama. Proper musicians use music to express themselves and she's got a lot to sing about now.' It added: 'No-one outside the tabloids has it in for La Winehouse. That casualness - her sulky disdain for opportunities that other singers would throttle their grannies for - has given Amy kudos.'

Despite the positivity of these reviews, Amy's performance sharply dropped again the following day at the Hammersmith Apollo. Tickets or the hotly tipped event had sold out and were reaching hundreds of pounds each on auction websites. However, buyers were to be sorely disappointed. The *NME* reported: 'Winehouse arrived on stage 45 minutes late, by which time some fans were already demanding refunds for their £30 tickets. Many sections of the crowd were booing before Winehouse took to the stage.'

Perhaps with that less than warm welcome, an already unstable Amy's reaction was unsurprising. 'Midway through the performance Winehouse seemed bored and walked off stage, leaving a backing singer to step forward and take vocal duties,' the review claimed. It was reported that hundreds of disgusted fans left the venue halfway through her performance and were spared the sight of the encore, where Amy left halfway through 'Valerie', never to return again.

Amy's next stop was an uneventful gig at the Brighton Centre. After the show, she and a friend hailed a taxi back to London, an action which had a sense of permanence about it. Was Amy so insecure that she couldn't stay away from home for one more night – or had she decided to put a stop to the tour altogether? Prophetically, *The Times* had written a few days earlier: 'Those with her best interests at heart say that now is the time for Winehouse to quit the stage and deal with her demons.'

The following day, the news broke that Amy had cancelled the remainder of her UK tour. A record company spokesman revealed: 'Amy Winehouse has cancelled all remaining live and promotional appearances for the remainder of the year on the instruction of her doctor. The rigours involved with touring and the intense emotional strain that Amy has been under in recent weeks have taken their toll. In the interests of her health and well-being, Amy has been ordered to take complete rest and deal with her health issues.'

Apologising profusely, Amy added a personal message: 'I can't give it my all on stage without my Blake. I'm so sorry, but I don't want to do the shows half-heartedly – I love singing. My husband is everything to me and without him it's just not the same.'

Fans were stunned. One particularly poignant message on her official forum read: 'Amy chasing after her man and everyone else chasing after her does capture a lot in one image. She's a sensitive soul and, if we assume she was hurt a lot by her parents' divorce and has fears of abandonment and low self-esteem as a result, that would explain a lot about her behaviour. I do wonder a lot about what is the underlying cause of her pain and distress. I hope she gets help to address that. I don't think just treating the symptoms is going to be enough. [She has] an ability to turn pain into beauty. I think of her as super-human in some ways, but incredibly human and fragile in others.'

At around this time, the *British Journal of Psychiatry* released the results of a study indicating that the probability of drug addiction or mental illness was significantly higher in a group of jazz musicians than in groups playing any other musical genre. It suggested that Amy was drawn to performing sad songs because she lived these traumas wholeheartedly. Her father had once remarked: 'For Amy, writing a song is like ripping her heart out.'

Her on stage persona that month was perhaps summed up best by a fellow musician who described her as 'an angry kitten'. He anonymously remarked: 'She was feisty and yet incredibly vulnerable and fragile at the same time. The way her life was playing out was so ugly, yet there was a great deal of beauty there too.'

Yet Amy had once begged to be allowed to attend stage school and her personal essay had read: 'I want people to hear my voice and just forget their troubles.' Tragically, these early words seemed almost entirely forgotten as a drug-addled, love addicted and thoroughly exhausted Amy was reduced to tears time and time again on the stage. It was now time to put a stop to the public humiliation, for Amy to finally admit that she needed help and submit to recovery.

The cancellation of the tour was costly – the 17 concerts were expected to have earned Amy £1,125,000. Unfortunately for Amy, she was neither ambitious nor particularly materialistic, and so the loss didn't provide the wakeup call people might have hoped for. However it did offer a respite from the harsh criticism of the media, her fans and her detractors, as well as a much needed opportunity to rest. Amy also received support from her brother during this time. Mitch revealed: 'The bond between Amy and Alex is unshakable. He's very protective of her and always will be. He doesn't like seeing her hurt or upset. He's upset by the current criticism of Amy, as we all are, and has asked her critics to be a bit more understanding in view of her youth.'

While he shielded her from the newspapers, some more gentle sympathies were also being broadcast. Mary J Blige spoke out to say that Amy was 'the future of music' and that 'she needs someone in her life to say she is too beautiful for this. It's going to take years. It's not overnight. These things take a lifetime.'

Friends such as Kelly Osbourne rallied round, offering her self-contained accommodation on the grounds of her family's sprawling country mansion in Buckinghamshire if she needed to recuperate privately. This was an opportunity for her to escape from the temptations of Camden's drug scene. Former class-mate Billie Piper supported her too, claiming: 'I love Amy. I hope there's a happy ending, particularly because she is so talented. Her lyrics are so painful and angst-ridden, beautifully written, well-observed stuff.' She added, in a hint at the drug culture of showbiz, 'I'd almost certainly never go back to the music industry. There were aspects of it which I didn't care for at all.' Amy might have breathed a sigh of relief at Billie's latter admission, as she remained opposed to her brand of 'cheesy pop'. Meanwhile, her parents were longing for a snide joke about Billie or one of the others she scorned musically – or even about them – as it would symbolise a return to the cheeky Amy they had known and loved – and lost.

Katy Perry also had her say, claiming that the one celebrity in the world she did not want to be was Amy. 'I think everyone would probably say that,' Katy claimed. 'As much as I pray for her, if I can get over to the UK faster, I'm going to get in a white van and throw her ass in there and get her to rehab and watch over her and babysit her. Who cares if she tries to hit me in the face? I'll hit back.'

Even Girls Aloud, a group that Amy pitied and despised, lent their support, with Cheryl Cole expressing regret that 'the talent has been overshadowed by her personal life'. Finally Roger Daltrey, lead singer of rock group The Who, made a personal call to Amy's father to offer his support and discuss his own struggles with drug addiction over the years.

However, some offers of help were a little less wholesome. Rumours arose that Pete Doherty, a long time friend, had made a pass at distraught Amy and professed his love for her, only to be rejected. At a subsequent concert, he altered the lyrics of a song to: 'I won't be Amy's dildo no more.' Allegedly smarting from her friend's betrayal, Amy tried her best to move on.

However, she didn't have to do so alone. While Mitch had told the *Huffington Post* that he wasn't a violent guy, he assured the paper that he 'knew how to protect my family'. The following week, *The Sun* claimed that Amy's enraged father had hit Pete with a guitar backstage at a show. An eyewitness revealed to the paper: 'He told him to leave Amy alone, saying that he was the last person she needs at the moment. Pete was smirking until Mitch turned and attacked him.' The paper added: 'If I was Pete, I'd look twice before crossing the road from now on. You never know when a taxi might suddenly appear.'

It was clear that Amy had the support of family and close friends. However, setbacks were revealed when she was seen braving the freezing December weather to walk the streets in skimpy sleeveless tops. On one of these outings, she purchased a family sized carton of Ice Pop lollies. 'She was struggling under the weight of it,' a bemused onlooker recalled. This led newspapers to come to the conclusion that she had been smoking heroin. Addicts of the drug are said to experience hot flushes and sudden changes in body temperature that users struggle to regulate.

Hairdresser Alex Foden confirmed their suspicions when he told The Mirror: 'Because heroin depletes the sugar levels in your blood, she used to mainly survive off sweets. At one point, she was basically sponsored by Haribo. They would send us about £200 of Fangtastics and Starmix bags – we had a 4ft high cupboard crammed with the stuff.'

Amy was not only craving sugar to sustain normal levels in her blood, but she was burning up so badly that she was reduced to wandering around in skimpy tops on freezing cold winter nights. 'Unfortunately, Amy had an obsessive personality,' Alex claimed, before adding: 'At her worst, she could get through about £1,000 worth of gear in 24 hours. Her limits were incredible.'

Not so incredible, however, that she wasn't suffering. The same evening, Amy made a distress call to her new friend Sadie Frost, former husband of actor Jude Law, who arrived at her home at 6am to comfort her.

And, in spite of the best intentions of her support network, on one December night Amy hit rock bottom. She had moved to a friend's home in Bow, east London to escape the harrowing memories of the flat she had shared with Blake and to avoid sleeping alone. Yet even there the paparazzi seemed to be hounding her. Unable to resist the prospect of images of bloodied ballet pumps, heroin-fuelled romps with multiple lovers and the tearstained dramas that played themselves out on every street corner, photographers followed her every move. Amy's messy life unfolded before the eyes of the public as if it was a soap opera, its sole purpose to entertain.

One photographer struck gold when pictures emerged of the singer wandering outside the house in just a red bra and underpants. Dozens of flash lights had gone off as a confused, dishevelled looking Amy retreated back inside. An onlooker recalled: 'She came out and started stumbling around. She popped her head over the fence like she was looking for something. It was freezing and she had no shoes on and just a red bra. She was mumbling something incomprehensible. It wasn't the behaviour of someone in the right state of mind.'

Yet was there more to this drama than there seemed? Rumours instantly began circulating that unscrupulous photographers had been relentlessly pounding on Amy's windows, desperate to get a reaction. When she had rushed outside, still half-asleep, to locate the sound, they had pounced and she had become the victim of a profit-fuelled bid to humiliate her.

Friends claimed she had been 'sound asleep' when she heard the noises and had thought a friend she'd spent the evening with was returning to collect some forgotten belongings. Meanwhile a spokesperson for Amy simply said: 'The constant harassment by certain agency photographers at her home has increased anxiety and caused disturbance.'

One paparazzi photographer, known by his pseudonym liveon35mm, launched a passionate fight against her exploitation, telling the author: 'Search for Amy Winehouse on Google images and 900,000 hits pop out. A very small percentage show you a singer. Most portray Amy as a drug addict, a desperate, alcoholic junkie.' He continued: 'Most photographers are not born rich but have a mortgage or a rent to pay, same as anyone. Photographers shoot what people buy – fact. A picture of Amy using drugs is worth thousands of pounds and a picture of Amy doing her gig onstage is not worth a penny. Literally, not a fiver, not a single penny. Photographers' options aren't a lot – either we do another job so we can put the concert pictures for free on our blogs, or some have to hang out in Camden's Tesco trying to snap Amy shopping for alcohol at 4am to cover the February mortgage with a blunt, small, grainy snap on a Metro cover. That people love to see.'

He questioned of the public: 'Why do you find it interesting to look at Amy drunk – even better if she is half naked and looks miserable? Does it give you a relief? Does it tell you that you are not like her? Or does it feel a relief to know that even rich and famous celebrities use drugs just like you? Is there a personality void you have to fill with heroes and anti-heroes to feel better? Tabloids will stop paying big money to see Amy drunk if no-one cares – ideally they will also start paying for images of her doing what she can do best – singing. Amy wouldn't be caught up in this mechanism that at the same time as making her famous put her on the edge of cracking up. Paparazzi will stop running after celebrities for any kind of miserable image and will be forced to concentrate on taking good pictures.'

The debate raged on between those who argued that photographers were simply satisfying public demand and making a living the best way they could and those who saw them as ruthless and calculating, cashing in on private pain.

Publicist Max Clifford added his opinion with tales of ruthless journalists, claiming: 'If they can assassinate them and sell newspapers, they will. The sad thing is, bad news is news and good news isn't. When I started out in the business in 1962, it was all about promotion. Now most of my job is protection – protecting celebrities from an ever more vicious media.'

Fellow musician Annie Lennox concurred: 'It's harrowing to see Amy spiralling out of control like a car crash. I wish somebody could just put a stop to everybody taking pictures of her and get her out of the spotlight for all the wrong reasons… I wish somebody could just get her the help she so desperately needs to save her life. It's so not right.'

Her words were echoed by Jeff Zycinski, head of radio at BBC Scotland, who was so passionate about Amy's plight that he'd wept at pictures of her. He told a conference that viewing photographs of Amy's self-destruction was 'a form of pornography'. According to him, the public's attention had shifted from Pete Doherty because he 'wasn't dying fast enough' but that viewers could just as easily satisfy their curiosity in any city-centre, where 'the streets are full of 24 year old women destroying themselves on drink and drugs'. He accused viewers and paparazzi alike of being 'complicit in [Amy's] destruction'.

Yet shooting Amy continued to be a lucrative business. No matter how much of her life was in the public domain, and no matter how easy it was to locate Amy in her usual haunts of the Hawley Arms, or her local Bow high street, the public's appetite for more and more debauched scenes never ceased.

However, did she bring on the chaos herself? Despite her growing fame, she seemed undeterred from visiting her usual haunts – small north London pubs that hid nothing from the paparazzi. For the most part, Amy had shunned offers of time out in the countryside away from the prying eyes of the media, who would always be keen to earn some money from filming her misfortune. Yet now it was becoming too much and she had started to lash out at photographers in frustration.

It was perhaps little wonder that Amy fled London for Christmas, spending the holiday season on the island of Mustique. But even a break away couldn't hope to cure her. She had been invited to join rocker Bryan Adams at his luxurious holiday villa and her parents were delighted, thinking it would give her the chance to recuperate. However, this was far from an innocent detox break. According to hairdresser Alex Foden, who was planning to accompany her until her management banned him, she had £2000 worth of heroin concealed in her stomach.

'I watched her as she swallowed seven £300 wraps of heroin before boarding the plane,' he revealed to *The Mirror*. 'It was a crazy, stupid thing to do. If even one had opened inside her, she could have died – but, at that stage, her addiction was so bad, she didn't care.'

After two weeks, Amy returned to the UK, ready to make amends. Plans had even been made for her to work with Bob Marley's son Damien and write new songs together. Plus her heart was full of renewing her wedding vows as soon as her husband was freed.

Fortunately for Amy, she hadn't been implicated in the blackmail plot and, by January 5th, had been formally cleared of all charges. The Crown Prosecution Service released a statement saying: 'The evidence building is purely circumstantial at this stage and it is not enough to charge Amy with anything. If she did give money to her husband, this is not a criminal offence and is not enough to prove she was involved in a conspiracy. Unless new evidence comes to light, it is most likely the charges against her will be dropped.'

Those in Amy's camp breathed a huge sigh of relief at the news. However there was more sensation in store when a video emerged on the internet of Amy smoking crack and snorting a potent cocktail of cocaine and powdered ecstasy. Mumbling incoherently as she took several hits of crack, she told friends she couldn't go out on the town with them, claiming: 'I'd be useless to you because I've had about six Valium.' A friend who took her cat into the drug-ridden and noisy atmosphere of her house party was chastised with the words: 'If I was that cat, I'd leave of my own accord. I'd call a cab. It ain't right, this ain't Toyz R Us. They took my cat!'

Alarmingly, Amy revealed that this was a quiet night in for her, as she needed to be awake by 8am the following morning for a court appearance featuring her husband. Painfully, this wake up call could have been a blessing in disguise as her destructive lifestyle was now out in the open for all to see. As the video, hosted by *The Sun*, circulated around the internet and was seen by millions by viewers, a humiliated Amy now had the motivation for getting better. What had at first seemed to be a cold-hearted betrayal by a trusted friend could actually have turned Amy's life around. The video ate into her denial and proved that she had a tangible problem.

Two days later, on January 24th, she voluntarily admitted herself to a private drug addiction clinic, Capio Nightingale, on London's Harley Street. Without Blake around, Amy's resistance was decreasing and her family had managed to persuade her that rehab was the best option for her. A statement released by her management gave the news: 'She has come to understand that she requires specialist treatment to continue her ongoing recovery from drug addiction.'

It was a timely decision, as she had just received six nominations at the prestigious Grammy Awards in the USA, dwarfed only by Kanye West who had received eight – for a British artist, this was an unparalleled feat and her goal was to get better quickly enough to perform at the ceremony. Amy gushed: 'I'm honoured to have my music recognised with these nominations. This a true validation from people I respect and admire.'

4am start due to time differences in LA, but she would make it. 'I appreciate I'm being given a second chance,' Amy revealed. 'I'm raring to go and really excited to be performing at my first Grammy Awards.'

By this point, Amy's popularity in Britain had soared so much that Conservative MP Boris Johnson, a candidate for the position of Mayor of London, invited her on board his political campaign. Fellow celebrity Elton John had publicly backed Liberal Democrat rival Brian Paddick and Boris was keen to get in on the action. He had hoped to recruit Amy to sing the controversial line: 'Ken Livingstone – no, no, no.' However, he had some tough competition on his hands for Amy's affections – the then Labour leader Gordon Brown was also a huge fan, believing that – like him – she was 'misunderstood'. Whilst she'd clearly become a spokesperson for Great Britain, heralded as one of the UK's biggest singing talents, would America be so willing to set aside her colourful personal life?

Just weeks previously, industry mogul Lucian Grange had told Amy she wouldn't be releasing so much as another album, let alone attending the Grammys, if she couldn't sort her health out. What was more, her father had even considered having her sectioned under the Mental Health Act in a bid to save her fragile life.

Chris Willman, an influential music critic for national magazine *Entertainment Weekly*, believed that Amy's only saving grace was that the video of her smoking crack had surfaced after the voting had ended for the Grammys. 'The Recording Academy's support for substance abuse programs might give voters pause for thought about handing top honours to the major artist who's been in the news the most for alleged drug abuse,' he warned. 'The only thing that might save her from a shut out is the fact that voting closed before the alleged crack smoking video showed up. Let's face it, sympathy goes down when you not only appear to be smoking crack, but you're openly allowing someone to film you, knowing you're posing for the YouTube video of the week.'

Amy's team insisted she had been filmed without her knowledge or consent, but Willman had some more bad news to impart. 'As much as the Grammys like to have a belle of their ball, they want to have one who's likely to show up to be coroneted, not just make it to [the venue] but be beaming and coherent when posing with all those statuettes,' he added. 'Amy doesn't have a real hunger for awards and doesn't lust after increasingly massive success the way most singers do and that's admirable, but there is always a subconscious impulse for most voters in any field to want to give a prize to somebody who actually wants it.'

At times, Amy could be openly contemptuous of lavish award bashes and her casual demeanour in Germany the previous month when she picked up the Artist's Choice Award proved that accolades didn't always impress her. Yet according to Monte Lipman, the president of the American division of her record label, such nonchalance might have worked in her favour. In a world of artists with a rabid hunger for publicity, Amy's disinterest might have made her seem mysterious, modest and the antithesis not just of shows like the *X-Factor* but of American culture altogether. 'We're living in a world of sell, sell, sell and here's a girl who just didn't care,' Lipman enthused. 'People found that refreshing. We decided not to press so hard on the commercial aspects.' Had she gone from a sensitive soul who didn't go in for the hard sell to the other extreme – someone who just didn't care – or had she struck a perfect balance? Only time would tell. Lipman also believed her candour was a perfect recipe for success with American audiences. 'The public responded to her honesty on this album. She and Blake were having rough times and she exposed her heart in such a vulnerable way that she could say "I'm no good" and "I'm not ready for rehab".'

Joe Levy, the editor-in-chief of *Blender* magazine, also had words of support for Amy, despite the shambolic interview she had done for the publication which had seen her fall asleep mid-sentence. For him it was all about the music – and with that, he believed she had already won voters over. '*Back to Black* is what the Grammys absolutely love, a record that sounds like an old record,' he enthused. 'It's a very smart update on classic sounds, applying a hip-hop DJ's logic to old soul and R & B grooves, very simple and effective. She connects with songs about the pains of living and loving, songs that all evidently have to do with her real life. She's the closest thing to a musical and cultural sensation we have here. Whether she wins or loses, she's the story of the Grammys.'

It was true that Amy had captured the nation's attention. *USA Today* had claimed that her rock and roll antics made Courtney Love seem over her drug revelations, the effect of the cocaine fiasco had eventually been to make her more notorious, chic and powerful than before. In fact, one 2007 study revealed that 23% of teenage girls saw Amy as a leading influence and that both her and Kate were more influential on girls' lives than teachers or politicians. Rehab had become the world's new buzz word and Amy's songs and behaviour had epitomised that growing trend. As Mark Ronson had insisted, a song like 'Rehab' – despite its old-school sound – could only have come to fruition in modern times.

Singer Natalie Cole, the daughter of soul legend Nat King Cole, was one of Amy's loudest detractors. She told *People* magazine: 'I don't think she should have won. It sends a bad message to young people trying to get into this business, trying to do it right and keep themselves together. We have to stop rewarding bad behaviour.'

She added a little more generously: 'I think she is gifted, her performance was fine. I just feel she's stepping into a place she hasn't earned yet. She could die. This isn't something that's cute and fun to throw around in the press. Those of us who have been in the business long enough know the sacrifice it takes. You don't just get to do your drugs and go on stage and get rewarded.'

Opinion was divided between fans who thought they detected a hint of jealousy in Natalie's rant and those who felt her voice was one of seasoned experience. 'I've been in this business over 25 years and I sacrificed five years of my own life on drugs and almost lost my life because of it,' Natalie confessed. 'So I take great offence to almost see someone getting glory out of being in the position that they're in – she needs to get her life together and embrace her craft. She will lose it if she doesn't get it together. Rehab is no joke. I was there for six months.'

However, those who had been listening carefully questioned whether Natalie was a hypocrite – despite being a user of LSD, cocaine, heroin and the sedative Valium during her career, as her 2000 biography divulged, she too had won awards at the Grammys.

Amid rumours of jealousy, Janet Jackson had her say in support of Natalie. 'I could see her side of it, for sure,' she told E! Entertainment. 'It's kind of a catch 22 because it does feel like someone is being rewarded for a negative act and drug addiction… It's real close to my heart because I've been in relationships where that's been really heavy.'

Perhaps Amy had been partying a little too hard. Cleaners at London's Riverbank Plaza hotel in Tower Bridge revealed that the scene of her suite after checking out of rehab had been 'carnage'. According to reports, champagne and red wine had been spilled all over the wooden hallway and the bath-tub had been stained black after she dyed her bee-hive there. Finally, a large mirror had been detached from the wall and placed on the floor, leading to fears that Amy's cocaine use was on the rise again. However, she had completed a course of rehab and had achieved her dream of singing at the Grammys. Whatever critics might have said about Amy, one thing could not be disputed – she had come a long way.

CHAPTER 13

It might have seemed to Amy as though she was public enemy number one, with even the United Nations stepping out of the shadows to publicly denounce her. Francisco Santos, Vice President of Columbia, was furious about the repercussions of drug use on his nation, claiming: 'Amy's a mess. I don't think she understands the harm cocaine does to my country.' He raged 'people in the UK think it's a victimless drug – but that's not true. The effect is not just on the individual who takes it. Not only does it kill, displace and mutilate people in Columbia, it destroys our wonderful forests. The damage is catastrophic.'

An area of Columbia as large as Wales – over 7,700 square miles of primary rainforest – had been slashed and burned to produce cocaine. Had Amy become a scapegoat for the seemingly endless troubles of the South American nation? Figures published that year suggested that one in 20 Brits took cocaine recreationally, around 80% of which was produced in Columbia. Yet it seemed as though Amy was being singlehandedly blamed for the UK's plight as the tiny island stood accused of having the highest number of cocaine users in all of Europe.

Santos had insisted: 'It's time to send Amy into rehab', but she was already there. What was more, tabloid newspapers were reporting that despite attending the clinic, Amy's troubles had only just begun. One newspaper told of a repeated meltdown where she had deliberately self-harmed with a cigarette lighter, screaming, 'My life is a shell of what it was. People talk to me and I just zone out. It's like the whole world is now still-born. Colours aren't as bright, love doesn't feel real and I just feel numb.' If the reports were to be believed, Amy found herself self-harming in a desperate attempt to feel again and had scarred herself with lighter burns. Experts believed that this was all a part of weaning herself off drugs, but friends remained concerned. 'Amy has been up and down in a way she never was before,' one reported. 'One minute she'll be fine, the next she'll be in a heap on the floor, screaming she can't go on. She feels that rehab is turning her into some sort of zombie with no emotion.'

Biologically, it was probably was. According to scientists, years of drug abuse gradually desensitises the receptor sites in the brain involved with regulating mood and experiencing happiness, leaving the addict with impaired pleasure thresholds. The user eventually requires more and more of the substance to achieve the same high. During withdrawal – without the drug to artificially stimulate a good mood – the problem peaks, often leaving a recovering addict numb and virtually unable to feel pleasure. In severe cases, it can take years of abstention to repair the damage to brain chemistry. Consequently, while conquering her drug demons should have been a defiant victory, she was now feeling lower than ever.

However Amy held her head up high and was as victorious in the UK as she had been stateside when she made an appearance at the Brit Awards on February 14th. She was still heavily reliant on prescription drug methadone but was well enough to pay tribute to her incarcerated husband on Valentines Day.

Amy took to the stage with Mark Ronson to perform 'Valerie' and mouthed 'I love you' to Blake in her second song, 'Love is a Losing Game'. However, a source told *The Mirror* that it had been touch and go. 'Amy was atrocious in the final rehearsals – she kept falling over,' the source revealed. 'She had had a couple of large drinks before she went on stage and she seemed out of it. At that stage we were seriously considering pulling her out of the show.' Arrangements had hastily been made to extend Paul McCartney's set at the end of the show if Amy hadn't been able to pull through. However – yet again – she had sung with an intensity the media had described as 'near flawless' and had stolen the lion's share of the press attention.

Of course there was still unwanted intrusion – *Evening Standard* journalists even resorted to rifling through Amy's rubbish to discredit her. The drugs each week including crack cocaine sprees for breakfast, and binged on 10 chocolate bars at a time before making herself sick with his tooth-brush. Divulging deeply personal information, he claimed: 'It was my job to look after her, but it was impossible. I thought she wouldn't survive the year with all the drugs and self-harming. Cutting herself was her favourite pastime.' However the couple's main source of friction turned out to be Amy's obsession with Blake. 'She would go on about him and her being together forever straight after we made love,' he revealed. 'I sat there in disbelief. We had a few bust-ups over it.'

Amy denied the affair but behind the scenes it was reported that Blake had angrily tried to cut a tattoo with her name on it out of his flesh after the allegations. Rumours circulated that he was threatening to divorce her for her affairs not just with Alex but with a tee-total photographer three years her junior by the name of Blake Wood. Self-harm, suicide attempts and bitter arguments were among the stories in the media of how Blake had reacted to the news of her infidelities. The night of her show-down with Blake, Mitch had attempted to get his daughter sectioned for her own safety. Despite Amy's protestations to the contrary, there were indications that the couple were now frosty with each other. A German model had taken Amy's place at court appearances, mouthing 'I love you' and telling curious journalists that the two were 'best of friends'. Yet a spokesperson insisted that Amy and Blake would divorce themselves from drugs, not separate from each other.

Meanwhile it emerged that Alex was not the picture of innocence his employers had first thought. After a video was published of the 'geeky schoolboy' smoking crack, he was sacked from Amy's team alto-gether. Island Records hired surveillance to keep away the 'waifs and strays' from her door, her friends were vetted carefully and it seemed as though things were finally looking up for Amy.

Her lyrics even appeared in a Cambridge University English Litera-ture exam, a sure sign of her widespread notoriety. Candidates were asked to compare and contrast the words of 'Love is a Losing Game' to a work by the 16th century poet Sir Walter Raleigh. One student exclaimed: 'I wouldn't consider a controversial pop singer and literary figure', but Amy had made her mark. Another marvelled: 'I think it's cool poetry doesn't have to mean Keats and Byron.'

Amy continued to be recognised for her musical achievements too and, on May 12th, a stunned Mitch found himself accepting an Ivor Novello award on her behalf. She had won the gong for Best Song Musically and Lyrically for 'Love is a Losing Game'. Awkwardly, he had explained that Amy couldn't make it, but she had unexpectedly burst in during the ceremony to hug her family and tell concerned guests 'I'm fine – really well.'

However, the following month, she had a major relapse. The pressure of her husband's trial had built up and on June 16th, just a week after Blake pleaded guilty to GBH and perverting the course of justice, she was admitted to hospital with another life-threatening seizure. After collapsing at her flat, she was rushed to an emergency ward in the back of her father's taxi and was placed on a drip. Under the watchful eye of a team of doctors, she slept for three days solid. Her last words to her father were: 'Don't worry about me, Dad. I know I've got to stop taking drugs now.'

However her grim-faced father learnt something that would break his heart as Amy clung to life in her hospital bed – that she was suffering the early stages of deadly lung disease emphysema. Normally an affliction suffered by elderly or middle aged heavy smokers, it was almost unheard of in someone as young as Amy. The degenerative disease, which kills 40,000 Brits a year, can lead to heart and brain damage, collapsed lungs and – for singers who rely on their voice – a complete loss of vocal range. That wasn't all – Mitch told *The Mirror*: 'This is her last chance. It won't be just her career that's over if she goes back to crack cocaine. It will be her life.'

He continued: 'To think this could be my beautiful 24-year old daughter's life is preposterous... it's in its early stages but had it gone on for another month they painted a very vivid picture of her sitting there like an old person with a mask on her face struggling to breathe... she's got 70% lung capacity.'

Doctors also medicated Amy for an irregular heart-beat. Mitch recalled: 'I was messing around and picked up a stethoscope and listened to her chest myself. It was all over the place. But they've sorted that out now with medication. That was likely to have been the drugs. But one step back and it could be fatal.'

Amy's grand-mother Cynthia had died of lung cancer just two years earlier and had struggled to breathe on an aspirator in her final hours. Mitch warned that, like Cynthia, she could 'die a slow and painful death, gasping for air'. Meanwhile doctors alerted him that Amy could be confined to a wheelchair within a month, might lose the ability to hit the high notes on her much-loved songs and could eventually need a permanent oxygen mask to stay alive – if she survived at all.

Amy was due to appear at a number of events that month, but it was now a question of not when but if she could sing again. She was photographed emerging from the hospital and instantly lighting a cigarette, causing concern about whether she understood the seriousness of her condition.

This was a disregard for her own health that seemed to border on insanity. It was painful for those around her to watch Amy wilfully discarding an obvious talent and metaphorically bursting into flames in front of their eyes. What were the causes of her seemingly motiveless self-sabotage? Lighting up seconds after being told she had a potentially career-haemorrhaging and life-threatening illness seemed to be an unspoken suicide wish. Meanwhile her behaviour leading up to that moment had been just as bad – drunkenly mumbling her way through concerts, if she bothered to turn up at all.

Perhaps she self-sabotaged because she was afraid of failure. Amy may have absorbed messages unwillingly imparted to her by her parents that she couldn't sing – messages that were delivered as early as her childhood audition for Annie. Her mother had castigated her for being tuneless, while her father had remarked to his new wife that, while she was proving herself to be a disastrous singer, at least she might succeed as an actress, There was no indication that Amy's parents were being intentionally cruel, but perhaps the result was that – deep in Amy's subconscious – she now felt unworthy of success.

According to psychoanalytic theory, not trying to achieve something protects oneself from the pain of trying and failing. Alongside the fear of failure is the belief that 'I don't deserve to win' – something psychologist Leon Seltzer, who has a PHD in Clinical Psychology, terms 'passive-aggression towards the self'.

He explains, 'You'll experience guilt and shame for sins never committed and routinely snatch defeat from the jaws of victory. It's fundamentally about self-punishment. If you're self-disapproving, don't much like yourself and have never been able to fully embrace yourself (flaws and all), your ultimately counter-productive behaviour will reflect this negative self-regard. It's as though you've given, let's say, your overly judgmental parents permanent residency inside your head, with the inevitable result that these perennial authority figures constantly remind you that you're not good enough, that you can't live up to their expectations. Sadly, in the recesses of your brain, their critical voice has become your own.'

Without extensive experience of Amy's day-to-day interaction with her parents as a child, a definitive analysis would not be possible – but Amy's rocky relationship with her parents could be a contender for explanations of her self-sabotaging instinct. Leon continues, 'The battle is far less with others than between the adult part of you (which, being your rational self, would like you to be effective and succeed) and the child part of you, which has its own "logically illogical" reasons for methodically undermining your efforts. This is reactive – negatively and hyper-sensitively responding to the memory of circumstances that occurred many years or even decades ago.'

The self-saboteur may be stubborn towards and even have contempt for authority figures, perhaps explaining Amy's steadfast refusal to submit herself to rehab in the past. On that first occasion, Mitch – perhaps not wanting to acknowledge his daughter's demons for fear that he would have to accept there was a problem – told her she didn't need intervention, that things hadn't gone that far. As Any telling mentioned in 'Rehab', 'If my daddy thinks I'm fine...'

Blake too was reluctant to face up to the fact that they both had a problem. In a 2007 interview that the couple did with *Spin*, he spoke of how he and Amy had made a pact to tell each other straight away if their hunger for hedonism ever got out of hand. In the same interview the pair joked with each other, 'You wouldn't tell me – you'd wait until I had a needle hanging off my eyeball!'

They made light of the issue – perhaps in an attempt to convince themselves as much as anyone else. Yet burying their heads in the sand could be dangerous. Amy's father and her husband – the two most important male figures in her life – both told her at the start that she didn't have a problem – something all three of them desperately wanted to be true – and so the delusions continued.

With that, of course, came the scars of self-sabotage. Amy was struggling to marry up her enormous success with how she felt inside. The more adoring crowds praised her, the more insecure she felt. Underneath her persona of fame, she was the same 'contemptible' Amy she'd always been – and she felt like a fraud.

Perhaps because she felt undeserving of applause, she was reluctant to get on stage and receive it – explaining why she'd previously told the media that her sole reason for attending award shows was ' to please my parents'.

It also seemed that her primary motivation for writing music was to lose herself in song and forget her pain – not to become successful and famous.

Then there was the prospect of having her worst fears confirmed – that she really was talentless. As Leon Seltzer elaborates, 'If you party the night before, you can then shrug off your performance. You have an excuse for not doing well. Instead of facing the fear that you're not good enough or smart enough, you can chalk it up to too many beers.'

The fact that Amy's self-destructive weapons of choice didn't stop at alcohol, extending instead to the highly addictive crack cocaine and heroin, only served to complicate things further. Amy was not punishing herself actively (with self-harm) and passively (with self-sabotage). And yet now that she was toying with her life, her self-sabotage her reached a whole new extreme.

Even worse, Amy was living her life under the pressure of intense public scrutiny, with the lenses of half a dozen cameras never too away. Her every mistake would be documented, analysed and amplified in newspapers and on TV stations around the world. It seemed as though the public thrived on her misfortune, watching her take life to the limit in a way that Joe Public would never dare to do. Did Amy's success and multi-million pound fortune validate her behaviour, making a refreshing change for Mr Average to escape from his mundane life by reading about her daredevil exploits?

The public could also be cruel – when the consequences of an addiction that had been emblazoned across every tabloid's entertainment pages finally turned ugly, the affections of the general public turned just as quickly. Amy found herself the victim of contempt as onlookers jeered, booed and mocked her, chastising her for being a poor role model.

She found support in the words of journalist Julie Burchill, who wrote a feature about her demise for *The Sun*. 'Bestriding the music scene like a pouting, beehived fag ashed King Kong, she is the anti-Madonna; lividly young, extravagantly unhealthy and magnificently talented,' Julie enthused. 'And whatever the state of her lungs or other parts, she makes it clear to us exactly what has been missing from the soft parade of female vocalists – passion, skill and God given TALENT... she makes the contemporary female singers seem pointless and phony.'

Warming to her subject, she added: 'Amy went to the Sylvia Young school as a child and could have become one of the legions of professional irritants who burrow into our lives with all the determination of a show pony in tap shoes – talent-free girls driven by ambition alone. But what good is talent if she will be dead by 30? I don't have the answer to that but I do know we're so used to female singers who are ambition-led rather than talent driven that we seem to have forgotten how truly gifted singers behave.'

Indeed, Amy had very little ambition at all, talking to anyone who would listen of her desire to have five or ten children with her beloved husband and retire from the music industry altogether. However, it was too late – millions of people had been seduced by her talent and they wouldn't give her up without a fight. Julie continued: 'Edith Piaf, Judy Garland, Billie Holiday – for some reason, women who have a great talent for singing also have a great capacity for reckless behaviour. Whereas if your talent is an itsy-bitsy, teeny weeny sickly little thing (see Madonna) then you have to behave the very opposite of recklessly in order to preserve it.'

She concluded: 'I think it's rather tragic and cretinous to expect entertainers to be role models – the clue is in the word entertainer... However it ends, she is a legend, living or dead... like star-crossed lovers from one of her songs, if we truly love her, we won't try to change her and we'll set her free. And one day, if we love her enough, maybe she'll come back.'

Embarrassingly for Amy, just a few days after her touching dedication, tabloid newspapers revealed that Blake had been writing X-rated letters to fellow prisoners. Perhaps her loyalty had been misplaced. Melissa Goldstone, who was serving two and a half years in Surrey for conspiracy to supply Class A drugs, struck up an unlikely friendship with Blake after writing to congratulate him on his efforts to stay away from heroin. Referring to his failed love affairs, Blake allegedly wrote: 'When we really needed them, they got wrecked and fucked other people. It's their loss.' He told Melissa his explicit fantasies, including an unnatural sex act and a four page 'disturbing S & M fantasy' that was deemed too offensive to be printed in a family newspaper. He also hinted at the prospect of a threesome with Amy, despite telling his new friend that the pair had broken up. He also invited her on a six month break in Thailand, boasting: 'We can just sun ourselves, I can fuck you all over the country and the gear there is fucking unreal.' The letter suggested that Blake had not been successful in conquering his drug demons yet.

And while Amy had been counting down the days to her husband's release, her family were terrified that she would relapse when that day came and that the two would fuel each other's addictions. According to Mitch, one more cigarette or illicit whiff of crack cocaine could kill Amy. Now just a lowly toilet cleaner at his segregation block, once out of prison, Blake could be responsible for the death of one of the UK's biggest musical talents.

Mitch had begrudgingly admitted that he wanted to help, telling Radio 5 Live: 'Blake has apologised to me for getting Amy into drugs and said he's going to try to put it right. He wants to go from zero to hero. It's very hard for him being in prison, but at least he's trying.'

Amy denied that her husband had sent out the provocative letters, telling OK magazine: 'Does that mean we both see other people? No way. We're absolutely obsessed with each other. We both pinch ourselves daily. It's unbelievable that the person that you're obsessed with is the person who loves you most in the world,' she gushed. If Mitch had designs on separating the two on Blake's release while he rehabilitated, he would have a very hard job on his hands.

However it was far from the end of the story - Blake's behaviour was to have even more painful repercussions for Amy than ever before — and this time they were on tape. In the younger years Amy had been able to laugh off her verbal blunders, insisting: 'I won't ever be a mass artist, so I don't think I'll ever have to apologise for the things I've done!' Little did she know — and her instincts were to be proved dramatically wrong when an incriminating video emerged in the tabloids of Amy and her husband indulging in racist chants.

The scene of the crime was a hotel room, which *News of The World* would describe as a 'crack den'. Drug paraphenalia including crack pipes, loose powder and discarded aluminium foil wraps were carelessly strewn around the room. A clearly intoxicated Amy appears in the video along with her friend Sarah and is egged on by Blake to abuse her singing voice by belting out a racist chant to the tune of children's nursery rhyme 'Head, Shoulders, Knees and Toes'.

Amy sang out: 'Blacks, Pakis, Gooks and Nips!' while squeezing her breasts lewdly for emphasis. She continued: 'And deaf and dumb and blind and gay!' The evidence is followed by a smirking Blake who insists: 'I'm not filming!' Amy feistily replies: 'You liar!', but continues nonetheless. The two then dissolve into giggles.

The video would prove inflammatory to many, and would fuel the already rife complaints that tracks like 'Stronger Than Me' were homophobic. Even if Amy was inebriated and unable to think straight, it didn't look good for her. *News of The World* also recovered over 100 photos, including one where Amy pleasures Blake by gripping his penis in one hand while holding the phone with the other. In one clip, Amy performs oral sex on her husband in a hotel stairwell, remarkably uninterrupted by passersby. The former friend who leaked the material claimed: Blake's clearly the instigator behind the idea of them having public sex. It looks like the camera was a new toy and he wanted to test it out.' She added: 'But to risk all Amy's achievements and her future by committing this sort of material to camera is beyond the pale.'

Some argued that Blake was exploiting her vulnerabilities, while others questioned why — if the anonymous friend was as concerned about Amy's reputation as she claimed — she had released the material to the public herself. However, Amy had already shown elements of the footage to one bewildered interviewer already, quipping: 'Do you like my slide-show?' The astonished journalist found the screen filled with images of decadence. In one photo, Amy openly smokes a crack pipe, in another she and Blake passionately kiss, while in a third, they pass what appears to be Ecstasy tablets between each other's tongues. Drugs were clearly at the centre of the pair's relationship.

For anyone else, it would have been painfully embarrassing car-crash viewing, but to Amy it was merely testament of their love for one another. She assured terrified friend Remi Nicol, who objected to her crack use, 'These things are more casual for me than they are for you, babe.'

Amy soon found herself having to explain her actions to a group of photographers gathered outside her flat, demanding to know if she was a racist. 'I don't want to play anything down, but I'm the least racist person going,' she insisted. She added that the footage had been a product of 'really happy times'. Yet Amy had also been caught on camera making racist comments when a car pulled up at a service station with her in the passenger seat. She had been buying food for passersby, bombarding them with KFC, before shouting to a young black man who approached her car. Leaning out of the window, she had asked to see the gold brace-let on his wrist and when he showed reluctance, she protested: 'Don't worry, I'm not going to steal your jewellery – I am a white girl!'

In spite of that, Amy had dated African men on numerous occasions and had fed herself a musical diet in her youth that was almost exclu-sively ethnic. Yet the race debate scarred Amy's reputations and cast a dark shadow on her scheduled public appearances that summer.

Putting a brave face on, Amy arrived at Glastonbury on June 29th to face the music. Was she ready to face the unforgiving public? Only time would tell. Dressed in a blue sequinned peacock style dress, Amy shakily took to the stage on the day for an increasingly erratic performance. *The Guardian* lamented: 'Organisers were claiming Amy Winehouse drew the biggest crowd of the night, but she also opted to scat her way through the set instead of sing, tell the audience about the time an ex-boyfriend hit her round the head with a cricket bat and treat an audience member to what looks suspiciously like a quick succession of punches.' The review continued 'Covers of the Specials' 'A Message to You Rudy' and 'Hey Little Rich Girl' were almost reduced to instrumentals as she neglected to use her most impressive asset, her voice… the main message of the night was an incoherent up yours to a crowd who, for the most part, just wanted to sing along to a version of Valerie that they recognised.'

The show proved to be disastrous for Amy's dwindling reputation. Fans crowded internet forums to complain about a shoddy performance. Some who had been looking forward to seeing her live for the first time described her as 'over-rated' and 'out of tune'.

However it seemed that the BBC had been to a different show altogether. The Entertainment section of the website raved: 'She is talking, joking, dancing and looking every inch the super star with not a worry in the world. Is this really the same Amy Winehouse we know from the papers? The dangerous wreck who's in danger of throwing it all away? Not tonight, she isn't. She's engaging, in good voice and not looking too bad for someone who's just been let out of hospital for the night. She hasn't had any trouble keeping the party atmosphere alive.'

XFM joined in the praise, setting it aside from the 'questionable performances of the past'. 'She was on time, looking healthier than she had in a long time, cracking jokes and gushing about how indescribably happy she was to be there. More importantly, she was sounding fantastic. This XFM reviewer was truly warmed to see such a stellar start. So when she punched a fan in the audience, you could hear the visible groan emanating from the crowds as everyone knew that that would be the only thing people remembered or talked about [afterwards].'

Had Amy's talent been overshadowed by sensation, disguising a brilliant performance? Blogger Catherine Tuckwell also had only good words to say about the set. 'Although she had four cocktail umbrellas in her hair, she couldn't have been drunk – her beehive was so top heavy that in those four inch heels she would have been flat on her face quicker than a punter driving into a formerly unspoiled pool of Glastonbury mud… Given recent events in Amy's life there was something almost heroic about her diminutive frame tottering and dancing about the stage, belting out her songs in her wonderfully soulful, sultry and powerful voice while still making it look effortless.'

However, incredulous fans questioned whether the reviewer had even been to her concert. One anonymous fan claimed: 'Amy mumbled and slurred her way through the entire set. 'Rehab' was perhaps the worst: barely intelligible, shameful... I am so disappointed words almost fail me.' Another insisted 'This review bears no resemblance to the train wreck of a gig that I witnessed. This woman embarrassed herself in front of a massive audience and presumably will find it hard to find a promoter willing to risk putting her on a stage in the near future.' Responding to a claim in the review that she had remembered the words to her hits, a furious reader hit back: 'A performer who knows their own material? What an achievement! How low are our expectations here?'

The concert had clearly attracted diverse opinions, with official reviews awarding a range of marks from 3 to 9.5 out of 10 across various media sources. Amy's on stage banter had shocked some as she claimed: 'Jay Z has got some front to come here, with tunes you don't even remember' as a snipe at the headliner. In front of a 80,000 strong audience, Amy also degraded Kanye West when she changed the lyrics to 'Some Unholy War', instead singing 'At least I'm not opening for a cunt like Kanye'. The feud had been ongoing since Amy's first demos and Kanye responded publicly on his blog: 'Amy Winehouse hates me! Now I've really made it!'

She told any audience member who declined to dance through her set that she felt sorry for the partners who had to have sex with them. She also grinned lewdly while cupping her breasts, before punching an audience member three times in a row as she sang the final track, 'Rehab'. Glastonbury founder Michael Eavis spoke out in support of Amy, insisting: 'The fan deserved it. He grabbed Amy's breasts as she went past him.' A fan argued, 'Most people were quite horrified when she lashed out and punched one fan who dared to touch her outstretched hand.'

The Guardian sarcastically added that Amy had 'taken crowd control to a whole new level'. '"We love you Amy!" screamed the crowd. "Smack!" replied Wino after appearing to wallop a crowd member in the front row,' the report claimed. As it turned out, the fan in question laughed off his assault as part of the breathless, crowded Glastonbury experience. James Gastelow told the newspaper: 'I saw a hat being thrown from behind me and it hit Amy's beehive. She looked down, saw me looking up, and her elbow went for me... at the end of the day it was all part of being at the front and being pushed by thousands of people... I'm just pleased I got to see her.' Bandying a huge bruise about the size of the singer's fist as a dubious trophy, he was nonetheless pleased as punch and certain he'd be seeing her again.

However, The Arctic Monkeys were not so keen, snubbing Amy's set to drink beer backstage until headliner Jay-Z arrived. Guitarist Jamie Cook told XFM disapprovingly: 'Only a week ago she was seriously ill and now she's performing at gigs. She needs to take a break from performing and sort herself out.' Their harsh words echoed public opinion – Amy had publicly humiliated herself as onlookers both praised and criticised her in equal measure. She had joked: 'I like festivals because if I fuck up, no-one can get a refund.' This parody was now becoming true to life. The show had failed to be the indisputable success previous concerts had awarded her with – and that night, a defeated and exhausted Amy made her way back to hospital.

Once there, she made a stand, refusing to leave until her husband was freed. She had once denounced rehab as a place for 'people who like to be babied' but it seemed that was just what Amy craved and needed now. Her mother revealed: 'She likes it at the clinic and feels more secure. She doesn't have any worries while she is in there.'

The previous year Amy had told *Rolling Stone* magazine: 'I've never been to rehab. I mean, done it properly. I'm young and I'm in love and I get my nuts off sometimes.' Yet in the space of less than a year, that status of young, fun hell-raiser had irrevocably changed. It was not her career but her life that was now in the balance, something her family hoped she valued more. After some time in hospital to lick her wounds, Amy eventually discharged herself.

Her next performance would be her very own club night named Snakehips, taking place at the Monarch pub in Camden. On the night, there were more journalists than revellers and Amy had to repeatedly beg the crowd to 'put away your cameras and have a good night'. However, her protests were in vain. Billed as a musical battle between Amy and DJ Bioux, Amy's role was to draw the crowds and select the tracks, while her more technically minded friend mixed them. She chose 1960s pop tunes with a

It looked as though the blackmail plot might never have been uncovered. However, two other men had stepped in to sell their story to the tabloids and, believing James was also responsible for wrong-doing, he was held for eight months in jail waiting to be cleared.

'I've lost my home, a successful business and how I'm sleeping on friends' floors with everything I own in six prison sacks,' he added. 'I think Blake and Amy are evil… the pair of them have wrecked their lives and now they've wrecked mine.'

Amy had been devastated to learn that her husband was suspected of perverting the course of justice, which carried a maximum sentence of lifetime imprisonment. Blake had almost served his sentence now, but the story heaped fresh humiliation on her, portraying him as a brutal thug rather than a pitiable and innocent victim of drug addiction.

Even worse, the public began to lose sympathy for Amy, tiring of her daily dramas. A survey of Londoners revealed that almost half of those questioned found the news updates 'boring'. To them, her problems seemed a world away from the reality of the recession and struggling to make ends meet. A spokesperson for the study confirmed: 'At a time when many people are watching the pennies, it's not surprising that the public have become tired of news about rock stars being odd… the fact that Amy Winehouse is seen as six times more boring than the economy this summer illustrates this perfectly.'

Yet whether the public was looking on or not, her lifestyle didn't change. Even innocuous charity events became riotous where Amy was involved. A fundraiser to earn money to repair the Hawley Arms, which was burnt down several months previously in a fire, ended in catastrophe when Amy's security team allegedly punched a pack of waiting photographers, knocking several to the ground. Amy also stood accused of assault on three fans in just two weeks, as well as an attack on her bodyguard.

As Amy's world went into meltdown, she was a no-show at the Rock en Seine festival in Paris on August 29th. Her absence cost her almost £100,000. She was also scheduled to play Bestival on the tranquil Isle of Wight on September 6th but it was billed as her last gig for the foreseeable future.

E-Festivals reported on her trauma filled performance, claiming: 'She looked like a frightened rabbit caught in the headlights and did her best to hide from the audience behind the enormous guitar, which she sporadically played, and her drummer's kit… while Amy is talented enough to get through a show on about 10% effort, this was just uncomfortable viewing. The crowd barely clapped between songs.' Despite the fact that she was headlining the main stage, it looked as though her appearance had been a tragic mistake. The review continued, 'She was gaunt and painfully thin, no amount of makeup could disguise the mess of her skin and no amount of showmanship from her awesome band could hide the fact that she needs to take a rest right now. Rumour has it she will fulfil her current live commitments and then take two years off to recover and get herself back together again. I sincerely hope that this is true. Amy Winehouse is one of the most talented singers this country has ever had and I live in hope that one day I will see her actually fulfil her obvious potential as a live performer. She has an amazing set in her somewhere. She just has to find it.'

This mixture of glowing praise and tender concern came in the wake of reports of yet another drug overdose. She had collapsed, hallucinating and vomiting uncontrollably. Mitch had desperately blamed an adverse reaction to medication and then a drink spiked with ecstasy, but a friend close to Amy's side had a different story. 'She had smoked an inhuman amount of hash which resulted in acute cannabis poisoning. You have to take a shitload of pot to suffer that severe reaction,' she claimed. It was alleged that after a 36-hour binge of staying awake and chain-smoking, she had suffered fits and convulsions 'like a scene from *The Exorcist*'. Doctors believed the mammoth overdose could have left her with brain damage, referring her to a psychiatrist to discuss multiple personality traits indicative of schizophrenia. According to those in the know, Amy was now a suicide risk.

Meanwhile the grandfather of a teenage boy whose first experience with heroin injection led to death hit out at Amy for normalising substance abuse. 'Young people see the likes of Winehouse taking drugs and think they'll do it too and it'll be okay,' bereaved Christopher Preece claimed, 'but that's far from the case.'

visibly shake their heads and groan. Their luxury break in paradise has just turned into hell. One woman immediately gets up and leaves, declaring 'Oh no! I can't sit through this again!' Whilst not to everyone's taste, this flamboyant Amy was a long way from the drug-addled victim portrayed in Perego's sculpture.

Amy's casual clothes stood out a mile in the elegant lounge, much to the horror of the bejewelled women in ball-gowns who shared the room with her – but she was there to stay. And while she might not have fitted in with the sedate atmosphere of a romantic five star get-away, she was clearly well on the way back to health. Amy's spokesperson had defended her from the macabre sculpture in her absence, claiming 'The artist seems in thrall to a tabloid persona that is not the real Amy'. Who was the real Amy? Residents at the luxury Le Sport hotel were about to find out.

For her, the holiday was not about drugs but music and merry-making, with Amy playing guitar on her balcony and breaking into song in the piano lounge. She played renditions of Puppy Love by Donny Osmond, Cry Me A River by Julie London and the Beatles' The Long and Winding Road. By her side was ex-public school boy Josh Bowman, who had embarked on a passionate but brief affair with her during her stay.

'He couldn't be more different from my husband,' Amy had enthused to News of the World. 'Blake was rubbish in bed. Almost every time I slept with him, it was like I was dead. When I'm with Josh I don't need drugs to feel good because he makes me feel so amazing.'

Countering sceptical journalists who believed she had merely skipped from drug addiction to love addiction, she continued: 'Before I came out here I looked at a photo of myself in the newspaper and was horrified. My skin was a spotty mess and I was so pale and skinny. I thought to myself, "Girl, you got to sort yourself out or you'll be dead soon." I was depressed, doing drugs and had no life in me at all. Coming here has changed everything… I just don't want the holiday to end.'

She added: 'Home is hell for me – I've escaped for it. There are drugs everywhere. I can't do anything without everyone thinking I'm off my head on drugs – although half the time they were right, I WAS. But here I feel so calm and peaceful and for the first time I can definitely say I AM off the drugs. I haven't touched anything since I arrived and I feel the best I have in years.'

Amy had replaced her beehive with a new short hairstyle and was spending her days swimming in the ocean and riding horses along the beach. However, Amy being Amy, she had been up to a little mischief too. She dismissed claims that she had thrown a glass of water over a newly-wed bride on her honeymoon, saying 'If that's the worst that's happened, I'm not complaining. For me, that's good as gold!'

Unfortunately, the agitated honeymoon couple didn't agree and the hotel's managers had to step in and negotiate a peace deal to persuade them not to call police in. Amy also had an encounter of the intimate kind with a lesbian woman who was holidaying with her girlfriend. The woman's distraught partner allegedly walked in to find Amy on the bed with her lover. Amy nonchalantly shrugged when caught in the act and simply asked the other woman to join them. After declining, she updated her Myspace profile to say 'Amy Winehouse asked me for a threesome and I said no, no, no!' She added 'Amy shouted at me for not joining it – it was a weird night.'

Sex scandals aside, Amy surpassed all expectations on the holiday when she became another woman's heroine. A fellow guest had been taking a sailing lesson when a six foot wave sent her flying out of her boat, crashing painfully onto some jagged rocks. Victim Louise Williams recalled: 'I was bowled over by her kindness. She ran over immediately and said "Let's have a look at you". She picked me up and took me across to the showers and was constantly asking "Are you alright?"' Amy then obligingly washed the victim's wounds clean.

Days later, the good Samaritan struck again, rescuing a six year old boy from possible death when she found him about to eat a raw cashew nut. She had been advised earlier that the nuts were coated with naturally occurring cyanide and came with a health warning. A friend of Amy's told the author 'When she's off the drugs, her maternal instinct gets going and she can be so sweet. I wish more people saw this side to her. She feels her media persona has gone too far and that she'll never be able to break free of the stereotypes. As for me and her other friends, we hope it's not just a case of looking after everyone but herself and that respect for her own health will soon follow on.'

Meanwhile reports suggested that she had been crawling on all fours under guests' tables and snatching their drinks after resort staff refused to serve her, as well as offering sex to random strangers. Yet according to friends, her antics were nothing more than alcohol-fuelled fun on a much deserved break. Even her casual, drunken renditions of Puppy Love had guests transfixed – it seemed as though she was finally returning to her first love – music. 'Amy hasn't lost her mojo,' the friend continued. 'She just sometimes hides it!'

Amy had also been writing song lyrics and poetry, inspired by the tranquil Caribbean surroundings. A source said 'Pete Doherty once told her that poetry was a good way to express yourself, so she thought writing a book of poems about her life would be a fine start. One of them is called desire and is based on her yearnings to be loved and give love.' Amy had been inspired most of all by the Nat King Cole phrase 'The greatest thing you'll ever learn is just to love and be loved in return.'

Amy then briefly left her island idyll to return to London, sparking concern that – with a thriving drug scene on her doorstep – she would return to her former ways. However, it was more worthy pursuits that occupied her mind – she was about ton open her own record label, Lioness.

It was founded as a way for her to lash back against the 'soulless', 'talentless' manufactured pop acts that she felt unjustly dominated the music scene and as a bid for her to promote what she considered to be genuine and more worthy talent.

It was an ambitious project to embark upon for someone who, just months earlier, had been seriously ill, but – following the adage that the devil finds destruction for idle hands – those closest to Amy were fully supportive. Allies on her label, Island Records, not only gave the project their full blessing, but financially invested in it too.

The aim was to follow in the footsteps of Berry Gordy (who founded Motown Records) or The Specials (of 2 Tome Records fame). Both were artists Amy admired who'd taken their career to the next level by making themselves responsible for not just their own musical output, but that of other talented singers and musicians around them.

The label's unusual name was originally devised in honour of a lioness pendant Amy's late grandmother Cynthia had given her. However, if rumour was to be believed, it was also intended as a tribute to Blake's pet name for her – a worrying sign that she might not have moved on as much as she thought.

However, the lioness also represented female power in its fieriest form – and Amy was primed to show that she was back in business and, unlike before, fully in control.

Her first signing was her 13-year-old god-daughter Dionne Bromfield who had aspirations of her own musical career. However Amy knew how cut-throat the music industry could be and how daunting it might seem to a new arrival.

Dead-set on protecting Dionne from failure, Amy began to help her compose an album of 60s Motown style classics, a musical diet she had been exposed to by her god-mother for many years already. This focus was a good distraction for Amy, who had asserted: 'I'm cleaning up my act for Dionne. She needs someone responsible around her to promote her career.' Unfortunately, her attention did not extend to the business side of things – and she was making no pretences otherwise. 'The record company director is me, but all me and Dionne do is creative – we're not good at dealing with business. That's not us. That's bullshit,' she dismissed.

Speaking of the affectionate relationship the two shared, prioritising love over money, she added: 'Me and Dionne are best friends. We're not just god-mother and daughter – we're best friends. All I do with Dionne is play guitar with her, sing with her and kiss her and cuddle her.'

Yet she was willing to share the love around, too. Following Dionne's signing, she quickly added best friend Juliette Ashby and backing singer Zalon Thompson to her label as well. Not only was this a display of loyalty, but she felt both were extremely talented. Darcus Beese told the BBC of their ventures: 'Whether we're sitting here in a year's time breaking open a bottle of champagne or licking our wounds, I don't know, but I know that no-one could ever tell us it was never about the talent.'

As Dionne left for LA to work on her voice with top singing coaches, Amy too jetted off – back to St Lucia. She had been looking for a property to purchase and was also looking forward to a hotly topped performance at the island's jazz festival – her first live appearance of the year.

However, her recovery was marred by the divorce that was looming in the background. It seemed that her ex had an axe to grind when a local London resident found the couple's wedding album abandoned in the street next to a skip. Alongside it lay a pile of used needles, syringes, a broken TV and a guitar, which had been smashed to pieces and left by the roadside. The message was clear. Blake seemed to be removing every trace of Amy from his life – and if he was resentful of her family, the feeling was mutual.

'I want her to get divorced.' Mitch announced protectively. 'I want Blake and his family out of our lives. I just hope Amy can stay away from him. This is the man who openly admitted he introduced her to Class A drugs. Amy nearly ended up dead thanks to him. This is the man who kicked a barman so hard he needed his face rebuilt. [And] he's after £5 million. Does he think we're idiots?'

Blake was allegedly staking his claim financially based on the belief that he had inspired the heartbreak that had seen Amy pen *Back to Black* in her darkest moments. Yet was hurting his girlfriend and sending her 'back to black' – into the depths of depression – really something to be rewarded, or indeed to feel proud of?

Stuck in the middle between the two divorcees was close friend Sophie Schandorff, a German model who'd been implicated in their breakup. She was keen to set the record straight, telling the author: 'I met Blake through my ex-boyfriend – they were best mates and Blake was kind of the third person in our relationship, good and bad. But we're just friends.'

Her affection for Amy was equally strong. She claimed: 'The Amy the media portrays and the real Amy are miles apart – same with Blake. What else can you do to keep some privacy? When you meet her, you instantly love her vulnerability and the more time you spend with her, the stronger that grows. She's a trouble-maker, so with her you always end up doing something naughty. She is a very special girl and has a big place in my heart.'

Talking of the alleged acrimony that characterised their split, she said: 'Blake was Amy's light and Amy was Blake's – they believe they were soul-mates. They didn't part in anger or because they didn't love each other. I guess they just knew staying together would make things worse. I think they probably still love each other as much as ever.'

She continued: 'They were in love, on top of the world, both with addictive personalities. They both followed their heart, no matter the pain it put them through. They lived wild, hard and to the full.'

Yet the pair's party lifestyle had finally come to an end and Amy would have to pick up the pieces. On learning of gossip that Blake had impregnated a fellow heroin addict and ex-prisoner, she was said to have thrashed her chest wildly and cried out in pain. She then quickly recomposed herself, telling astonished guests at the Cotton Bay Village Resort: 'I'm so glad he's having a baby! That is so amazing. I'm not sad, you know, I'm excited. I knew Blake and his new girlfriend would be able to have a normal life.' She added: 'I couldn't give Blake a whole wife because everyone knows me and everyone wants a piece of me so I have to share myself about.'

Sophie, who called herself 'an enemy of the media', agreed that the interest of the paparazzi was partially responsible for the relationship's demise. 'The way the media made Blake out to be is so far from the reality that Amy and I had to stop reading it – it upset us so much. Above all, Blake loves Amy and it was always so obvious to those who knew them. When they slagged off Blake, it pissed us all off.'

On May 1st, Amy secured a landmark victory in her battle against the much-hated media, receiving a court order preventing paparazzi from photographing her or approaching her within 100 metres of her home. The injunction also prevented photographers from following her out of the house to take sneaky snaps in public places.

Amy continued to party the pain away in St Lucia, even taking lessons in circus skills. A fellow trainee, Nancy Bird, reported: 'Amy was very good at the trapeze. She looked healthy and was beginning to get tone back into her muscles… she told me that she herself came off heroin and not at rehab. She said she just woke up one morning and couldn't remember what she'd done the night before, so decided there and then. I think the circus skills were helping her with her recovery. There is no doubt that her time on the island was doing wonders.'

In spite of that, Amy took a tumble backwards as the stress of her divorce raged on. After suffering from what Mitch described as alcohol-related 'backwards steps', she collapsed by the pool at her hotel and spent a night recovering in hospital.

'Amy's willingness to show up in her sick condition is a testament of her love for the country,' he defended. 'She could have been a no-show but instead she mustered the courage and commitment to make her presence felt. She looked pitiful... in her inebriated condition, but she came.'

In fact, he took his support a step further and claimed she might provide valuable tourist bucks and publicity for the island, just as Rihanna had done for Barbados. 'She is still a big catch when it comes to pulling a crowd,' he claimed. 'People want to see Amy on stage, drunk, dazed or sober.' He encouraged locals to have empathy for her plight, claiming: 'The country is wasting precious time in a daily orgy of badmouthing, instead of using her presence on the island to its maximum effect. Amy's love affair with the island is no accident. Consider her a lost soul if you care but... forget the naysayers, Amy Winehouse is literally fighting for her life, battling demonic addictions and yet she has found solace in the bosom of St Lucia... Are we missing out on a glorious opportunity to highlight the virtues of the island that has drawn this ingénue to our shores?'

In contrast, former government official Jeff Fodee depicted Amy as the devil herself, telling the same newspaper: 'We cannot put the future of our country in jeopardy [with] a character that will draw to St Lucia untold human suffering.'

Among those calling on the island's Tourism Minister to resign over booking Amy, he was outraged. To him, her performance had reduced one of the island's premier tourist attractions to a laughing stock. He wrote: 'Evidently, to our tourism officials, a notorious reputation for obnoxious behaviour and not necessarily musical ability, was the main criteria for including Amy in the jazz line-up. For me, it was a stomach-wrenching experience to witness a reptilian looking character with a skeleton frame, staggering on to the stage, barely fitting into what appeared to be a size zero dress, cut just above an unsightly crotch... my first thought was that if a St Lucian artiste appeared on the stage in such a state, the morality police would quickly get her off stage. I thought Amy Winehouse should be locked up, be put into compulsory rehab and force fed to put some flesh on her insect frame.'

Was there some resentment on his part that Amy was allowed privileges of bad behaviour that he perceived would not be allowed of his own people? Did he see her as a wealthy young playgirl and a bad influence? Either way, he wasn't happy. To him, Amy was less of a legend and more of an embarrassment. He continued: 'Amy's disgusting performance was compounded by a misguided Tourism Minister who, instead of admitting a major faux pas, defended the indefensible – that Amy Winehouse had performed as expected. Based on her performance, she is an overrated artiste beyond her abilities, causing untold damage to the youth with her outrageous antics.'

However, Nicholas Joseph hit back in his own newspaper feature, claiming: 'Where is the outrage when Saint Lucian fathers impregnate their own children? Hypocrite!' and urging onlookers not to be 'sanctimonious' but to 'have some compassion'.

In the midst of these eyewateringly negative reviews, and the debates about whether Amy was even a worthy candidate for the stage, she continued to try to improve her life. Still inspired by the place she called her 'second home', Amy was still trying to purchase a house on the island. She also planned to work with the charity African Impact, delivering medicine to sick children on the island, preparing meals for them and providing emotional support to their families. Whilst this was hoped to heal Amy, distract her from her desires for self-destruction and satisfy her maternal instincts, this gesture too was met with disapproval. Jeff Fedee countered: 'The effrontery of this character who reminds me of a tattooed reptile, offering to help St Lucian youth when it is Winehouse who needs help.'

However, it turned out that those who branded Amy good for tourism hadn't been mistaken. Her healthy appearance after jetting back to London from the island on several occasions, shocked national newspapers into writing special features in their travel sections, with the implication that if it worked wonders for poor, tortured Amy, what might it do for the rest of the world? It was this publicity that Nicholas approved of – and it was the same thing that Jeff despised. He didn't want St Lucia's reputation to be of a rehab centre, one where heroin addicts would be encouraged to stay to recuperate. He wanted to ensure the island's reputation remained pristinely clean – and its visitors likewise.

Yet Amy was determined to prove her detractors wrong and change attitudes towards her. She even took part in a Hope Not Hate anti-racism campaign, which might be a step towards making amends for the video released earlier that year featuring her singing racist slurs in nursery rhymes. She wanted to make it clear that colour was no barrier to her and that she felt sincere remorse for her actions.

On a brief return to London, Amy was expected to perform at a promotional concert for her record label, held at the Shepherd's Bush Empire on May 1st. However, not for the first time at that venue, she was a no-show. Mitch explained that whilst her recovery was slow, she was making progress. 'She's a recovering addict, he said. 'We are a million miles away from being cured, but we are getting close to a resolution where she can live her life in a dignified and controlled manner.'

Yet some demons from her past would come back to haunt Amy, when she stood accused of punching a dancer at a Prince's Trust Charity Ball in 2009. Professional dancer Sherene Flash, who had worked on tours for the Pussycat Dolls and Take That, alleged that the drama started when she asked Amy to pose for a photographer with her. She claimed that, despite agreeing, Amy had suddenly and without warning, lashed out. She told the court: 'She punched me forcefully in the right eye with her fist. I started crying. I was shocked.' In a phone call to the police, onlookers reported seeing a tearful Sherene screaming into her mobile that she had been assaulted – 'by Amy fucking Winehouse of all people!'

Demurely dressed in a grey pinstripe suit and accompanied by her protective father to shield her from the press, Amy told a very different story. She claimed that the dancer, whom she had denounced as an impatient fan, had refused to wait a few moments for her photo opportunity until her god-daughter Dionne's stylist had left the event, so that she could say goodbye. She said: 'The woman insisted that we had the photo immediately, she kept insisting we have the photo taken together. The woman started to put her arm around me. I was offended by the woman's rudeness. I felt intimidated. I'm slight and she was considerably bigger than me.'

She continued plaintively: 'I meant to just get her away from me. I was scared. I thought: "People are mad these days, people are just rude and mad, or people can't handle their drink".' She added: 'It was just intimidating. Suddenly out of nowhere, she's got her arm round me, her face next to mine and there's a camera in front of me. I'm not Mickey Mouse, I'm a human being!'

Whilst Amy was often typecast as a thug devoid of all morals, her friends and family thought otherwise. The longing for her estranged husband, the emotional distress of recent events and her ongoing recovery from drug addiction had left her nerves frayed. She had begun to react to the slightest trauma or most imperceptible provocation, by lashing out. Amy hoped to portray to the courts that she was suffering, anxious and simply misunderstood.

Was Amy being treated like a performing monkey and had she been overwhelmed by the sheer volume of unwanted attention, or was she wilfully violent? Prosecutor Lyall Thompson rejected her pleas, saying she had reacted with 'deliberate and unjustifiable violence; and that 'there was nothing accidental about Winehouse's actions. She reacted badly to a polite request.'

However, much to Amy's relief, the evidence was insufficient to press charges and, perhaps showing a glimmer of sympathy, the judge formally cleared her of all wrongdoing.

Amy made a second visit to court that month - but this time to annul her marriage. It had been one of the nation's most high profile love affairs - and perhaps among the most toxic, torturous and all-consuming too - yet it was about to come to an end.

Vocalist Remi Nicole had spoken of her respect and admiration for Amy's 'heart of gold' and her belief that she loved 'wholeheartedly'. Her feelings for Blake had certainly run deep, but it was time to cut the ties.

Mother Janis had spoken of his infidelity, fathering a child with a fellow addict he had met in rehab - a drug program which Amy had paid for. 'Amy needs to be hurt by him in order to see him for what he really is,' she told News of the World. 'In a way this will be good for her as it will open up her eyes. I just hope that this revelation helps to get the divorce moving.'

It had helped - yet not everyone was as sensitive to Amy's plight. Surprisingly, ex-hairdresser Alex Foden wrote a sarcastic message on his Facebook account, questioning: 'Wonder what the pay-out will be for about eight affairs and numerous beatings in a court of law at this date in time. Hmm... me is thinking someone could be poor.'

Yet Amy's divorce went ahead, with the couple officially separating on July 16th 2009. To Amy's embarrassment, Blake wasted no time in lining up interviews for lucrative front-page tell-alls in the press. The tabloid revelations saw him confess that he had introduced his wife to hard drugs and now blamed himself for her addiction. He admitted that eyewitnesses who had reported Amy crouching under the table in restaurants had in fact witnessed her taking sneaky hits of crack cocaine there. It seemed that all of the worst rumours were true - and that it was the ultimate betrayal.

To some, Blake was a creative inspiration and a caring husband who was ready and available to rescue Amy from the brink. To others, such as Sun entertainment editor Gordon Smart, he was 'a manipulative disgrace responsible for introducing Amy to Class A hell'.

Who-ever was to blame, the relationship was over. In desperation, Blake told *The Sun*: 'You can't have a relationship and be a heroin addict. You can't sustain love for each other when you're constantly fighting over a bit of gear. I was fighting for attention with her drug-taking, eating disorders, the fame and the record company. In the end, I just couldn't take it any-more - we were killing each other.'

CHAPTER 15

Amy had started a new chapter in her life but breaking the addiction to Blake would prove to be almost as difficult as freeing herself from drugs. She poured her heart out backstage at the V Festival on August 23rd, telling reporters as she clutched a pack of cards: 'You see this ace card right here, this one is for me and Blake. It's our lucky card. He's my man. We can make it. We're so strong together.'

Against all advice, the two had begun communicating again, this time with Amy befriending him on Facebook with a profile belonging to her cat. Yet Amy had recovered from her emotional outburst later that night when she took to the stage with the Specials for the songs 'You're Wondering Now' and 'Ghost Town'. Less impressively, she also made an appearance at Pete Doherty's live set, bounding on stage to kiss him on the lips. While she urged the crowd to 'Put your hands apart and back together for the amazing Pete Doherty!', he returned the favour by dedicating Libertines track 'What A Waster' to her. A dubious accolade it might have been, but – fired up her performance – Amy left Chelmsford that night with a smile on her face.

Pete Doherty wasn't the only song writer to dedicate a tune to her – Boy George penned a track entitled 'Your Pain Makes A Beautiful Sound' in her honour while languishing in a jail cell for shackling a gay escort to the wall of his flat. In the song, he called Amy both a 'genius' and a 'car crash'. Her struggles with drugs were something he could relate to and the unlikely pair also found common ground when he discovered they had a mutual favourite song in common – the 1962 Carole King tune 'He Hit

Me (It Felt Like A Kiss)'. The song was frequently covered by rock girl Courtney Love in the 1990s and it was on both singers' turntables.

Juliette Ashby had also written a track believed to document her friend's troubles, called 'Falling Out Of Love'. It talks of a friend whose body is getting weaker and who she feels she is about to lose. She also mentions that the mystery friend's family have been 'begging' her to help – but to no avail. Rumour had it that Amy disapproved of the lyrical content and the 'fuss' her loved ones were making, but it was Juliette's chance to reciprocate for the B-side 'Best Friends'.

Meanwhile her family were about to make an even bigger 'fuss' when Mitch was invited to join a Home Affairs committee inquiry into the cocaine trade, advising MPs on how to improve facilities for drug users. Amy's hairdresser Alex Foden seemed incensed, writing on his Facebook wall: 'Alex Foden has just read the most ridiculous thing ever. Apparently the kind of enablers, Mitch Winehouse, is giving drug advice to a select committee for the government. I've never heard anything so fucking pathetic!'

A friend of Alex's on the social networking site responded: 'What the fuck does he know, ain't be crack-head's dad?' In reply, Alex continued: 'The guy enables her to take the fucking shit. If he's got the face to sit there and give advice when he knows who and where all of Amy's supplies come from and he keeps them close, he's a hypocritical loser. If this is what he has to do to give himself peace for having a drug addict as a daughter and turfing her out like a product instead of treating like the blood connection that she is to him, then go for it, Mitch. Wonder who he'll blame this time? Or was she already spiked?'

Perhaps Alex was irritated that Mitch had singled him out as one of a group that Amy had to stay away from if she wanted to recover, meaning he was no longer touring with her. It later emerged that Alex had been through rehab himself, using an estimated £130,000 of Amy's money.

Meanwhile Steve Rolles of the Transform Drug Policy Foundation was equally cynical stating: 'This reflects politicians'' concerns with tabloid obsessions more than anything else. There are drug wars in Columbia and we must move on from what Amy does on weekends.'

While people jeered at Mitch's lack of expertise in the industry, rather than theorising, he had direct first-hand experience to draw on and that was exactly what the Committee was looking for. He talked frankly, telling the committee: 'People are committing offences just so that they can get the chance of getting treatment. For non-offending addicts, the NHS has a one year waiting list. Last year, the government spent £400 million on drug rehabilitation, yet for anybody who wants to come off drugs voluntarily there's little help available to them. The vast majority of the money is being taken up by the criminal justice system, such as burglars who are offered residential treatment as an alternative to a spell in prison. Law abiding people are losing out and finding it almost impossible to get help. [Committing crimes] is the only hope of getting any kind of rehab at all.'

At the time of his comments, Mitch had also been helping to produce a documentary where addicts had spoken personally to him of those who offended to get help to beat their vices. Yet the National Treatment Agency for Substance Misuse denied his claims, offering statistics that 93% of addicts received help within three weeks, including rehab programs if required. Yet Mitch had support from professor Neil McKegany of Glasgow University, who countered: 'We wouldn't have one of the largest drug problems in Europe if our drug prevention policies hadn't been successful.'

Mitch continued of his own family: 'We were very fortunate. We were able to afford the best doctors and rehabilitation services. But for most families of addicts, there are very few facilities available. I find it very frightening.'

His comments followed talk that Amy would not have succumbed to addiction if it hadn't been for the 'drug infused music industry' with its 'club culture'. Mitch's other controversial statement was that he believed heroin users should be offered the drug free on the NHS to reduce violent crime and robbery from desperate addicts. He claimed that this move would 'make communities safer'.

Ironically, while the debate raged on, Amy seemed to be getting better. No longer were there tales of collapses and seizures emblazoned across the tabloids – in fact, the biggest scandals in the news were Amy's occasional catcalls about rival artists – and that was nothing unusual. To her delighted friends, in fact, a bit of trademark bitchiness merely signalled the return of the old Amy they knew and loved. While Rihanna gushed about how much she'd love to tour with Amy, for example, she responded with a complaint about her swiping the song name 'Rehab', claiming: 'Rihanna, you owe me!'

Soon afterwards, Amy shrugged aside her contempt for reality TV shows and talent contests to appear on Strictly Come Dancing as support for her god-daughter – young singing prodigy Dionne Bromfield. She believed in her so much that she refused to take part in the show – despite the desperation of bosses to sign her up – unless Dionne could perform too. In the event, on October 10th, Dionne took centre stage for a rendition of 1960s hit 'Mama Said', while Amy was merely her backing dancer. Yet things seemed to be looking up for Amy, although she might have needed a few lessons in self-confidence. She had claimed: 'When I look at Dionne, she reminds me of myself. Look where I am now. I'm a mess – but this girl has everything ahead of her.'

Amy clearly believed in Dionne, but what about her belief in herself? Nevertheless, her appearance had the desired effect for Dionne, instantly propelling her into the public eye by proxy. She then took part in a series of interviews, which she bravely fielded without Amy or her own family present, claiming: 'I can hold my own, I'm not stupid – I'm not gonna say something I'm not meant to say!'

She could leave that to Amy instead. Her usual outspokenness had first reared its head earlier that year at the Q Awards on July 28th. Asked why she'd arrived late, she apologised by snapping: 'What's it to you? I was doing my hair. Fuck off!' The age-old excuse of 'I'm washing my hair' might actually have had some authenticity for Amy – her awe inspiringly high beehive did take some time to perfect.

She had struck again a little earlier in the year at the Wireless festival on July 4th, when she had accosted Prince Harry from the side of the stage. The royal had been watching Jay-Z and trying to be inconspicuous, when she ran straight into his path, yelling: 'Oi, 'Arry! Oi, 'Arry!' She continued raucously, 'How are you, luv? I only wanted to sau hello to 'Arry!' Shocked onlookers in the VIP area included Beyonce, Gwyneth Paltrow, Kate Moss and Madonna. Shunning the celebrity guests she despised, Amy had made a beeline straight for Harry, but concerned festival organisers had stepped in to ban her from accessing her. Meanwhile, one onlooker had jokingly accused her of sounding like Frank Bruno.

So far, it had all been harmless taunts or indiscretions, but her acid tongue took a turn for the worse over the Christmas period when she was arrested again on suspicion of a new assault. She'd been invited to a theatre production of Cinderella in Milton Keynes on December 19th to see her friend Anthony Kavanagh in action as Prince Charming. However, Amy being Amy, a quiet night at the theatre could never be just that – and before she set out, she'd already downed five vodkas.

As preteen children sat in the wings and their angry parents looked on in horror, Amy let loose a string of obscenities, screaming: 'Where's Prince Charming, where is he?' and then 'He's fucking behind you!' All normal theatre banter, until she called: 'Fuck Cinders, Prince Charming, marry me!'

Following complaints, front-of-house manager Richard Pound attempted to move Amy to a private box, something that she initially accepted. On the way, she asked to use the toilet and was escorted by security staff – only to pass a bar. An anxious Mr Pound responded to her requests for yet another vodka and coke with the words: 'Don't you think you should have a glass of water?' - and, by all accounts, Amy exploded. She stormed into the toilet, shouting: 'Fucking cunt!' behind her. On her return, she was asked to leave, when she saw red again, kicking Mr Pound in the groin, pulling his hair and screaming 'Who the fuck do you think you are?'

Moments later, she and a legal adviser were voluntarily attending a local police station to defend her conduct. What had begun as a drunken bid to embarrass a friend to heckling him from the audience, had turned into a nightmare which ended in her arrest.

What was more, her court appearance was no ordinary one. On the day, she was hounded by dozens of curious photographers jostling for a snap of the accused. However, she looked the picture of innocence as she arrived at the court with her father, dressed down in a demure grey skirt and pale pink satin ballet pumps. According to her lawyer, Paul Morris, Amy had acted uncharacteristically. 'She felt embarrassed and patronised [by the refusal to serve her alcohol] and, with no premeditation, grabbed the theatre manager's hair and pulled,' he told the court.

The book alleged that Mitch believed his daughter had more than just a debilitating drug addiction, but mental health problems too. While Mitch confessed in his interviews that he 'wasn't a doctor or a psychiatrist', neither was Daphne. Yet throughout the book, she psychoanalysed Amy's behaviour and motivations down to the very last detail – and it would make for uncomfortable reading.

Daphne, who had built a career out of interviewing public figures such as freedom fighter Nelson Mandela and tyrants Robert Mugabe and Saddam Hussein, had appeared as a friend of her father's and had filmed Amy, initially without her prior knowledge of her plans for the material.

Daphne portrayed Amy's father as 'needy' and 'lonely' – although many would argue that was hardly surprising for a man whose daughter seemed to be slowly killing herself with drug abuse – and her mother was described as equally lonely and 'grateful for any attention'.

She seemed to imply incest between Amy and her father when she made a disapproving mention of Amy kissing him 'full on the lips'. She also revealed that Mitch was allegedly terrified to leave her alone with Amy in case, due to her 'psychiatric problem', she became violent towards her. She told of an evening when he burst into her villa unannounced at 4 a.m. and begged and pleaded with her to leave the resort with him the next day, rescheduling her homeward bound flights to do so.

Some parts of her account were criticised for not being relevant to the topic – that is, of saving Amy. For example, she printed scandalous text messages exchanged between Mitch and Blake, where the latter allegedly wrote: 'I'm not going to leave your daughter like you left her and her mother' and subsequent texts, which she implied were a blackmail plot on Blake's part, seemed to promise to leave Amy alone for good if he would agree to deposit money into his bank account for a few months rent.

Daphne went on to berate Amy's parents for not managing to break her heroin addiction when it began, questioning: 'Why did they seemingly stand by and let their daughter flounder on alone?' She also seemed to pass judgement on the interaction within the family, asking: 'So it's okay for Mitch to kiss his daughter on the lips, but not for Amy to suck her thumb in front of the camera?'

After a failed performance on stage in St Lucia, she put Mitch's parenting skills under the microscope too, asking: 'Why on earth would you put your frightened daughter on the stage? Why on earth is Mitch letting a manager choose what's best for his own daughter?'

Controversially, she also depicted a tense argument between herself and Amy, when – not content with being given one designer dress as a gift – Amy allegedly tried to steal a second, exchanging it for what Daphne referred to as an unattractive 'Jewish bar mitzvah dress from the 1940s... made from a curtain.'

Some fans criticised the author's stance as 'self-important' when she revealed that she had snapped at Amy – the face of two multi-million selling albums – 'You're not the most interesting person in the world. In fact, you are becoming very boring. I am more known in some countries than you!' Many felt that as a potentially sensitive recovering addict – who, by Daphne's account, constantly seemed insecure and begged for reassurance – she needed the kid gloves treatment. Surely, they asked, harsh and cruel words would have been counterproductive? Not only that, but was Daphne really in a position to place herself above an award-winning singer who'd been described as the best vocalist of the 21st century by some newspapers?

Episodes like these translated into bad reviews for Daphne. Some were straight to the point about the book, arguing: 'It wasn't an attempt to help. It was a sleazy tell-all that made the News of the World hacking scandal seem classy.' One Amazon reviewer added: 'This is a truly terrible book, replete with more references to the author than Amy Winehouse. It is disconnected, disjointed and thoroughly disappointing... it reads like the deranged twitterings of a narcissistic gadfly instead of telling me anything important about Amy. Saving Amy? More like Starring Daphne.'

Another reader dismissed her words as 'self-indulgent rambling', claiming: 'It fails miserably to achieve the in-depth analysis I was expecting... if you want a book about "Saving Amy", trust me – this isn't it.'

One irate reader even challenged: 'The book is meant to be about SAVING our beloved songstress, but Daphne seems to imply that Amy cannot be saved, and this won't be the opinion of the majority of readers. She alienated herself from her entire fan base with that attitude. Daphne portrays her as an out of control spoilt brat or a naughty child who isn't fit to play a show or set foot in a recording studio. She comes across as insensitive and unfeeling and I don't see how airing Amy's dirty laundry in public is going to help the crusade to save her – it's more likely to take the problem a step back. Is this woman jealous that, even with a heroin addiction, this woman's star still shines brighter than her own?'

These comments echoed the beliefs of many fans, who felt that the book was a sensation-seeking expose calculated to increase publicity for the author at the expense of finding a solution to Amy's problems.

The media world seemed equally uncomfortable with the title. The Observer, for example, claimed: 'Barak seems to be cosy with the Clintons, has done Mugabe and Mandela and was tight with Benazir Bhutto. She knows little about London cabbies, however, and does not contextualise Amy's self-destructive behaviour in the jazz tradition. Even more damningly, she fails to interview anyone of Amy's generation, who might shed better light on Amy's demons than, say, Jane Winehouse, Mitch's current wife.'

Amy herself remained tight-lipped about the revelations; although Mitch stepped forward to legally enforce a ban on a planned TV documentary featuring the video footage shot in St Lucia. His PR company made reference to the unseen footage on Twitter, explaining that her 'unauthorised' book had been released because she'd been refused permission to go ahead with her proposed official documentary. Yet why had Mitch allowed several hours of filming, allegedly without his daughter's knowledge of the project, if he condemned the idea of the documentary? Answers were in short supply.

For Amy's part however, she set out to prove the slights against her were wrong when she did make it to the studio after all – and began recording with legendary producer Quincy Jones. 77-year-old Quincy, best known for his work on Michael Jackson's Thriller album, recorded three tracks with Amy for his forthcoming covers album. Contrary to Daphne's insistence that she wasn't fit to hit the studio, he countered: 'Nobody sounds like her. She's been going through a lot of stuff, but she came through, man. Everybody was saying: "You'll never get her" and all that stuff. You know how the press is today – it's lethal with all the haters and negative shit. But she… did it. She has a great voice. She's from another planet.'

Amy had won that round and was displaying brief flashes of brilliance, but it was a never-ending battle to keep her on the straight and narrow. Amy's family hoped that, far from just a holiday destination, the top would be a permanent position for her. After agonising about the string of unsuitable men she fell for, they were relieved to see her finding comfort in the arms of a much more sensible prospect – film producer Reg Traviss. There was just one problem – like many of Amy's past beaus, he was already attached.

Blonde burlesque dancer Raven Isis stepped out of the shadows to reveal that they'd been in a relationship for years – and that he'd cheated on her with Amy to further his career. According to her, he was an unfeelingly ambitious man desperate to score publicity for his films. Dating a high profile public figure like her would lift him from anonymity into the public domain – and, sure enough, within days of getting together with Amy, his photograph was splashed across the tabloids. Raven insisted he'd told her that it was her he really wanted – and that as soon as he'd advanced his celebrity status, he would come back to her.

Amy – described by close friend Aisleyne Horgan-Wallace as 'naïve' and 'trusting' had a history of being exploited by lovers, who seemed to be with her for the wrong reasons. According to Mitch, Blake too was a culprit who'd been in it for the fame. 'He started seeing her on a casual basis just after Frank came out,' he had claimed. 'But, of course, after six months the interest in the album started waning a bit and so, it seemed, did Blake's interest in Amy. He didn't turn up again until Back to Black was No. 1.'

In Reg's case, his friends were on hand to dismiss Raven's claims as 'nonsense' – but was he just seduced by the spotlight or was he genuinely enamoured with Amy? Were Raven's words part of a jealous rant by an ex who couldn't let go or was she sincerely exposing him as a love cheat?: Reg's presence in Amy's life seemed to bring her out of her shell and she was soon doing impromptu performances at gigs and having the time of her life again. At the Proud Galleries on June 2010, she leapt on stage without warning to treat the audience to a duet with Professor Green on

In October 2010, Amy played a secret gig at an East London branch of clothing store Fred Perry in Spitalfields to promote her new fashion line. The chain had been launched in 1952 by a famous English tennis player of the same name and had since sold clothes designed by Damon Albarn of Blur and Gorillaz, Paul Weller and Terry Hall of the Specials. Now that Amy was on board, the line featured skirts with 'dangerously short' hemlines and tight Capri-style leggings with a punk twist. There were also classic polo shirts in Amy's favourite shades of black and pink. A spokesman claimed of her line: 'Collars are most definitely raised and ready for action – and yet, for every tomboy twist, there's a deeply feminine twirl. It's Amy all over – sharp, clever, sexy, lots of attitude – but stays true to the Perry aesthetic and unrivalled heritage.'

Amy was not a typical candidate for a fashion line at that time. That year, she'd been named and shamed for being photographed wearing the same skirt five days in a row without changing it. Her signature ballet pumps had been worn even when stained with blood. She might have had a penchant for indecently small dresses – sometimes rolling up or trimming already short miniskirts to maximise the impact – and she liked open toe heels to feed her 'foot fetish', but – nonetheless – she wasn't exactly knowing for her burgeoning sense of style. The Amy that stuck in the public's minds was a girl with an unkempt, slightly ruffled beehive, blackened fingernails and vest tops with the bra straps showing.

Plus, even as a multi-millionairess with a sizable estate, Amy was still prone to wearing fake Louis Vuitton earrings and bags rather than the authentic product – market-stall chic. However, while she was undeniably a down to earth girl, her line reflected that, with a cropped trench-coat – the most expensive item in the range – setting the buyer back just £100. She wouldn't be the only unconventional fashion icon to front a line either – famously voluptuous Beth Ditto from rock band The Gossip, at size 22, had designed for plus-size store Evans.

What was more, the clothes really did represent Amy. Not only were they sporty and practical, but one woollen jumper dress with a triangular pattern had looked almost identical to one she'd donned back in 2003 for her first ever CD signing for Frank. A spokesman confirmed her involvement, claiming: 'We had three design meetings where she was involved in style selection and the application of fabric, colour and styling details.' While it might have seemed as though celebrities were mere puppets to plump up the sales targets of a fashion house – R&B star Rihanna confessed to the press that labels had asked her to take a cheque to be part of lines she hadn't even designed – Amy was too single-minded and stubborn to conform to that.

As the similarities of her line matched her personal style, it was clearly something she believed in. Her spokesman described her as a 'loyal fan' and she was indeed loyal to the brand, almost never venturing out without a dress or top featuring the distinctive logo. At the concert itself, she was fully kitted out, playing four songs to a select audience of 20 competition winners, ending with a jazz rework of the Oasis track 'Don't Look Back In Anger'.

Amy was no stranger to the therapeutic effects of music so she took to the stage again the same month for the Nordoff Robbins Music Therapy charity. Around 100 people crammed themselves into the tiny Hawley Arms pub to hear her sing 'Tears Dry On Their Own' and Specials cover 'Message To You, Rudy'. Following that, she tried her hand on the guitar, together with Sadie Frost's ex-boyfriend Kristian Marr. The concert was a relief to those worrying about her plummeting weight and issues with anorexia and bulimia.

Hairdresser Alex Foden had shared her anguish with *The Mirror*, revealing: 'She loved food, but she'd either have binges – eating loads before running to the toilet and getting rid of it all again, or she'd go for up to four or five days without eating, surviving on alcohol, drugs and sweets. Often when she got sent clothes, they'd be too big for her. I'd have to ring the designers and tell them to adjust the dresses and measure them up against a seven-year-old child. She had a 21in waist – at times, smaller.'

However, at this concert, perhaps owing to Reg's calming influence and anti-drugs stance, she was back on form, telling the crowd: 'I'm putting on weight, you know. It was even a struggle to get into these jeans. I don't know how I'm going to get them off again.' She also had an indignant message for anyone who'd questioned her ability to make it back from the brink, claiming: 'Don't let anyone tell you you're wrong and you can't do it. Keep going. You can make it. Everyone tried to hold me back, but look at me – I'm back!'

CHAPTER 16

Sadly, Amy's confidence wasn't to last for much longer. Shortly after her charity gig, the Causeway – the Essex rehab clinic Amy had attended at the height of her addiction – found itself facing a very public criminal prosecution.

On the outside, it had seemed like the perfect place to recuperate from addiction or even just exhaustion. Harassed celebrities such as Take That band member Mark Owen, big screen actor Jonathan Rhys Meyers and, allegedly, Robbie Williams, had all briefly called it home, while some of the world's most aristocratic families had been guests. The clinic had boasted higher weekly rates than the Priory in a bid to cement its status as both a rehab venue and a luxury hotel all in one. Owned by Sugababes producer Nigel Frieda, the clinic came complete with a recording studio on the premises – one that had once been used by Bob Marley. Despite its £10,000 a week price tag, it wasn't difficult to see why it appealed.

Yet, according to a High Court judge, Mr Cooper, the clinic was not only unlicensed, but its standards would 'shame a third world country'. He continued that the clinic was 'scandalously negligent, if not downright misleading and fraudulent'.

A scandalous court case ensued, revealing that patients were allowed to sign for large batches of medication unsupervised and suicidal victims slashed their wrists with nail clippers in a bid to end their lives, while 'busy' nursing staff apparently turned a blind eye. One drunk woman had been forcibly tied to a boat to prevent her escaping en route to the island, while an acclaimed Channel 4 producer had committed suicide just months after the Causeway had refused to treat her for being 'disruptive'. One guest suffering post-traumatic stress and hallucinations claimed she'd even seen a therapist who 'couldn't speak English very well and wore a hearing aid – it was pointless'.

The legitimacy of what had once been the rehab clinic of choice for every self-respecting yet underperforming celebrity, was now being seriously brought into question. Most concerning of all, it emerged that patients were being treated illegally without the scrutiny of the regulating body, the Care Quality Commission. Prosecuting barrister Paul Spencer spoke of the injustice of 'the death of a young lady discharged from the Causeway without any proper assessment because she was considered a difficult patient' and spoke of the 'significant danger' to the public, in particular to those who spent huge sums of money to enter for treatment.

Amy and Blake's case proved his point – they had successfully smuggled valium and a heroin substitute into the clinic but had gone undetected by staff. What was more, their short stay in rehab had done little to curb their desires for illicit drugs. Those running the clinic were ordered to pay £38,000 in compensation. Yet as the illusion of a perfect rehab clinic shattered, so did the belief that Amy could get better without a fight. If her recovery had seemed too good to be true, that was because it was.

She'd been successful performing at a Russian oligarch's party in Moscow for a £1 million price tag, which – at just 40 minutes long – had earnt her an incredible £25,000 a minute. As 2011 arrived, she had also been booked for concerts in Dubai and Brazil. The first night of her Brazilian tour, in Florianopolis on January 8th saw concert-goers report a return to form and Amy was even seen drinking from a bottle of Evian on stage, for perhaps the first time ever at a concert. The following night however, she slipped back into alcohol abuse and the bad reviews began again.

What was more, friends claimed that Amy didn't enjoy travelling abroad and that she'd rather play intimate gigs in her hometown in the jazz tradition. Many miles from home, she appeared lost and awkward on the stage, interrupting her usual banter to hug herself for comfort. She cheered up slightly with a visit from Rolling Stones buddy and fellow recovering alcoholic Ronnie Wood, who'd be holidaying in nearby Uruguay, though.

Meanwhile Amy's concert in Dubai on February 11th to promote Gulf Bike Week was met with an equally frosty reception. Stories emerged that she appeared on stage intoxicated, although the strict Islamic emirate had a low tolerance policy for any amount of alcohol. Amy, with her loose tongue and insatiable appetite for vodka, was an awkward match for a country as reserved as the UAE – and some might warn that it was a recipe for disaster even when she was on her best behaviour. Nevertheless, performing her first official gigs in almost three years was a milestone in her recovery. The five shows in Brazil alone had netted her £5 million but, more importantly, they would build up her confidence and her management had high hopes that an album release and a full European tour would soon follow.

Amy had been in the studio with Ceelo Green and her idol Tony Bennett, excitedly telling the latter: 'I'm just happy to be there. It's a story to tell my grandchildren to tell their grandchildren to tell their grandchildren.' Sadly, while Amy's legacy would live on, the chance to pass down that story was not to be.

Meanwhile, by February 28th, Blake was back in trouble, seeing himself charged with burglary and possessing an imitation firearm. He and an accomplice had thieved £4,000 worth of jewellery and electrical appliances, intending to sell them on to buy heroin. After he was bailed the following month, his mother took him in, only to turf him out again when she discovered he and a heavily pregnant Sarah were still abusing heroin.

The crime supported Mitch's theory that drug users deliberately offend to be in with a chance of attending rehab on the NHS – although Georgette thought otherwise, simply believing he was looking for cash to get his hands on more drugs.

The Sun then published a feature revealing that, over the last decade, 21,000 heroin addicts had been living on benefits, costing the British tax payer more than £1 billion. Georgette, who had closed a successful hair salon due to the stress of rehabilitating Blake, told the newspaper: 'He disgusts me. I lost my business because I was too frightened to go to work while he and Sarah lived here [with me]. Why shouldn't he go out to work? I've given up on him now… what the government is doing is giving [people like Blake] money to feed their addiction.'

She claimed that he received £91 per week in disability handouts alone, adding: 'I fought for him and he humiliated me… but the door is finally closed now.'

When it seemed as though even Blake's mother had given up on him, Amy still cared – and those close to her were fearing a relapse, particularly when it emerged he'd been jailed for 32 months for the burglary and fake firearms offence. She had been in constant contact with Georgette throughout the pregnancy, urging her to use her influence to separate Blake from his girlfriend, who she insisted was 'fit to burn'.

However, she also had ulterior motives for wanting a separation – she had been making posts on the internet about still loving Blake, and deep down, friends believed she still longed for reconciliation. Could his downfall have been sabotaging Amy's own recovery? Since her marriage, her performances had been erratic – she had seemed vacant on stage, regularly running off between songs for a quick kiss with her husband or, as he had later revealed, a hit of crack cocaine. Yet Blake's 2007 prison sentence for assault saw Amy's shows hit an all-time low. She stumbled her way through shows that punters deemed 'diabolical' before giving up altogether, explaining that she 'couldn't give it her all' without Blake beside her. Now, her management feared a repeat performance – Amy seemed to need to be weaned off Blake as much as she did from any drug and, if reports were to be believed, she hadn't taken the news of his second incarceration very well.

'Amy was crying her eyes out,' an anonymous source had revealed. 'She's totally in denial over their breakup and still feels a huge emotional attachment to him.' This spelt disaster for Amy's comeback. Tabloid reports emerged that Amy was now 'obsessed with having children' and was doing 'everything she could' to make that happen, including changing her lifestyle. Yet was it just a rebound reaction to comfort herself after the trauma with Blake?

By May, Amy had been admitted to the Priory for in-patient treatment, where she spent two weeks weaning herself off alcohol. However, eyewitness reports suggested she was not taking her treatment seriously when she was sighted buying a bottle of vodka on her way to the clinic and downing it all in one gulp. Did Amy see rehab as just a temporary break from alcohol to clean out her system so that she could start afresh abusing her body? Or did she truly want it to be a permanent solution to a problem that had been plaguing her?

Her management hoped for the latter when she arrived in Belgrade, Serbia on June 18th to perform the first of her comeback shows. As a precautionary measure, the floor of the hotel where she and her entourage were staying were alcohol free zones, with staff forbidden from delivering booze there. However, had a persuasive Amy bribed or cajoled someone into buying it from the bar for her and smuggling it up to her room?

Friends reported she had shared nine bottles of Jack Daniels whiskey before taking to the stage for her last official show – one that would be described by local media as 'the worst in history' and one that most of Amy's fans would dub the worst of her career.

However, according to backing singer Ade Omotayo – who'd known Amy for almost a decade and shared a stage with her every night on the Back to Black tour – her comeback had been ill-fated from the very beginning. Her return to showbiz had got off to a promising start initially with a widely-applauded show at London's 100 Club the previous week, and he'd been impressed by her vocals. 'For me that performance was quite encouraging,' he recalled. 'I felt we had a tour on our hands, but what happened next was just so sad.'

Firstly Amy had been unhappy with the material on her set-list. According to Ade, at rehearsals earlier in the year, she'd refused to sing most of the tracks from Back to Black, complaining that they reminded her of Blake. Even with Reg on her arm, the wounds of losing her ex-husband had never healed and performing scores of tracks she'd penned about him, one after the other, was proving too much for her to take. 'There were many songs she didn't want to do because they reminded her of the relationship, especially 'Me and Mr Jones', 'Tears Dry On Their Own', 'Back to Black' and 'Wake Up Alone',' Ade recalled to the author.

The problem was that Amy had only recorded two albums and Back to Black – which was full to the brim with Blake-inspired tracks – had been by far the most popular. She was even reluctant to perform 'Rehab', feeling that as a fully recovered drug addict, it didn't correlate with the new phase in her life. 'She'd say "I'm not doing drugs anymore",' Ade continued. '[She'd claim] it wasn't relevant to who she was as a person by then.'

Ironically, when the going got tough, one habit from the past did rear its ugly head – the rehearsals saw Amy clamouring for alcohol. 'She wanted to have a drink but they wouldn't let her,' Ade recalled 'They wanted her to get through some rehearsals.'

Yet in Amy's state of mind, even that was proving to be a problem. Despite being firmly behind bars by that time, Blake still had a hold over Amy. While she was keen to get back on the stage, she wanted to erase tales of drug addiction, depression and difficult ex-husbands and wipe the slate clean. To do so, she was determined that the tracks performed for her comeback should all be covers instead.

'She wanted cover versions in there,' '50s jukebox things like 'Shimmy Shimmy Coco Pop' and 'I'm On The Outside (Looking In)' by Little Anthony and The Imperials, 'Lovers Never Say Goodbye' by the Flamingos and 'Boulevard of Broken Dreams' by Tony Bennett. It was like her obsession with '60s tunes by people like the Shangri-Las when she first recorded *Back to Black*, but she was going further back into the archives,' Ade revealed. 'She wanted to replace the *Back to Black* songs. They didn't fit. It was a place she really didn't want to visit.'

Her management, however, were dumbfounded. 'Rehab' had been one of Amy's most popular tunes – it had sold over half a million copies in the first year of its release alone – yet she was considering banishing it from her set-list altogether. Ade wasn't exactly surprised though. 'Amy always fought for doing what she wanted and she never followed someone's orders,' he insisted. 'I never got the feeling there was an outside influence at all when it came to her material. I don't think she really listened to people if she didn't want to.'

Yet to some of her team, a gig full of cover versions could have spelt career suicide. Where were the tracks her fans knew and loved? In fact, it mirrored the time when they had vetoed her plans to change her musical style beyond all recognition. 'It was reggae-tinged singing with a Caribbean accent,' Ade recalled, 'and the label didn't want it. They didn't think it was the right way to go because it was a very drastic departure from what she used to be doing.'

vocal – the crowd would help her sing anyway – [but] that show was the first time when there was a unanimous disappointment, everyone at the same time, like "This is really bad!"' Ade grimaced. 'We played some bad shows but this was the worst ever – nothing was right about it.'

Whatever the underlying problem was, it made for uncomfortable viewing. Amy had announced that she was 'the happiest girl in the world' one minute before throwing down her microphone and dissolving into tears the next. She hugged herself protectively while tears brimmed from her eyes, and – as she pouted and defensively folded her arms across her chest – she looked more like a toddler having a tantrum than a worldwide musical icon. Amy looked lost, lonely and terrified.

To add insult to injury for gig-goers, the average cash-strapped Serbian barely scraped £65 per week, and the ticket price represented almost half their weekly wages. The equivalent in British terms would have been paying £250 for the show. Frustrated music fans began to boo and jeer, as Amy cowered tearfully on the stage – yet many had little sympathy.

One Croatian fan argued: 'That was not singing. She was mumbling and holding her hand before her mouth. I'm really mad as I don't know why I paid 40 Euros to see that.' Another raged: 'She promised to sing some new songs, but, God, she could not sing old ones or [even] remain on her feet.'

Many shared her sentiments, with locals taking to Facebook, Twitter and Youtube to express their outrage. She was dubbed a 'liability' who made for 'train-wreck viewing' and even national newspapers joined in to brand the affair a 'scandal'. Amy had not just tripped drunkenly on the stage – she had also tripped into a media circus. While tabloids created a sensation, the defence minister of Serbia, Dragan Sutanovac, was only slightly more cautious, describing the event as 'a huge shame and a disappointment'.

However no-one was more mortified than Amy herself. By the time news of the disastrous show hit British newspapers, she had already cancelled subsequent shows in Istanbul and Athens – and the entire tour was axed soon after.

'It was a relief,' confided Ade. 'It was painful. This is someone we love and respect, so we felt like "We can't continue to go through with this". We knew it would be the last tine to play a show unless we could be a hundred percent sure she was clean.' Tom him it had been a repeat of the tour she'd performed when Blake was incarcerated for the first time, where there'd been 'no point in carrying on' – but little did he know then that Amy's situation was now much, much worse.

However, her plight didn't protect her from the full force of media disapproval back home. One newspaper, *The Mirror*, described her on stage fall, before jeering: 'She clawed herself back upright with all the elegance of a rhino on ice'. Meanwhile, *The Northern Echo* took a more serious view, branding Amy the 'architect of her own misery' and asking: 'How many more skull-splitting hangovers will she endure before coming back to her senses? The alternative is too awful to contemplate.' It added prophetically: 'How much longer can Amy Winehouse go on like this before she kills herself?'

While reports like this brought Amy's problems into further clarity, some newspapers had different views. Shining the spotlight on the theory that tabloids were hyping up her meltdown to improve their own ratings and capitalising on her reputation as a 'car-crash liability' to drive up their sales, *The Guardian* questioned whether her show was 'really that bad'.

It asked whether she was being unfairly targeted when other musicians seemed to get away scot-free. For instance, Noel and Liam Gallagher of Oasis had often played up their sibling rivalry with drunken and furious bust-ups both on and off the stage. Meanwhile, according to the paper, 'when Bob Dylan renders his back catalogue unrecognisable, as he did in London's Finsbury Park last weekend, people think he's a maverick genius.'

The review added: 'Winehouse is now typecast as a troubled diva – yet watching Saturday's rendition of 'Back to Black' on Youtube, to my ears it's not even that had – if the people of Belgrade wanted note-perfect versions, perhaps they should have stayed at home and listened to the records.'

That was the fate that met the people of Greece and Turkey as well as several other countries scheduled to receive Amy during her comeback, when her management announced it was axing the tour. 'Despite feeling sure that she wanted to fulfil these commitments, she has agreed with management that she cannot perform to the best of her ability and will return home,' a press statement read. 'She would like to apologise to fans expecting to see her at the shows, but feels that this is the right thing to do.'

Amy's shows had never been polished displays of perfection – there were no elaborately sequined costumes, pyrotechnic effects or carefully choreographed dance routines a la Beyonce. Instead, her shows were low key prop-free affairs, designed to showcase her voice alone. In place of a full face of makeup and a glittery leotard, Amy had always arrived on stage in a stained vest top and skinny jeans, with a mere swoosh of her trademark black eyeliner to colour her face.

The fact that Amy could sell out arenas without any gimmicks was testament to the quality of her singing voice – but that meant it was all important for a show. Britney Spears might have had a pass for miming, but there was no way Amy could get away with the same. Fans at shows craved an authentic 'live' experience – one they couldn't get from listening to her albums alone – and back in the day, she'd provided it with a combination of no holds barred on stage banter and reworked interpretations of the public's favourite songs.

With Amy, however, every show was a gamble. Earlier that year in Brazil, she'd delighted listeners with an impromptu performance of Tony Bennett's 'Boulevard of Broken Dreams', but by the time of her Serbia show just a few months later, she left the entire track to her backing singers while she slouched incomprehensibly by the side of the stage.

In the past, drunken antics and wobbly walks were written off as an endearing part of her stage routine, although it had now gone so far that she could barely sing a note – and in most people's eyes that was one step too far.

Fans had come to expect a high standard from Amy, even when her belly was full of vodka and her senses numbed by deadly crack cocaine – in the early days, she'd simply been able to get by on semi-consciousness. Journalist Julie Burchill had argued in *The Sun* that, unlike celebrities such as Madonna, Amy hadn't needed to keep her voice in shape because her 'God-given talent' rendered that unnecessary. Yet, while Amy was still pleasing fans in 2007, smoking crack backstage but still delivering concerts that would achieve rave reviews, her personal issues had now taken things way beyond that stage - and she was truly incapable of performing.

What was more, she had embraced the jazz tradition, as previous managers had commented. She was more at home at a low-key London supper club crooning her favourite tracks than abroad, out of her comfort zone, playing to tens of thousands of screaming fans who were desperate to catch a glimpse of their international idol in action.

According to Ade, travelling far afield actually frightened Amy. 'Europe she could deal with, but I don't think she was ever big on going to places that were far out – I don't think we'd ever have played in Australia or Asia because she wasn't that excited by it,' he explained. 'She wasn't crazy about breaking America like most artists are, either. She was like "I've made an album. If they like it in America, that's fine. If they don't, they don't." I think she just wanted to hang out with her mates.'

Indeed, the closest Amy would ever get to Australia was an interview with a website down under called *Get Music*. Even then, she'd spent part of that interview waxing lyrical about her infatuation with London. 'I'm really soppy, you know? When I fly home, I literally come off the plane like [breathes in deeply], like London is my first love!!' she claimed. 'I'll always go back to London.

To Amy, she wasn't an idol. She was no glamorous international jetsetter with dreams of world domination - instead, she was a heartbroken talent who'd rather be drowning her sorrows with the jukebox of a Camden pub. In one of her earliest interviews in 2003, she'd even told a journalist: 'If my career should die right now, I would be a lounge singer. I'd do that every single night for the rest of my life and be completely happy.' She'd wanted to sing, record albums and be heard, but it seemed that - to Amy - the intensity of her fame had been an unhappy accident.

For all of these reasons, listeners who'd hoped to catch a legendary comeback show ultimately felt like guilty voyeurs of a desperately unhappy woman struggling not just to claim the stage, but to get her life back. It was clear to everyone that this tour was over.

For his part, backing vocalist Ade was shell-shocked. Two days afterwards, he received a call from a remorseful Amy, who wanted to meet up for dinner in Istanbul. 'She was extremely apologetic,' he recalled of their reunion. 'Reg was with her and she was sober, completely sober. No drinks, nothing. She was coherent, she was funny. I flew back with her on her private jet and that was the last time I saw her, when we said our good-byes. [Despite the bad show] I thought she was going to be alright. Any-thing elsc didn't occur to me at all.'

He gave his soulmate in music a warm embrace at the airport, little imagining that it would be the last time he'd ever see her alive again. For now, a shame-faced Amy had returned to her beloved London and waited for the recriminations to begin.

Some blamed Amy for the disaster, with the *Daily Mail* claiming: '[She] may be lost, but what about a moral responsibility to the young girls who admire her and want to copy her? Those who think that she still looks cool and daring [although] she is the toxic role model to end them all.'

The reviewer compared Amy to indie rock singer and guitarist Pete Doherty, who had in the past distributed drugs to his fans at shows and even held impromptu concerts for up to 50 people - usually women - at his own home. Despite 25 drug convictions, 15 court appearances and a scandal when he seemed to have been filmed injecting an unconscious woman with heroin as she lay on the floor of his flat - not to mention the dubious credit of allegedly introducing Kate Moss to cocaine - the paper believed he was still idolised by many and was setting a bad example. After all, in spite of his troubles, he had fame, notoriety, column inches in music magazines and - at one point - a supermodel girlfriend.

Even wife of French president Nicholas Sarkozky Carla Bruni - who famously declared that monogamy was 'boring' and that physical passion with one person lasted a mere two to three weeks - struck up a close friendship with Pete. Perhaps with all of his musical successes and links with high profile people, fans wondered if he was really a waster or if this was proof that hardcore drug use was actually cool and the way to go.

It might seem preposterous to imagine young, sober fans looking on in admiration as singers like Pete and Amy spectacularly self-sabotaged, destroying their voices and stumbling drunkenly around stages, but the *Daily Mail* cited 18-year-old Freddy McConnel as proof of the adora-tion. The teenager had died weeks after his 18th birthday to a heroin overdose, while his father held Pete responsible, claiming that Freddy had 'idolised' him. Did impressionable teenagers indeed see drug use as a route to fame and fortune – or, at least, a way to get ahead in the social stakes and bag a gorgeous model of their own?

More to the point, had Blake's parents – who, at the time, had been dismissed as jealous, mean and petty – had a point when they called for Amy not to be rewarded with trophies at award ceremonies any more due to the message it might send both to herself and to her millions of fans? Perhaps rock and roll excesses of jaw-dropping proportions would be seen as obligatory in the music industry from now on – a mere way of honouring an age-old rock and roll tradition.

Yet, while the *Daily Mail* candidly blamed Amy both for her troubles and for being a bad influence, stating: 'She makes it her business to keep people around her who will allow her to carry on... that is her misfortune and also her fault', others believed that she was blame-free and far from in control of her addiction. Rumours began to circulate that bodyguards had pushed Amy on stage against her will after she had second thoughts, realising she wasn't ready. Some members of the public had been echoing author Daphne Barak's thoughts when she asked incredulously how her management could put her on stage when she was clearly unwell and still suffering.

However, close friend and *NME* journalist Alan Woodhouse described a woman 'consumed' by unwanted fame and believed the concert had merely been a mistake. 'Her management wasn't pushing her to go back to the show,' he insisted. 'I think what possibly happened is that they'd seen she was maybe getting it together a little bit. Apparently she'd been a bit healthier recently and maybe they thought getting her on stage would inspire her again. Obviously it was the wrong thing. It was just a disaster.'

Backing vocalist Ade concurred, insisting: 'One thing's for certain, whether she was in the right state of mind or not, she wanted to do those shows. She requested them. The management wanted to meet up with those requests so they booked the European shows. [It's just that] there's a difference between wanting them and actually executing them.'

Manager Jazz Summers, who had been responsible for acts like The Verve, who'd produced tracks such as 'The Drugs Don't Work' was also supportive of the efforts of Amy's management. 'I've dealt with artists who are addicts,' he revealed. 'You're dealing with the addiction, not the

now. I literally woke up one day and was like: "I don't want to do this anymore".'

If reports were to be believed, she hadn't just cut out drugs either - she was on a mission to stay away from alcohol too. Ze Silva, who owned the A Baia Cafe in Camden recalled her begging to be kept away from booze. 'In the last two of three weeks [before her death] she didn't drink,' she revealed. 'She said she had given up - she just had a Coca Cola. She told me, "I'm not drinking. Don't give me anything to drink if I ask for it. I mustn't have it!"'

Not only that, but - according to Mitch - Amy was the 'happiest and healthiest she'd been in years' the month that she had died? What had gone wrong? There were plenty of people willing to try to answer that question. Prior to the post-mortem, gossip forums and newspaper headlines buzzed with speculation – and that was nothing compared to the murmurings in Amy's inner circle.

One theory was that Amy had committed suicide, determined to die a legend. Since 2009, she had been known to read morbid poetry and forecast her own death, telling mother Janis: 'Mum, I've a feeling I'm going to die young.'

That fear might not come as a surprise, due to the extreme limits she'd been pushing her body to, but hairdresser Alex Foden took it a step further, insisting that she relished the idea of dying young. 'Amy always told me she thought she would die young and that she knew she'd become a member of the 27 Club,' he claimed. 'I think she almost needed to die a legend.'

The 27 Club - a group of deeply troubled musicians and vocalists who'd all died in tragic circumstances before seeing in their 28th birthdays - included Nirvana singer Kurt Cobain, Rolling Stones member Brian Jones, rock icon Jimi Hendrix and feminist vocalist Janis Joplin. Most of the club's members had suffered depression or fallen prey to temptation and become embroiled in drugs or other vices.

Meanwhile an anonymous friend confirmed: 'She was past the point of caring whether she lived or died. Amy never wanted to die in obscurity, to die having never made a record as good as Back to Black. It was almost as if she wanted to die young, to leave a legacy and to be remembered for her music and her voice. Sadly she was all too aware of the 27 Club and was never afraid to join it.'

Was Amy's death a suicide attempt driven by fear of failure? After her disastrous show in Serbia, had she been unable to live with the idea that she seemed to have peaked at just 27 and might never regain the power in her voice, with lungs ravaged by emphysema? Was ending it all better than the alternative: facing up to a life in which she'd destroyed her talents through drug abuse?

Others might have argued that Amy barely needed or wanted the notoriety - and that she spent most of her career hiding from the lenses of cameras and longing to be left alone. She'd once fantasised about strangers hearing her voice and taking pleasure from it, but she'd quickly discovered a darker side to fame. Did she really care to make a dramatic exit?

Alex Foden maintained that she did. 'It is heartbreaking that she appears to have gone through with her plans [to join the club]', he elaborated. 'Amy knew her limits. I truly believe she knew this final binge might have killed her.'

The binge he'd been referring to was an alleged final hours drug marathon which some claimed had taken place as a result of fighting with much-loved boyfriend Reg. A source told *The Mirror*: 'Reg found out Amy and Blake had been chatting and got upset. The pair had a fight and Reg walked out... she was upstairs injecting heroin on a self-destruct mission. The fear is she deliberately took more than usual because she was past the point of caring.'

Whilst these words were later proved false by toxicology tests, the tales of an argument with Reg seemed more likely. Photos of Amy with her boyfriend Tyler James – whom she hadn't formally dated for five years – emerged on his private Facebook account showing the pair kissing on the lips. Tyler had posted them in 2010, over the Christmas period, with the subheading 'My baby'. As she was at that time meant to be in a committed relationship with Reg, the pictures spelled trouble for her. Could it be that Amy had been bed-hopping again, following the same patterns of infidelity as her philandering father, the ones she'd bemoaned in 'What Is It About Men?'

However, according to Ade Omotayo, Reg had nothing to worry about. 'I always thought Tyler was gay,' he mused. 'He was just taking care of her and he probably knew her better than anyone else. At one point she was regularly having seizures and he knew when she was about to have one and he'd help her. He could tell when one was coming on because he said she'd get a certain look in her eyes – then he'd get her to take her drugs, because she had medication for it.'

So she and Tyler could just have been extremely good friends – why then did Amy have to seal their friendship with an incriminating looking kiss? Like everything else in her life, it was complicated. Either way, there was now a much more serious problem afoot.

Her parents were shell-shocked by the allegations of drug use. To them, their daughter had been making a speedy recovery - but Camden-based Anglo-Italian fixer Tony Azzopardi came forward to contradict that, claiming he'd helped Amy find drugs the night that she died. His story had held added weight in many people's eyes because he risked a possible revenge attack from the dealer who'd supplied Amy after volunteering to help police with their enquiries. What was more, by speaking out, he was at risk of a custodial sentence himself.

However, seemingly wracked with guilt at facilitating what many believed was Amy's fatal dose, he claimed: 'I want Amy's parents to know the truth about what happened. I want to help them out - but I'm scared for my safety.'

According to his account, Amy – who, along with Blake, had been a friend of his – pulled up in a taxi outside his home and implored him to help her score some heroin. Astonished, he told her: 'I thought you were off all that now', only for Amy to respond: 'I dabble a bit'. The pair then took a cab to West Hampstead, where he used a local telephone box to contact a well-known dealer. According to his story, Amy was aggravated that Blake had been 'hassling' her with constant calls from his prison cell. When the dealer arrived, she handed over £1200 and was given half an ounce of heroin and half an ounce of crack cocaine. Azzopardi had revealed: 'She looked good, like she'd been clean for a while and filled out a bit. I couldn't believe it when I found out she was gone.'

However, some of Amy's friends blamed the company she'd been keeping for her relapse, thinking that - in a moment of weakness - she'd been tempted back into her old circle of drug-taking buddies.

Plus, according to one source, they were fair-weather friends who leeched off her fame. 'It was awful to see her being taken advantage of,' the source claimed, who believed photographers were paying to be tipped off about her location. 'These so-called mates would even go so far as to manufacture a kerfuffle with the paps to make it look like Amy was attacking them... Amy was so naive and trusting that you couldn't tell her any different.' She added: 'I know for a fact that the arseholes she bought drugs from would automatically triple the price just because it was her. She didn't have a bad bone in her body and thought others were the same.'

Meanwhile, she maintained emotional ties to another possible fair-weather friend: Blake, the man who had egged on recovering alcoholic Ronnie Wood to cast aside his treatment plan and have a drink regardless. When he and Amy had been intoxicated together, they'd often felt invincible – the highs had reinforced the feeling they had of the two of them against the world. As for the lows, in their increasingly unstable world, they had all too easily been forgotten. Even when they were apart, and Reg had replaced his role in her life, Amy had continued to think of Blake and they had maintained mutual friends. With people around her who still believed that abstinence was something to disregard or poke fun at, what chance had Amy had?

Tyler James had historically pulled her back from the cliff-edge, but after her death, events occurred that made the skeptic wonder just how much of a true friend he had been. For instance, he had repeatedly refused to speak to the media about Amy throughout her life but, when he became a contestant on TV talent show *The Voice*, had suddenly begun to regale anyone who would listen with his stories of love for her. The driving force behind his musical career, he insisted, was her. Was his change of heart about discussing Amy with the media altogether innocent – or was he using her name as a convenient means of gaining attention for his own solo career?

Either way, the irony was obvious – Amy had been blessed with many close friends but seemingly no-one who had been able to help her. Was it those with whom she surrounded herself that had led her into a death trap?

With an army of hangers-on close by, who didn't have her best interests at heart, some believed that she hadn't stood a chance.

Opinion was divided between those who thought Amy had accidentally overdosed from overindulgence, those who thought that she had deliberately topped up her dose to fatal levels after an argument with Reg, and those who felt that Amy had simply tired of life and opted out.

Alex Foden had told *The Mirror* her capacity for drugs was almost without boundaries, exclaiming: 'At her worst, she could get through about £1000 worth of gear in 24 hours. Her limits were incredible.' However, police failed to find any drugs in the house, suggesting that – if she had been indulging – she would have finished off her £1200 supply since purchasing it the night before. If so, it would have exceeded all of her previous limits – and perhaps the exceptionally high dose had been the last straw that had killed her.

What was more, she had already reached rock bottom. A source revealed: 'Her health was in a very bad state and she had been admitted to hospital by ambulance on a regular basis, suffering seizures. Her nervous system was shot to pieces. The last time she was taken to hospital was about two weeks ago after the collapse of her latest tour. She was found in the street and taken to a private London clinic.'

As Amy had been off the touring circuit and away from the prying eyes of the media, the events described had gone unpublicised. Dark warnings about Amy's death had once been commonplace, but in the end she seemingly died quietly and peacefully in her sleep when everyone had least suspected it – apart, of course, from those in her inner circle.

But were their accounts to be believed? Amy's parents had strikingly different memories of her last moments. They dismissed claims that she had bought drugs hours before her death as 'nonsense', rejected the drug fixer's claims on the grounds that his timings were wrong and insisted that in the weeks leading up to her death, she had been making an unprecedented 'fantastic recovery'.

In fact, it was Mitch's belief that it was her newly clean-living lifestyle that killed her. He felt that a sudden withdrawal from alcohol, instead of a gradual reduction in her intake, could have been fatal. A family friend told *The Sun*: '[Mitch] said doctors had told Amy to gradually reduce her intake of alcohol and to avoid binging at all costs... [but] Amy told him she couldn't do that. It was all or nothing and she gave up completely. Mitch said the shock of giving up, after everything she had been through over a bad few years, was just too much for her to take.'

Renowned doctor Carol Cooper backed up his beliefs with medical evidence, claiming: 'The heaviest drinkers have a particularly severe form of alcohol withdrawal called delirium tremors, or DTs. They may fall into a stupor and sleep it off, or lapse into a coma - and have dangerous seizures.'

Without the sedative effect of alcohol to calm the damaged body, adrenalin can flood through it with dangerous consequences. However, recovering addicts are often given sedative drugs to avoid sudden changes that can otherwise be crippling to the nervous system. In spite of that, revellers at the Roundhouse earlier that week claimed they had spotted her taking over the bar. One insisted: 'She downed gallons of gin before drinking the bar dry.'

Another source believed that whether or not Amy had indulged in drugs recently was irrelevant - and that her body was already destroyed. According to him, the effects of hard living had already caught up with her. She had allegedly developed insomnia - on one occasion tweeting 'Oinka, oinka, oinka, why you still awake?' at 3.35am a couple of days before she had died.

While 'oinka' might have been dismissed by many as the ramblings of a confused addict, it was actually a private joke dating back to happier times, when she would 'snort like a pig' with laughter. 'Amy and I went to see the film Borat in Cambridge while we were on tour and she wouldn't stop laughing – pretty loud as well,' backing vocalist Ade recalled to the author. 'She'd laugh and then she'd have this little oink at the end of it, which I'm sure people in there didn't appreciate!'

However, years on, her jokes were caused not by mirth but by crippling insomnia.

She'd also begun to hallucinate, seeing people emerge from mirrors and white mice scuttling around her feet. For her friend, it was a sign that the end was near - and that it was irreversible.

'The hallucinations were truly terrifying for Amy,' he recalled. 'The line between reality and fantasy were increasingly blurred and she found it absolutely intolerable at times. No-one can really appreciate how tough it has been for her. Even if she never touched drugs or alcohol again, she knew that her health had been ruined. There was only so much battering it could take and these side effects were a sorry testament to that. Physically, she was a wreck.'

Not only that, but earlier that year Amy's hard partying had even left her paralysed. After one particularly intense drinking session, she had fallen unconscious and couldn't be revived. Those around her had thought she was out for the count, but – as her terrified friends debated calling an ambulance – she could hear every word. An ex-lover and friend until the end told the author: 'She was paralysed. She couldn't open her eyes, move or speak – but she later told us she could hear everything we were saying. She was locked inside herself – it was as if she was brain dead for a few minutes.'

He added: 'I don't even think that partying is the right word for what she went through at the end because that would suggest she was actually having a good time. She went way beyond that point.' With an episode of what had seemed to be locked-in syndrome in her not so distant past, it seemed that even party nights had become painful towards the end.

As the family awaited for the post-mortem results to tell them what had killed her, it was an increasingly tense time. Mitch had often spoken of her good health, but had he been in denial? Or was Amy simply fluctuating so quickly that no-one could keep a handle on it? She had been due to attend a family barbecue on the day of her death and had kept bonds with relatives and friends intact - but, nonetheless, few had suspected this sudden turn of events. However, following a mother's intuition, Janis had allegedly spoken to a friend of her rapidly deteriorating health, confiding: 'Amy was completely out of it [the day before she died]. She was in such a state the guys minding her had to help her down the steps. It looked as if she had been out drinking the night before and was still drunk or hungover.' She added: 'She was seen drinking in the bar at the Round-house that evening. But how much she drank and what happened next is a mystery. I just think she put her body through too much - there is only so much it can take.'

As the news of her death broke, a world went into shock and a reported 20 million people exchanged messages on Twitter about it the very same day. Amy had again hit headline news for all the wrong reasons. Instead of discovering that she'd won another award or finally released her long awaited third album, the public were confronted by images of her tiny frame being carried away in a body bag. The street outside her house quickly became a shrine, where followers left bouquets of flowers, artwork, tributes and messages on heart-shaped notepaper. Alongside the tributes were a few empty vodka bottles - a twisted attempt at irony.

The most noticeable gift of all was a large spray painting of Amy, complete with her beehive, stiletto heels, one of her signature thigh-skimming dresses, and angel wings to mark her departure into heaven. A winged unicorn flew alongside her. Rumours began to circulate that it was a Banksy painting - the cult artist's drawings had become legendary and could attract million-pound bids at auctions. Whether it was Banksy's work or simply a replica in his trademark style, no-one knew - the painting had appeared in Camden Lock overnight.

Speaking of the scores of tributes outside her home, Mitch told fans at the scene: 'Amy was all about love and it's incredibly touching to see all these tributes reflecting that. Her whole life was devoted to her fans and friends and all of you guys as well. I really don't know what we'll do without her. We are lost. I can't tell you what this means to us. It really is making things a lot easier.'

Meanwhile, celebrity fans took to Twitter to offer their condolences. Glamour model Jordan seemed to have forgiven Amy's taunts that she was just a 'poor man's Pammy' when she wrote: 'OMG, how sad, Amy Winehouse has been found dead. Tragic. My thoughts are with her family.' Mark Ronson, meanwhile, had put the feud over who had made whose career behind him to describe her as a 'musical soulmate' and a 'sister'. Lady Gaga, who'd dyed her hair blonde because as a brunette, she'd been mistaken for Amy countless times in the early days of her career, wrote: 'RIP... such a talented singer'.

Burlesque singer Dita Von Teese, who had once been granted a private gig told of how she 'sang for me for hours' and that she was 'devastated'. Close pal Kelly Osbourne posted an even more emotional tweet, claiming: 'I can't even breathe right now, I'm crying so hard. I just lost one of my best friends. I love you Amy, and will never forget the real you!' Rapper Professor Green, who'd had one of his shows cheerfully gatecrashed by an Amy on the mend the previous year on one of her stunning returns to form, warned: 'I don't wanna hear any chat about it's her own fault - addiction is a powerful demon.'

Fellow Brit School graduate Adele claimed: 'Amy paved the way for artists like me and made people excited about British music again whilst being fearlessly hilarious and blasé... I'm grateful to be inspired by her.' George Michael tweeted: 'It's a tragedy on two levels. The waste of such a young life and the pain of those who loved her, but it's also a tragedy that we won't be hearing the exquisite music she would have given us.' God-daughter Dionne, who'd been mentored by Amy for years, posted: 'I feel like a part of my soul has departed with the beautiful song bird Amy. Please say a prayer... she loved everyone.' Well-meaning fans also had their say, hoping that Amy was able to enjoy a glass of her favourite tipple in heaven.

However, the ultimate goodbye was scheduled to take place at her funeral. In the Jewish tradition, bodies must be buried within 24 hours of death. Due to toxicology tests and an extended post-mortem, that proved impossible - but Amy finally got her send-off on July 26th. The funeral began at Edgewarebury Cemetery where over 200 close friends and family members gathered to celebrate her life and mourn her passing. Mark Ronson and Kelly Osbourne were among those present, both of whom had flown in from the USA, dark sunglasses covering their faces.

All of her backing singers attended too and, for Ade, it was his chance to reflect sadly on the demons that had destroyed her talent. To him, she hadn't been herself for three years. 'The show at the 100 Club is the only time she sang even remotely like what she was capable of,' he told the author. 'Before then I don't remember her doing a good show since the

Nelson Mandela concert in June 2008. That's the last time I remember it really being all about the music. She really wanted to do well so was at the rehearsals and ready to go.'

Sadly that was an effort destined never to be repeated. 'There was a time when the spark left her,' he continued. 'I think addiction does that to you – it goes from being a fuel to becoming everything. From 2008 all the way up to her death, that's what we were looking for – could we ever recover that spark? And I doubt if we ever did.'

Yet why did Ade think she had been drawn into the dark world of addiction in the first place? According to him, it was more than riotous ex-husbands – he thought the death of Amy's grandmother, Cynthia, had driven her to drugs. 'She was very close to her and I think that might have made her spiral out of control,' he explained. 'Amy loved very hard, she wore her heart on her sleeve and she especially cared for her grand-mother. She spoke about her a lot and had this massive love for her. She always had stories that she'd told her about growing up in the East End and she used to keep telling me how close they were.'

Whatever the reason, Ade struggled to accept that, at a time when they should have been celebrating her third album and getting back on the road, they were instead burying her in the ground. This was the second time he'd been to Amy's funeral – although, on the first occasion he'd merely been an actor in the *Back to Black* video where Amy had come face to face with his own coffin. This time, sadly, it was for real.

Ade found it particularly hard to swallow due to the kindness she'd shown him. 'The Amy I remember, the one behind the headlines, was someone who was full of love and life who was really passionate about music – someone who was so kind and so good to me that I'll never be able to repay it,' he recalled. 'I wish I could have thanked her every day. Even at the Mandela concert, she always wanted us [the backing vocalists] there. She said: "I want you to see that you can do it too, if you want to do it." She was so supportive and had belief in our talents.' If only Amy could have had equal belief in – and respect for – her own.

Ade added: 'I hope people will realise she was just fighting to be nor-mal. It was the dilemma of trying to be normal but at the same time knowing it was never going to happen. She was fighting to have an ordinary life and probably end up being a wife and a mother, but at the same time she had a strong desire to make music. She wanted to make music but at the same time she wanted to be normal. She wanted to sell out Glastonbury but then go down to the Good Mixer pub for a pint – and it just didn't work that way.' Now Ade, like the dozens of other loved ones gathered at the funeral, was fighting back the tears that it hadn't.

Prayers were said in both English and Hebrew, including 'The Lord is my Shepherd' and the coffin - containing an immaculately made up Amy with her trademark black eyeliner and backcombed beehive hairstyle was carried out to the tune of Carole King's 'So Far Away'. Black and white photo cards of Amy's face were also handed out with details of the service and an address where the Shiva ceremony would take place. The tradition, known as 'sitting Shiva', it sees families of the Jewish faith spend a period sitting at their home in quiet remembrance. After the service, mourners were then taken to the Golders Green Crematorium to see her ashes scattered with those of Cynthia Winehouse, the grandmother she'd always cherished. However, there was a shock in store when photographers gate-crashed her send-off, climbing trees and standing on cars to be in with a chance of peering over the crematorium's high walls.

Her family was furious that the photographers were disrespecting Amy's memory by pointing their camera lenses into a private place of mourning. It seemed that she had no more respite from media intrusion in death than she had had in life.

Even worse, groups of drunken revellers had taken to spending the nights after her death partying hard on Amy's doorstep. Onlookers watched in horror as the scene of her passing was reduced to a bizarre tourist attraction. In direct contrast to the weeping Japanese fans who'd taken an eight hour flight to be at the scene, there were some who'd shown their appreciation in a more sinister way. What was more, irate neighbours weren't confident of getting a wink of sleep that week. Some fans celebrated her life with vodka bottles in hands and cigarettes in mouths - symbols of her demise which were then left littered across the nearby shrine of artwork and messages when they left. It was an uncomfortable lasting reminder of exactly what had caused Amy's death.

Many denounced their behaviour as callous and – seeing them dance in the street to her music – commented that they might as well have been dancing on her grave. Was a night of debauched partying outside the front door of the deceased really one of the lessons that should have been learnt from her death? National newspapers which disapprovingly spoke of 'a celebrity culture that worships self-destruction' might have been right.

As even one impartial local pointed out, 'Since when has it been appropriate to show respect for a recently deceased alcoholic with a drunken party?'

Others who seemed to be profiting from or belittling Amy's death – this time in the musical world – were named and shamed in The Guardian. Talking of a show where U2 had dedicated 'Stuck in a Moment' to Amy, the paper raged: '[It] would have been more touching if (a) Bono hadn't already claimed it was for Michael Hutchence (one dead singer is the same as the next, eh?) and (b) if Winehouse hadn't famously told Bono to shut up at an awards ceremony and therefore, presumably was not a U2 fan.' It added of the countercultural singer M.I.A., who had released a song called '27' to coincide with Amy's death, 'This makes the time you claimed Gaddaffi as "one of my style icons" look relatively tasteful.'

What with profit-hunting celebrities, drunken hangers-on and trespassing photographers – all present from the start of her career – it seemed that Amy had been at the mercy of vultures in life and was suffering just the same beyond the grave.

Meanwhile, those that did have her best interests at heart were still shocked to the core. Outsiders might have cynically tutted that, with the cocktail of drugs she fed herself, her death had been inevitable – but others had believed that, no matter what, she would always bounce back. To them, it had seemed inexplicable. Just hours after getting a clean bill of health from a doctor, she had died. She had been under weekly surveillance and it had seemed her nightmare of addiction was finally coming to an end – not her life. The night before, she had been banging on her drum set and playfully wreaking havoc among the neighbours – that was the Amy people knew and loved.

Yet it had been clear to others that Amy was no longer present on earth in spirit. Increasingly shambolic performances, where she clutched the microphone looking lost, desperation etched across her face as she failed to remember how to sing 'Back to Black', gave the impression that she was already gone. Her frame was slight, her eyes were glazed and she could no longer even sing. A mere shell of her former glory, Amy was mumbling as if on auto-pilot – and it was if the real Amy Winehouse had left the building a long time ago.

Tellingly, Amy predicted her own transformation back in 2007 in an interview on Popworld. The host, Simon Amstell, claimed that he missed the 'old Amy' – perhaps a reaction to her spitting on the floor of a live TV studio moments earlier – and was met with the curt reply: 'We used to be close, but she's dead.'

Now Amy was dead in body as well as in spirit – but what had caused the tragic turn of events? This wasn't just about one overdose – what was the root of the problem? One theory for her demise into addiction – where dabbling with drugs as many celebrities had done before her had turned into a full-blown self-destructive obsession – was that Amy had painfully low self-esteem. She'd run out of a photo shoot in America – after self-harming in full public view – because she 'didn't feel pretty enough'. She'd admitted to interviewers that when she felt less attractive or talented than her musical idols, or depressed because of a fight with a lover, she'd drink copious amounts of champagne and start slapping herself in the face with frustration.

However, artists like Jessie J had admitted to not feeling 'good enough' on her first stint in America, while surrounded by 'impossibly beautiful' model types – but while she'd occasionally succumbed to tears or anxiety, she hadn't reacted in such an extreme way.

That said, Amy had a long history of self-harm dating back to her pre-teen years. After all, she'd tried to end her life at age 10 and had threatened suicide a second time when Blake had been on the brink of leaving. Did Amy's suicidal tendencies all come down to one common denominator – men? Whether it was the absence of a father or of a husband, Amy had seemed to react the same self-destructive way.

Her behaviour also pointed to a self-loathing – perhaps in spite of her bravado, Amy hadn't believed she deserved her fame and was punishing herself. Or perhaps she was terrified she wouldn't live up to expectations. The average person might have seen fame as an ego boost, but for Amy, being made a worldwide icon at the centre of public scrutiny, when she was already so unsure of herself, could have made her demons even worse.

Perhaps it was fame itself that had caused Amy's downfall. The formerly anonymous girl who hadn't even sought recognition to begin with had found herself plunged into a world of drug shopping lists, free for all nose candy, showbiz parties with more chemicals than the average pharmaceuticals factory, binge drinking and blackouts. It was a world where septums plunged down plugholes, ravaged from years of cocaine abuse, where fingernails dug into weeping sores – she had entered the dark world of showbiz.

Arguably someone as vulnerable as Amy, who was looking for ways to bolster her already minimal self-esteem, didn't stand a chance. What might have begun as idle temptation or moments of curiosity had led to dependency. She had become reliant on drugs to give her the energy, not to mention confidence, to perform. As someone who ran off stage between songs to take a whiff from her crack pipe, perhaps it wasn't just the physical aspects of addiction that had plagued Amy, but the psychological ones – the belief that she couldn't put on a good show without them. In fact, the opposite was true – but this knowledge came too little, too late.

She'd started off writing songs as therapy for herself and then wanting the public to hear them – but she was no *Pop Idol* contestant, no media whore. While she could sing for hours on end, she was uncomfortable about being made into a lauded figure or being known for her personal life – and in interviews, she struggled to talk about herself.

She'd told many an interviewer, 'I think the songs speak for themselves.' But Amy ended up on the media circuit anyway, playing the game. While many would have soaked up the attention with a smile, it was evident that she was desperately unhappy. She would leave local pubs with tearstains around her eyes, oblivious to the adoration. Manager Raye Cosbert noted: 'She likes playing pool with the bar men in her local. If she could take the tube everywhere, she would. She feels deeply uncomfortable in the world of VIP celebrity.'

Indeed, even when flanked by bodyguards, Amy didn't create an 'us' and 'them' mentality. While she struggled to sign autographs or play the role of the gracious yet superior superstar with the public, she was happy to serve them drinks and make Cockney banter behind the bar of her local pub, the Dublin Castle.

Amy had never believed her music would be so popular, telling the press: 'I'll never be a mainstream act.' Yet how wrong she had been – and she was totally unprepared for the stream of photographers following her, thrusting microphones in her face and intruding on every aspect of her daily life. Could it be that, because Amy had made jokes about, for example, doing interviews with her beehive instead of her, that people had believed – wrongly – that she'd been coping with the way her life had turned out? It was part and parcel of showbiz – but had Amy predicted this, or had it gone too far and surged out of her control?

In spite of the struggles fame presented, Amy had on occasion made cups of tea and handed out biscuits to the press – and not disco biscuits either. It suggested someone a little more comfortable with the hype than they were letting on. Would a woman terrified by all the attention really encourage the large groups gathered outside her home by plying them with treats? Or would it be wrong to assume that, because she'd been friendly and polite, that she was 'asking for it'? In addition, to add to the confusion, hadn't she told Sylvia Young in her application for stage school – not a place for the shy and retiring – that her life's ambition had been to be heard and to make people happy with her voice? The media had helped her to achieve that – so could they really have been responsible for leading her to her death?

On the other hand, Amy was far more prominent than, for example, a singer in a West End musical. With that type of career, she might have fulfilled her ambitions to be heard while still remaining anonymous and leading a normal life. However, unlike other addicts, the media interest had guaranteed she couldn't recover in any kind of privacy. It was one thing saying she wanted her voice to be heard and quite another to be comfortable with her recovery – or lack thereof – splashed across the tabloids.

Her every relapse had been documented by the papers and a visit to a rehab clinic made the national news. Primetime footage on the BBC and CNN played out to millions of households across the country and beyond of a frail and exhausted Amy falteringly crossing the threshold to a safer place surely couldn't have been aiding her recovery. Later, reports even suggested that her phone had been hacked in to in order to find out when she'd be arriving at clinics - so were the media to blame that she hadn't got better?

On the other hand, perhaps Amy felt obligated to uphold an image of a rock and roll lifestyle. Arguably her management were cashing in on her reputation as a hell-raiser, giving away pint glasses and ashtrays with the *I Told You I Was Trouble* live DVD - did she feel she had to keep up the pretence - that she'd no longer be loved without that image?

Meanwhile, the showbiz circles she mixed in might have normalised drug use, legitimised it because others were doing it too and provided easy access to the poisons of her choice.

More to the point, some of the media had picked up on Amy's tendency to overindulge in its early stages and had made it part of her appeal and marketing act - did she end up feeling that she had to stage it?

For example, one journalist had disapproved - albeit jokingly - of a night when she showed abstinence, at the all-important 2007 Brit Awards. It was a time when she should have been hitting headlines for the trophy she'd won. Yet even the *Independent*, a respected and strait-laced broadsheet, complained: 'Amy just flatly refused to get drunk' and 'at no point did she pass out from drink, forget the words or punch her guitarist - it's just not good enough'. The review added that she had 'let the side down badly'. While the feature was obviously intended in jest, could this - one of several reviews in the same vein - have taken its toll on Amy?

One journalist, who'd interviewed her on the *Tonight* show, revealed that she often felt ashamed if she wasn't partying as hard as the others. She said: 'If someone goes, "Amy, let me buy you a tequila" and I'm like, "No, no, I'm not drinking" and they ask why, I always say that I'm on antibiotics. Because I'm ashamed to just go: 'You know, I'm just not drinking." I have to say that I'm on a course of medication because I feel ashamed.'

She later revealed that if she was living in a way that was completely healthy, life 'wouldn't be fun anymore'. However, more worrying was Amy's lack of resistance to peer pressure and fear of seeming a lesser person in the cool stakes if she didn't indulge. As someone in the public eye, her reputation would have been all-important to her, and perhaps in her desperation to appear shocking, she'd taken it too far and lost all control? Tellingly, the journalist interviewing her, Chris Willman, later commented: 'I suspect the problem I was having with her [in getting her to open up at the interview] wasn't that she was under the influence. It's that she WASN'T.'

In the jazz and blues tradition, successful artists were renowned for their alcoholism, Billie Holiday being the most famous example. The rock and roll greats also demonstrated a dangerous lifestyle that people across many genres of music aspired to and tried to emulate. Even country artist Kid Rock - an unlikely candidate for hell-raising if ever - talked in his single 'Rockstar' of staying thin by not eating and having a drug dealer on speed dial. These things, along with the cars, mansions and extravagant wealth he also boasted of in the song, were lauded as part of the perfect life. Had Amy fallen prey to the perceived glamour of that lifestyle?

Each time she had life-threatening seizures and public meltdowns, her album sales increased dramatically - and so did her press coverage. What was more, album sales increased up to 37-fold in the week following her death - meaning the message really did seem to be that she was worth more dead than alive.

Maybe in her lifetime, she had taken the media's jokes to heart and thought being herself was no longer enough. Perhaps her very self-esteem depended upon providing the drunken antics that in recent years had made her famous. The media fuelled her behaviour, giving her press attention on a scale she could never have dreamed of sober. But would Amy really drive herself to death's door just to appear fashionable? After all, she'd taken things to extremes far beyond the average performer - for someone who wasn't interested in endless press attention and in doing interviews, would she really care about what they said?

To some, it was the humiliation of being jeered at by thousands of Serbians on her first headlining return to the stage that had prompted her death. She had looked tearful, distraught and frightened - clearly unable to cope with the demands of a live concert - and she had become like a rabbit frozen to the spot by headlights.

What was more, the media had turned on her in her moment of weakness and made her an object of ridicule. *The Mirror* wrote of her first public appearance after the disastrous Serbia show - at the I-Tunes festival supporting Dionne - scathingly, saying: 'Amy Winehouse turned at up at Dionne Bromfield's gig and, um, "performed" with her. Only she didn't sing a note - which was fortunate, given the shambles of that horrific set in Serbia... at one point, Dionne offered her the mic. Thankfully, Amy refused. That tour was cancelled for a reason...'

Not only had she been met with boos and jeers abroad, she wasn't even free from the media's acid tongue back home. Had the criticism got her down and dragged her deeper into depression and therefore drinking? The one thing that Amy, with her ravaged self-esteem, had loved about herself and thought she was truly good at, was now being criticised. It had to have hurt.

In fact, Ade Omotayo revealed that Amy had felt desperate insecurity about her singing voice, dating back to 2008. The onset of emphysema had ravaged her voice, leaving her confidence of ever getting it back fully extremely low. 'I just wish she knew it was about the music and she didn't have to worry, she just had to sing,' Ade recalled to the author, 'because at one point she didn't feel like that anymore. She wasn't confident with her singing because of her emphysema and smoking a lot, which never helps your vocals. She wasn't sleeping much either – it gradually takes its toll on you. She'd sometimes say: 'I didn't sound too good tonight" – she knew it. It frustrated her, because all she wanted to do was perform.'

It was a constant battle between Amy's desire to be involved in music and the addictions that threatened to destroy that passion. Ade added: 'She was obsessed with music, I know that, but it died down as the years went by and other things took over. Her addictions had definitely taken over and it had affected her so much vocally. She wasn't being as productive as she used to be. When you become dependent on [drugs], that's all you think about.'

Before the ill-fated European tour, he believed Amy had been 'pretty much housed' in the awkward interim period when she tried to stay clean – and her first tour since her extended isolation was proving stressful.

Some painted a picture of a woman pushed on stage by bodyguards and security against her will that night – someone who'd known she wasn't ready but wasn't given the option of pulling out at that late stage. One fan claimed: 'Amy was a veteran performer – she'd done loads of shows. So if she'd had a change of heart at the last minute, it was hardly stage fright. It had to have been that something was really wrong – but no-one listened to her.'

Singer Mica Paris claimed: 'She was very fragile after that, she was broken', while camp entertainer Boy George added incredulously: 'You wonder who let her go on stage like that.'

Attention had turned to her management for failing to protect her, with even record label boss Darcus Beese publicly criticising Raye Cosbert and calling his decision to put her in the public eye again 'mad'. Meanwhile Raye switched into defensive mode, beginning to catalogue the help that Amy had been offered. Raye, who had obviously cared deeply for Amy, was spotted in tears, head in hands, at her funeral. Yet were his tears motivated in any part by guilt – and did he feel he could have done more for Amy?

Her friend Piers Hernu believed some of the events were Amy's own doing, claiming: 'She was seriously ill – she would tell her management she was ready, but would drink heavily in her hotel room and then go on and be shambolic.'

Yet many believed the Serbia show – which saw furious gig-goers demand refunds – was the fault of her management for booking her when she was not in the lucid state of mind associated with her making her own decisions. As they held a position of responsibility in Amy's life and were expected both to take care of her and to manage the expectations of her fans, it didn't look good for their reputation.

However, a spokesperson defended: 'Amy really wanted to do the show. It wasn't a gruelling tour, more fly in, fly out. She was a grown woman and it was her decision. She had performed a well-received warm up gig at the 100 Club in London and in those circumstances, the decision was not a bad one. She did lapse, but it wasn't seen as a major problem.' Yet it had been more than a major problem – and a few weeks later, it had turned into a worldwide tragedy.

Was Blake to blame, on the other hand, for introducing her to drugs – or did Amy have to be credited for being strong-willed enough to do only what SHE wanted to do – the good and the bad? Amy had once been an opponent of hard drugs, telling her father she felt people who took them were 'mugs' – and yet she idolised Blake. He countered her belief that taking Class A drugs was an act of stupidity – after all, the man she adored, who she was riding high on a romance with, someone who didn't put a foot wrong at times in her eyes, was a regular user. Could he have changed her mind? Or perhaps she was curious to get inside the mind of the man who, according to the laws of marriage, she should have shared everything with – and what was motivating his habit?

Amy's father claimed that taking hard drugs had coincided with her marriage but that Blake wasn't entirely responsible. 'I don't think he coerced her,' he explained. 'I wish he had, because she'd have said "I don't want to do it".'

Ade agreed, claiming: 'Blake may have brought out a bad side to her, but Amy was never a victim. I've never known her to be a victim. It wasn't ever a case of being controlled by anybody. I always felt like she did things to herself.'

However, the two had become hopelessly addicted – both to drugs and to each other. One of Blake's tattoos had showed a corset-clad burlesque dancer simulating a saucy routine in a giant champagne glass. She had a smaller glass of the tipple in one outstretched hand and a deck of cards beneath her, with the words 'Man's Ruin' emblazoned below. His tattoo seemed to be a symbol that drugs, gambling and women – all of the things he was at the time addicted to – were the root of all evil. However, it seemed as though it was Amy he was addicted to most of all. Each time she pulled away, neglecting to visit him at the prison and believing that the relationship might be doing them more harm than good, he begged and pleaded with her to come back.

It was a dangerous world of dependency, where he found himself resorting to self-harm and suicide attempts – as well as emotional blackmail – to keep her by his side. Amy would ultimately always give in and take him back – and he promised for his part that he'd never leave her either. 'It's that co-dependency thing,' he claimed in a Channel 5 interview. 'The more nasty she was, the more in love I became.'

That meant that Amy ending the relationship would make him more keen - and it was a vicious circle of trying to bow out of a self-destructive liaison and failing. What was more, it was exactly the same vice versa. Many believed that Amy would recover away from Blake, but was it too late in any case, once her addiction had taken hold?

Whatever the answer, it seemed as though Amy had never fully given up on Blake. Even when outward appearances suggested she'd fallen head over heels in love with the archetypal tall, dark and handsome man of her dreams - Reg Traviss - she couldn't let go of her ex entirely.

She'd wanted to be a traditional wife with a fairytale Jewish wedding – and Reg was her tall, dark and handsome other half, a fellow Jew from within her community. It seemed destined to be. Yet, perhaps scarred by her father's infidelities in the past, her self-destructive actions betrayed her desire for a happy ending. As much as she wanted one, her thoughts kept returning to the very man who'd made her unhappy. In technical terms, Blake was both a junkie and an ex-con – and the opposite of everything she needed – yet he still seemed to consume her thoughts.

In fact, some accounts insisted she was turning back to Blake completely. She was depressed when her comeback tour was a write-off, announcing privately that she was giving up on music altogether, and she might have turned to him in her moments of weakness, feeling he was the only thing she had left that she deeply cared about after heroin had wrecked her, the one part of her past that - after her crumbling singing career - she still had in her grasp and within easy reach. She was vulnerable and going back to him would have comforted her.

In fact, she was alleged to have told one friend that Blake was the only person who could save her. But he couldn't - he was languishing in a jail cell for a burglary and returning to his side could only mean pain, addiction and conflict. Yet Amy's mind was made up - and the heartbreak began afresh. What had happened to the wise girl who - at just 19 - had penned a song about someone who no-one could help if they couldn't help themselves? Had she made a mockery of her own song?

According to Blake's lover, Sarah, the two would talk for hours on the phone - so long, in fact, that she would put a DVD on when Amy called, knowing that the film might have finished before their conversation did. On one occasion, she claimed that Amy had slept in bed with Blake while she was relegated to the next room - while her relationship with him was still active and Amy was supposed to have been past history. It had all become a mess - and all parties seemed to lack lucidity and self-esteem.

There was one other thing, however, that could have been credited with saving her - and that was her love of children. Before her death, Amy had set the wheels in motion for adopting a 10-year-old St Lucian girl, Dannika, whom she'd adored. After spending months with her on trips to the paradise island where she was recuperating, their bond had grown too strong to be broken - and the young girl's mother - a single woman struggling to feed her - approved the adoption too.

While Amy had achieved in a few short years of her career what many could not have achieved in a lifetime, she had up to that point been denied the one thing she wanted most - and that was motherhood. It was believed that children had been a stabilising influence on Amy, giving her a reason to stay clean, as she would have the responsibility of someone to look after other than herself.

Dannika's grandmother, Marjorie Lambert, believed that if she had adopted her and stayed in St Lucia, her troubles would have been over. Telling of how Amy had arrived 'weak and skinny' and how she had mothered her back to health with good food and nurturing compliments, she recalled to *The Mirror*. 'She was drug-free and normal here. If she had stayed, I am convinced she would still be alive.' She added: 'Amy used to beg me 'I want to adopt Dannika'... she was prepared to move to St Lucia to be her full-time mum. Amy wanted to have a child so bad... there is no way she would have done what she did to herself if Dannika was with her.'

Meanwhile, the inconsolable youngster herself revealed: 'Amy was already my mother. I would call her mum and she would call me her daughter... I loved her and she loved me.'

It seemed in St Lucia Amy had found people who catered to her longing for family life - the girl she called her daughter and Marjorie, the grandmother she'd called her own mother. Marjorie had told of how she would never let someone near Amy who she believed might have had drugs. It seemed like the fairytale ending that was not to be, but did Amy have an unhealthy dependence on being looked after by the very children she was supposed to be looking after? It seemed that Amy herself was the one in need of parenting.

In an emotional phone call with Dannika's Germany-based father, she allegedly revealed: 'Dannika is taking care of me. I couldn't live without her.' She'd also told the media previously that her 13-year-old goddaughter, Dionne, was 'like a big sister to me' in spite of their age gap. She also called Marjorie her 'Caribbean mummy'. It seemed as though Amy may have suffered from chronic insecurity, using those around her that she affectionately called family as emotional crutches to keep her from falling back into depression. Was she fit to be a mother when she struggled in this way? Or would motherhood have lifted her out of the hell she'd been living in?

There was an inexplicable contrast between the traditional, home loving Jewish girl with a penchant for cooking meatballs and cleaning her home and her non-identical twin - the tortured party animal on a ruthless self-destruct mission. In spite of her obscenely voluptuous talent, her biggest dream was not to be a star but to be a mother and a wife.

Friends described her as a 'mother duck' and even those older than Amy called her 'mum'. She had washed the wounds of a stranger in St Lucia when she'd been in an accident and she befriended local children wherever she went. Yet there was another side to Amy - it was the girl who slapped, punched or verbally assaulted seemingly anyone who crossed her path some days versus the loving, kind Amy who would stop at nothing to nurture her loved ones - and the differences were not easy to reconcile. Would living with the children she longed for have curbed her urges to self-destruct and would it have deterred her from drugs for good? No-one knew the answer.

The finger of blame was also being pointed at Amy's own family - her father had left when she was a child, which some would argue had sparked her experiments with cutting herself - and some perceived that the week she died, she'd been abandoned by Mitch yet again. Two days earlier, an insecure Amy had bid him goodbye as he embarked on a jazz tour thousands of miles away in New York. That was where he had been when she drew her last breath – pursuing his own career. Was Mitch selfish, callous and uncaring?

Some fans thought so, criticising his tough-love approach. The previous year he'd told the *Mail on Sunday*: 'We [as a family] learned to say "We love you Amy, we're here for you, but we do not approve of your behaviour." It sounds callous, but you have to get on with your life.' He added: 'I don't believe that her mum or I could have done anything differently. Some people think I should be walking around in sackcloth and ashes for something happened to my daughter, but what would be the point? Anyway, she's on the mend now.'

Yet it seemed that Amy was desperately attached to him and had relied on his emotional support to keep her on the straight and narrow. In St Lucia, according to Daphne Barak's book, *Saving Amy*, she'd told him: 'Dad, thank you for pulling me out of drugs – you can do it again and stop me drinking.'

Perhaps as a sign of her appreciation, she had then sat down with her father to choose 40 album tracks, all of which he'd performed in front of her and her manager, before they whittled it down to 11 for his album itself. He confessed to the New York Times: 'I admit that if Amy wasn't my daughter, I wouldn't have a shot.' Yet now he was releasing an album.

One anonymous friend told the author: 'Amy's problem was that she was a kind soul, always helping people. She'd have done anything for her family. But even when she was in the depths of drug addiction, she was helping Mitch and Dionne with their careers, when she should have been focusing on getting herself better. if she'd had half as much respect for herself as she'd had for others, she would still be here right now.' Was this just wishful thinking, or did she have a point?

For Mitch's part, he insisted that she had been healthy right to the end, telling the *Mail on Sunday* in May 2010: 'Just because my daughter had addiction problems a few years ago, am I not allowed to enjoy my life today?'

In all of the press interviews that had taken part in leading up to Amy's death, he had repeated that she was getting better. Yet she wasn't. In the months before she passed away, she'd been weak and vulnerable, suffering regular heart palpitations and seizures. In May, she'd been admitted to the

Priory to do alcohol rehab, which seemed to have proved unsuccessful. In June she had performed a disastrous gig, dissolving into public tears after hapless attempts to remember her own lyrics. In July, she had allegedly blacked out three times in one week after alcohol binges. She was far from well.

The question was – had Mitch been wrong to leave his daughter to go on tour, or – as he'd said – was it impossible for him to restrict his life even further? His decision to pursue his career that week – one that Amy herself had made possible – had taken place while she'd seemed to need him the most. Had he let her down? The words he'd said to the press just a year earlier – 'You have to get on with your own life' – seemed to be coming back to haunt him.

However, another anonymous friend of Amy's told the author: 'Mitch tried everything, but him being around wasn't going to make a difference unfortunately, because she was so far gone. The addiction was stronger in the end.' He continued: 'Mitch had furious fights with Blake where he'd actually tell him that Amy loved drugs more than she loved either of them. This is a man who faked a heart attack to try and knock some sense into her. He really did try everything. Let's face it, even professional rehab clinics couldn't save her in the end – how could he have surpassed professional help?'

Ade Omotayo also supported Mitch, telling the author: 'He was well-meaning. He cared about his daughter and wanted her to do well and get better. He did everything he could, short of actually abandoning her, to get her off drugs.'

Meanwhile, Mitch announced plans for an Amy Winehouse Foundation, to be run from the home she'd spent her last hours in, to keep her legacy alive and prevent others from making her mistakes. The profits from a track a then smiling Amy had recorded with her idol, 85-year-old Tony Bennett, several months earlier, would be used exclusively to launch the foundation.

All of the things that had touched Amy's heart in her lifetime and represented who she was would be helped by the foundation – children, horses and – most importantly – fellow addicts. Amy had once jokingly predicted to an interviewer that, in 10 years time, she saw herself 'dead in a ditch' – and while the location had been a little more salubrious, everyone's worst fears had come true. Yet with both her music and her foundation, she would live on.

Early hiccups had seen Mitch's plans get off to a bad start when an unscrupulous internet user – who turned out to be an unemployed prankster – bought the domain name for the website and expected Mitch to 'come to an arrangement' with him to buy it back. The same man had launched a website in pop star Cheryl Cole's name the previous year and threatened to post pornography on it if she didn't pay up. He had become a force to be reckoned with, but the dispute was settled within days.

Blackmail plots aside, the foundation officially launched on September 14th – a day that would have seen Amy celebrate her 28th birthday. Meanwhile her duet with Tony Bennett, 'Body and Soul' was released concurrently.

A song about someone hopelessly in love who was prepared to surrender themselves completely to their partner, mirrored Amy's romantic nature to a T. In a glimpse of the Amy from the past that her friends knew and loved, she'd beamed with pride and pleasure at sharing the recording studio with one of her biggest idols.

Tony cast doubt over whether her love was fully reciprocated, however, when he revealed after recording a song with Lady Gaga, 'The Lady is A Tramp', soon after: 'I never met a more talented person in my life.' If Amy had been alive to hear it, the news might have bruised her ego a little. However, Tony still believed she was an indisputable 'legend'.

By this time, toxicology test results had been released proving that Amy's body had not contained any illegal substances. The only drug present had been alcohol. While this news salvaged a little of her family's lost dignity, the questions about the reasons for her demise – especially the psychological ones – and her state of mind in her final hours remained unanswered.

Amy: My Daughter, Mitch's literary account of the struggle of a parent who feared he was losing his daughter's very soul to drug and love addiction, aimed to bridge that gap. Yet like so much surrounding the enigma that was Amy, the book, published on July 5, 2012, raised as many questions as it did answers. While it was a candid and indeed poignant portrait of Mitch's feelings and emotions over the years, it introduced few new facts. Those who had been following Amy's progress in the newspapers might well have heard the same stories before. What many fans argued was missing from the narrative was an explanation of why an enormously talented young woman who seemed to have it all – someone whose fame might not even have reached its peak - would wilfully self-destruct.

However the book did reignite controversial feuds. For instance, Mitch had gently and diplomatically told of an episode when Alex Foden had discharged himself from rehab and moved into Amy's London hotel suite where she too been in recovery. 'With Foden staying,' he'd recalled ominously, 'I knew it wouldn't be long before there was trouble.' It seemed as though his worst fears had come true when, just as he'd predicted, within a couple of days Amy had started using heroin again. The episode perpetuated every stereotype he'd held about Alex – he hadn't moved past the all-consuming craving for the drug and, while he remained biologically dependent on it, he was at risk of relapsing and encouraging Amy to do the same.

Perceiving that Alex was a destructive influence on Amy, the last thing she needed, Mitch had hastily persuaded him to go back into rehab, agreeing to foot the bill out of Amy's *Back to Black* royalties. It was later claimed that it had reached an eye-watering total of £130,000.

In spite of Alex's previous acknowledgment that it had been Mitch and Raye Cosbert who'd "saved" him, the generosity was quickly forgotten when he read the passage in Mitch's book typecasting him as "trouble". Incensed by the claims, he argued privately, 'Amy's dad is a fame hungry, evil, egotistical pig of a man 4 the lies he's wrote! He wasn't even fuckin' there! Only I was most of the time!'

He added, 'She would be disgusted at the lies her dad has told in this book. I'm blamed for the demise. You believe that and you're a fool. That man never has and never did think of his work horse of a daughter that he put out on stage ever night and he's blamed me for her demise! He's spoke about occasion after occasion of lies upon lies of times and places he's been with us! The one I always remember was while Amy OD at home while he unveiled a wax work figure of her in the news! Fame hungry evil, evil man!'

Adding that Amy would be "fuming" with Mitch, he continued, 'I think many people who know that a father walked out on her so young and came back when she had a [record] deal knows [what kind of a person he is] and it's a sad thing to live with. My parents have always given me love, unconditional even though I put them through hell.'

In a final swipe to add salt to the wound, he claimed that Mitch's charity efforts were purely a bid to increase his own fame. 'Edward Zero Mitch does seem like a complete penis,' he went on. 'He's always seemed very keen to get himself famous too. Between his own music career (do we really need another dick singing fucking Frank Sinatra songs in this world???) and appearing on Four Rooms for "charidee", it seems that any good work he does, there is an equal percentage of doing it for his own gain. I'm sure that his band know how to play it, but Mitch certainly doesn't know the words to the song "Dignity".'

However, Alex's own record with Amy had been flawed too. The day after the woman he called his best friend had passed away, he'd given an interview to the Mirror, claiming that, at her worst, she'd spent £1000 a day on a cocktail of drugs. To add insult to injury in the eyes of some fans, he'd then been present at her funeral, the same day that his revelations were plastered across the front page of a national newspaper. The extent of her drug use was already well-documented, so was the tell-all theme of his interview ill-timed and inappropriate? Privately, many of those close to Amy wondered whether someone willing to divulge her secrets within hours of her death was really the true friend he claimed to be.

Another fly in the ointment was a documentary he had planned to front, based on his own struggle with drug addiction – not only would it feature his own life but he promised he would 'expose the real Amy' too. In the months before her death, he'd made his plans known to her, which caused a rift between the pair. 'When she heard what the press had to say about it, she assumed the worst,' a friend of Alex's revealed to the author. 'She misunderstood the nature of his plans to "expose" her. He wanted to show a side to Amy that the media didn't – the loving, caring side behind the drug scandals, which her friends saw at home. But she didn't want her private life exposed, and least of all by a friend. She didn't want him to do the documentary at all.'

Amy had been weak and vulnerable when the gossip hit the newspapers – in fact, her team had just made the announcement that, following the "disastrous" 2011 concert in Serbia, she would be withdrawing from all public appearances. However Alex pressed ahead with his documentary – described in *the Mirror* as 'a raw, hard-hitting account about Amy's descent into drugs'. Although the primary objective of mentioning Amy was to "make a plea to [her] to sort herself out", that the call to action was coming from a close friend who could have made his pleas privately made the program appear uncomfortably voyeuristic, sensationalised and sordid.

Tragically, after this revelation, relations between Amy and Alex were said to have remained icy until the end. It also raised questions about whether he was qualified to take the moral high ground over Amy's father.

It seemed that while Alex criticised Mitch for using his daughter's name to pursue fame, some might have seen him as guilty of the same. While he sneered at Mitch's charity efforts and belittled him as an unworthy publicity seeker, he too had planned a similarly named charity – the Alex Foden Foundation. Its aspirations were similar to Mitch's: to help those who were disadvantaged or struggled through drug addiction.

Bizarrely, he told the author that he had rushed through plans to start his own charity before it was too late - because he'd had an early premonition that Amy was going to die. 'After seeing her tragic performance in Belgrade, that was the moment that really gave me the strength to try and get her sorted,' he told the author, 'but it also gave me visions which I spoke to all my friends about, 3 weeks leading up to Amy's death, that she was going to die before I had got the charity set up because the government take so long with the registration process.'

Besides a charity, Alex had another objective in common with Mitch – he too was planning to write a book. After touting it to publishers throughout 2012, he bragged to the author, 'My advance was a large six figure sum, basically making me rich from one publisher but I had to put the work in for it. TV interviews and breakfast and late night shows in virtually every country with hardly any breaks for weeks. They want it launched worldwide and I definitely have the ambition and know that it will be a best seller.'

Going on to predict the as yet unwritten book as a 'sensational must-read on my addiction, my charity and success', he countered, 'I don't want it to come across up my own arse or snobby… I'm an open book which tends to get me into trouble, but for something like this it's perfect… I want the people that don't know me yet to not look at it like I've sold my best friend out. I want them to see that I'm bringing a message across.'

Unfortunately that desire might be, to coin an archetypal Amy phrase, a "losing game". He'd seemed extraordinarily motivated by money, telling the author that he'd ultimately turned down lucrative offers from publishers because the price wasn't right. He'd even complained that specific sums were "nowhere enough". For someone so keen to deliver two very important messages – a tribute to his much-loved friend after her death combined with a life-saving message about the perils of drugs – why would the financial side of the venture loom so large?

Could it be that, on his own mission for fame, Alex had lost sight of why he aspired to write the book in the first place?

He'd told the author, 'I want [the public] to see [me] through from being sexually abused from the age of 7-10, running away from home at 16 living in one of the roughest parts of Manchester stealing cars and living a life of crime to fend for myself, suing my boss for sexual harassment at 17 and moving to Spain for a year and a half with my first love, then moving to London to start my rise to my fall. A celebrity world full of glamour yet so dark and twisted. From smoking crack at John Frieda to dating Jodie Marsh at 21 even though I was gay. Living with Jade Jagger, working [as a hairdresser] in the film industry on films such as the first Batman through to Warhorse with Spielberg then how I ended up being friends and number one drug buddy to the most famous young legend of our time. I want all our happy stories as well as our drastically different, dark, messy, twisted world of drugs and death. I want everything in and nothing missed.'

Unbeknown to the public, Alex had also been moonlighting as an adult movie star and gay escort, becoming involved in prostitution to pay the bills after drug addiction temporarily wrecked his work in hairdressing. Claiming that his affiliation with Amy had cost him his career. He'd told the author, 'Because of me tarnishing my own name as the junkie hairdresser best friend of Amy Winehouse, I had to leave hairdressing for 2 years and work as a porn star and become an escort. [I was] top of the porn charts living in yet another twisted dark world that you stupidly think is all glamour.'

Yet there'd been light at the end of the tunnel. He'd added, 'Having a nervous breakdown a year and a half ago, being diagnosed with bipolar then changing my life for the second time after being clean of drugs for four years, [I was] giving something back, whilst at the same time trying to be a huge wake up call to Amy as to how different our worlds were now and how happy you can be clean. [Amy and I] were inseparable, dangerously, deeply entwined with each other and drugs, and I was with her [through] the deepest darkest times of her life. I want people to know the Amy that people only saw inside the home. The Amy that we as friends loved so much but also the shocking reality that addiction played in both of our lives.'

Yet if his true motivation was to tell the full story about his friend, helping others in the process, just why was the sum of money so important – why had a six-figure pay cheque that he'd perceived as insignificant been a deal-breaker?

On another note, had he genuinely felt Mitch was cold-heartedly capitalising on his daughter's fame to extract his own or did he, in reality, see him as competition for the fame he anticipated was to come his way? The truth about his motives would remain another unanswered question.

Whatever the reality, it couldn't change that Amy's chemical dependency had proved to be stronger than even the influence of the country's top rehab clinics. In spite of the best efforts of both the professionals and those that had loved her, she had slipped away.

In the years to come, her parents will pore over childhood photos of their baby, clad in the pink satin ballet pumps that would remain her trademark until the day that she died – and dream of the days when they'd still been able to protect her. They will wish they could turn back the hands of time to an era when she was blissfully untroubled, one where Blake never existed and the hardest drug Amy had ever seen was the beer her father sipped a glass of with dinner.

Yet the demons that drove Amy to her death were the same ones that drove her to write her most poignant songs – ones that had seen her net a Brit Award, four Ivor Novello song writing awards and a record-breaking five Grammys in one evening.

Like so many other passionate soul singers, Amy's talents were borne out of desperation, inspired by troubled times. Tragically, she was at her most creative when she was hurting. As Mitch had said, 'For Amy, writing a song is like ripping her heart out.' She was no bright, bubbly *Fame Academy* bimbo who wanted nothing more than to see themselves on screen – she was a real girl with a real talent, and all the problems that came with it.

However, Amy will be remembered. She once told *Heat World*: 'My greatest fear ever is dying without anyone knowing I made a contribution to creative music.' There was no fear of that – she was mourned by the millions who'd brought her albums.

RIP Amy – at least one of her wishes has been achieved.

ACKNOWLEDGMENTS:

● ● ● ● ● ● ●

Many thanks go to the interviewees who agreed to take part in the making of this book, namely:

Nathan Allen, Bill Ashton, Charley Baker, Ian Barter, Derrick Brown, Sammy Calixte, Jack Freegard, 'liveon35mm', Steve Nowa, Adeleye Omatayo, Sophie Schandorff, Stefan Skarbek, Charley Shults, Neal Sugarman and last but not least, all of the anonymous contributors who added their voice to the telling of Amy's story.

Extra special thanks to no-show Alex Foden for failing to call to postpone our appointment and leaving me waiting in six inches of snow.

Thanks also to everyone involved in the production and publicity of the book, including Andrew Lownie, David Haviland and Emma Donnan.

Finally thanks goes to Amy Winehouse for breaking the mould in a world of vacuous manufactured pop and for turning her pain into beauty the whole world could hear. Life might be fleeting, troubled and transitory, but music is forever.

For more resources and to keep up to date with the charitable work being done in Amy's name, visit the Amy Winehouse Foundation website at www.amywinehousefoundation.org

34849164R00193

Made in the USA
Lexington, KY
21 August 2014